Direct Marketing, Direct Selling, and the Mature Consumer

Recent Titles from Quorum Books

Cost-Effective Marketing Research: A Guide for Marketing Managers
Eric J. Soares

Corporate Philosophies and Mission Statements: A Survey and Guide for
Corporate Communicators and Management
Thomas A. Falsey

Strategic Executive Decisions: An Analysis of the Difference Between Theory
and Practice
Michael J. Stahl

Motivating Strategies for Performance and Productivity: A Guide to
Human Resource Development
Paul J. Champagne and R. Bruce McAfee

Innovation Through Technical and Scientific Information: Government and
Industry Cooperation
*Science and Public Policy Program, University of Oklahoma: Steven Ballard,
Thomas E. James, Jr., Timothy I. Adams, Michael D. Devine, Lani L. Malsa,
and Mark Meo*

Transformations in French Business: Political, Economic, and Cultural
Changes from 1981 to 1987
Judith Frommer and Janice McCormick, editors

Economics and Antitrust Policy
Robert J. Larner and James W. Meehan, Jr., editors

A Legal Guide to EDP Management
Michael C. Gemighani

U.S. Commercial Opportunities in the Soviet Union: Marketing, Production,
and Strategic Planning Perspectives
Chris C. Carvounis and Brinda Z. Carvounis

An Analysis of the New Financial Institutions: Changing Technologies,
Financial Structures, Distribution Systems, and Deregulation
Alan Gart

The Commercialization of Outer Space: Opportunities and Obstacles for
American Business
Jonathan N. Goodrich

Computer Power and Legal Language: The Use of Computational Linguistics,
Artificial Intelligence, and Expert Systems in the Law
Charles Walter, editor

DIRECT MARKETING, DIRECT SELLING, AND THE MATURE CONSUMER

A Research Study

James R. Lumpkin,
Marjorie J. Caballero,
and Lawrence B. Chonko

QUORUM BOOKS
New York • Westport, Connecticut • London

Library of Congress Cataloging-in-Publication Data

Lumpkin, James R.
    Direct marketing, direct selling, and the mature consumer : a research study / James R. Lumpkin, Marjorie J. Caballero, and Lawrence B. Chonko.
        p.   cm.
    Bibliography: p.
    Includes index.
    ISBN 0-89930-298-X (lib. bdg. : alk. paper)
        1. Direct marketing.   2. Direct selling.   3. Aged as consumers.
    I. Caballero, Marjorie J.   II. Chonko, Lawrence B.   III. Title.
    HF5415.126.L86   1989
    658.8'348—dc19   88-18519

British Library Cataloguing in Publication Data is available.

Library of Congress Catalog Card Number: 88-18519
ISBN: 0-89930-298-X

First published in 1989 by Quorum Books

Greenwood Press, Inc.
88 Post Road West, Westport, Connecticut 06881

Printed in the United States of America

∞

The paper used in this book complies with the Permanent Paper Standard issued by the National Information Standards Organization (Z39.48-1984).

10 9 8 7 6 5 4 3 2 1

Contents

	Tables and Figures	vii
	Acknowledgments	xv
	Preface	xvii
1.	Direct Marketing and Direct Selling	1
2.	Classification of the Aging Population	11
3.	The Study	23
4.	Buying Patterns of the Mature Consumer	31
5.	Determinants of the Patronage Decision: In-Home vs. In-Store	49
6.	The Mature Consumer and Direct Salespeople	91
7.	Perceptions and Preferences of Mature Consumers	115
8.	Profiling Users and Nonusers	139
9.	Reaching the Mature Consumer	177
	APPENDIX A	199
	TECHNICAL APPENDIX B: Discriminant Analysis	203
	TECHNICAL APPENDIX C: Perceptual Mapping	207
	References	211
	Subject Index	217
	Author Index	221

Tables and Figures

Figure 1.1 Direct Marketing . . . An Aspect of Total Marketing 8
Figure 1.2 Mail Order Growth Rate Estimation Indicators 9
Table 2.1 Population Growth Trends of the Mature Market 15
Table 2.2 Income Sources of the Mature 16
Table 2.3 Total Money Income of Aged Units by Age 16
Table 2.4 Income from Earnings by Age 17
Table 2.5 Income from Social Security Benefits by Levels of Total Money Income and Marital Status: 65+ 17
Table 2.6 Poverty and the Mature 18
Table 2.7 Top Ten States According to Percentage of Population 65+ 18
Table 2.8 Top Ten Chronic Conditions for Mature Persons (Rates Per 1,000 Persons) 19
Table 2.9 Ten Leading Causes of Death by Older Age Groups (Rates Per 100,000 Population in Specific Groups) 19
Table 2.10 Percent of the 65+ Population in the Community with ADL Limitations 20
Table 2.11 Marital Status of Persons 65+ 20
Table 2.12 Living Arrangements of Persons 65+ (Noninstitutionalized) 21
Table 2.13 Average Annual Expenditures: 1980-1981 21
Table 2.14 Weekly Expenditures of Urban Consumer Units by Age and Income before Taxes: 1982-1983 22

Table 4.1   Cross-tabulations of Direct Marketing and
             Direct-Selling Purchases   37

Table 4.2   Percent of Sales of Five Product Categories
             Direct Marketers/Sellers   38

Table 4.3   Top Product Categories in Each Shopping Mode   38

Table 4.4   Overall Top Ten Product Categories with
             Shopping Modes   38

Table 4.5   Direct-Marketing Purchasers Aged ≤ 49 and the
             Product Percentages   39

Table 4.6   Direct-Marketing Purchasers Aged 50-64 and the
             Product Percentages   40

Table 4.7   Direct-Marketing Purchasers Aged 65+ and the
             Product Percentages   41

Table 4.8   Direct-Selling Purchasers Aged ≤ 49 and the
             Product Percentages   42

Table 4.9   Direct-Selling Purchasers Aged 50-64 and the
             Product Percentages   43

Table 4.10   Direct-Selling Purchasers Aged 65+ and the
             Product Percentages   44

Table 4.11   Direct-Marketing and -Selling Purchase Profiles
             by Age Group   45

Table 4.12   Mean Willingness to Purchase across Mode and
             Age Groups for Three Product Categories:
             Direct-Selling User Category   45

Table 4.13   Mean Willingness to Purchase across Mode and
             Age Groups for Three Product Categories:
             Direct-Marketing User Category   46

Table 4.14   Mean Willingness to Purchase across Mode and
             Age Groups for Three Product Categories:
             Both User Categories   46

Table 4.15   Mean Willingness to Purchase across Mode and
             Age Groups for Three Product Categories:
             Neither User Category   47

Table 5.1   Importance of Shopping Characteristics by
             User/Age Groups   65

Table 5.2   Perception of Department Store Catalogues by
             User/Age Groups   66

Table 5.3   Perception of Specialty Catalogues by User/Age
             Groups   67

Table 5.4 Perception of Direct Mail by User/Age Groups 68

Table 5.5 Perception of Media Ads by User/Age Groups 69

Table 5.6 Perception of Telephone Solicitation by User/Age Groups 70

Table 5.7 Perception of Door-to-Door by User/Age Groups 71

Table 5.8 Perception of Party Plan by User/Age Groups 72

Table 5.9 Perception of In-Home Demonstration by User/Age Groups 73

Table 5.10 Perception of Retail by User/Age Groups 74

Table 5.11 In-Home Shopping Likes: 65+ Only 75

Table 5.12 In-Home Shopping Dislikes: 65+ Only 76

Table 5.13 Shopping Likes of Catalogue Users across Age 77

Table 5.14 In-Home Shopping Dislikes: Catalogue Users across Age 78

Table 5.15 Shopping Likes of Direct Mail Users vs. Nonusers: 65+ Only 79

Table 5.16 Shopping Dislikes of Direct Mail Users vs. Nonusers: 65+ Only 79

Table 5.17 Shopping Likes of Direct Mail Users: 65+ vs. <65 80

Table 5.18 Shopping Dislikes of Direct Mail Users: 65+ vs. <65 80

Table 5.19 Shopping Likes of Media Ad Users vs. Nonusers: 65+ Only 81

Table 5.20 Shopping Dislikes of Media Ad Users vs. Nonusers: 65+ Only 81

Table 5.21 Shopping Likes of Media Ad Users: 65+ vs. <65 82

Table 5.22 Shopping Dislikes of Media Ad Users: 65+ vs. <65 82

Table 5.23 Shopping Likes of Users of Phone Solicitation: 65+ vs. <65 83

Table 5.24 Shopping Dislikes of Users of Phone Solicitation: 65+ vs. <65 83

Table 5.25 Shopping Likes of Users vs. Nonusers of Phone Solicitation: 65+ 84

Table 5.26 Shopping Dislikes of Users vs. Nonusers of Phone Solicitation: 65+ 84

Table 5.27 Shopping Likes of Users vs. Nonusers of Direct Selling: 65+ 85

Table 5.28 Shopping Dislikes of Users vs. Nonusers of Direct Selling: 65+ 85

Table 5.29 Shopping Likes of Users of Direct Selling: 65+ vs. <65 86

Table 5.30 Shopping Dislikes of Users of Direct Selling: 65+ vs. <65 86

Table 5.31 Shopping Likes of Party Plan Users vs. Nonusers: 65+ Only 87

Table 5.32 Shopping Dislikes of Party Plan Users vs. Nonusers: 65+ Only 87

Table 5.33 Shopping Likes of Party Plan Users: 65+ vs. <65 88

Table 5.34 Shopping Dislikes of Party Plan Users: 65+ vs. <65 88

Table 5.35 Shopping Likes of In-Home Demonstration Users vs. Nonusers: 65+ Only 89

Table 5.36 Shopping Dislikes of In-Home Demonstration Users vs. Nonusers: 65+ Only 89

Table 5.37 Shopping Likes of In-Home Demonstration Users: 65+ Only 90

Table 5.38 Shopping Dislikes of In-Home Demonstration Users: 65+ Only 90

Table 6.1 Willingness to Purchase: Direct-Selling Users and Nonusers by Age Group Compared 99

Table 6.2 Perception of Extent to Which Consumers Perceive Direct-Selling Modes to Have Purchase Characteristics 100

Table 6.3 Shopping Orientations of Direct-Selling Users and Nonusers by Age Group 102

Table 6.4 Perceptions of the Importance of Source Traits by Users and Nonusers 103

Table 6.5 Perceptions of Salespeople by Direct-Selling Users and Nonusers 104

Table 6.6 Six Group Discriminant Analysis: Perceptions of Salesperson Traits across Buyer Categories 105

Table 6.7 Pearson Correlations: Salesperson Traits with Shopping Orientations 106

Table 6.8 Regressions of Age, Power, Shopping Orientation, and Sales Variables against Customer Orientation 107

Table 6.9 Regressions of Age, Power, Shopping Orientation, and Sales Variables against Job Orientation 108

Table 6.10 Regressions of Age, Shopping Orientation, and Sales Variables against Power 108

Table 6.11 Regressions of Age and Power against Customer Orientation, Job Orientation, and Power 109

Table 6.12 Regressions of Shopping Orientation against Customer Orientation, Job Orientation, and Power 110

Table 6.13 Regressions of Salespersons' Characteristics against Customer Orientation, Job Orientation, and Power 110

Table 6.14 Regressions of Selected Power, Salesperson Characteristics, and Shopping Orientation against Customer Orientation Controlling for Age 111

Table 6.15 Regressions of Selected Power, Salesperson Characteristics, and Shopping Orientation against Job Orientation Controlling for Age 112

Table 6.16 Regressions of Age, Salesperson Characteristics, and Shopping Orientation against Power 113

Figure 7.1 Perceptual Map of Direct-Selling Modes (vs. Retail Store) and Ideal Points (Most Preferred Mode) for Three Product Categories: Total Sample 119

Figure 7.2 Perceptual Map of Direct-Marketing Modes (vs. Retail Store) and Ideal Points (Most Preferred Mode) for Three Product Categories: Total Sample 120

Table 7.1 Mean Similarities between Modes: Four User Groups 121

Table 7.2 Rank Order of Similarity Scores: Direct Sources and Retailers Compared 122

Figure 7.3 Direct Marketing without Retail: Age-1 (≤ 34) 123

Figure 7.4 Direct Marketing without Retail: Age-2 (35-49) 124

Figure 7.5 Direct Marketing without Retail: Age-3 (50-64) 125

Figure 7.6 Direct Marketing without Retail: Age-4 (65+) 126

Figure 7.7 Direct Selling without Retail: Age-1 (≤ 34) 127

Figure 7.8 Direct Selling without Retail: Age-2 (35-49) 128

Figure 7.9 Direct Selling without Retail: Age-3 (50-64) 129

Figure 7.10 Direct Selling without Retail: Age-4 (65+) 130

Figure 7.11 Direct Marketing without Retail: Users-1 (Direct Selling Users) 131

Figure 7.12 Direct Marketing without Retail: Users-2 (Direct Marketing Users) 132

Figure 7.13 Direct Marketing without Retail: Users-3 ("Both") 133

Figure 7.14 Direct Marketing without Retail: Users-4 ("Neither") 134

Figure 7.15 Direct Selling without Retail: Users-1 (Direct Selling Users) 135

Figure 7.16 Direct Selling without Retail: Users-2 (Direct Marketing Users) 136

Figure 7.17 Direct Selling without Retail: Users-3 ("Both") 137

Figure 7.18 Direct Selling without Retail: Users-4 ("Neither") 138

Table 8.1 Cross-tabulation of Respondent Age by Residence 150

Table 8.2 Cross-tabulation of Respondent Age by Education 150

Table 8.3 Cross-tabulation of Respondent Age by Household Size 151

Table 8.4 Cross-tabulation of Respondent Age by Employment Status 151

Table 8.5 Cross-tabulation of Respondent Age by Income Category 151

Table 8.6 Cross-tabulation of Respondent Age by Marital Status 152

Table 8.7 Cross-tabulation of Respondent Age by Sex 152

Table 8.8 Cross-tabulation of ≤ 49 Users by Residence 152

Table 8.9 Cross-tabulation of ≤ 49 Users by Education 153

Table 8.10 Cross-tabulation of ≤ 49 Users by Household Size 153

Table 8.11 Cross-tabulation of ≤ 49 Users by Employment Status 154

Table 8.12 Cross-tabulation of ≤ 49 Users by Income 154

Table 8.13 Cross-tabulation of ≤ 49 Users by Marital Status 155

Table 8.14 Cross-tabulation of ≤ 49 Users by Sex 155

Table 8.15 Cross-tabulation of 50-64 Users by Residence 156

Table 8.16 Cross-tabulation of 50-64 Users by Education 156

Table 8.17 Cross-tabulation of 50-64 Users by Household Size 157

Table 8.18 Cross-tabulation of 50-64 Users by Employment Status 157

Table 8.19 Cross-tabulation of 50-64 Users by Income 158

Table 8.20 Cross-tabulation of 50-64 Users by Marital Status 158

Table 8.21 Cross-tabulation of 50-64 Users by Sex 159

Table 8.22 Cross-tabulation of 65+ Users by Residence 159

Table 8.23 Cross-tabulation of 65+ Users by Education 160

Table 8.24 Cross-tabulation of 65+ Users by Household Size 160

Table 8.25 Cross-tabulation of 65+ Users by Employment Status 161

Table 8.26 Cross-tabulation of 65+ Users by Income 161

Table 8.27 Cross-tabulation of 65+ Users by Marital Status 162

Table 8.28 Cross-tabulation of 65+ Users by Sex 162

Table 8.29 Demographic Comparison across Non/Light/Heavy Catalogue Users: 65+ Only 163

Table 8.30 Demographics of Catalogue Users Only across Age Categories 164

Table 8.31 Demographics of Direct Mail Users vs. Nonusers: 65+ Only 165

Table 8.32 Demographics of Direct Mail Users: 65+ vs. <65 165

Table 8.33 Demographics of Media Ad Users vs. Nonusers: 65+ Only 166

Table 8.34 Demographics of Media Ad Users: 65+ vs. <65 166

Table 8.35 Demographics of Users vs. Nonusers of Phone Solicitation: 65+ Only 167

Table 8.36 Demographics of Users of Phone Solicitation: 65+ vs. <65 167

Table 8.37 Demographics of Users vs. Nonusers of Direct Selling: 65+ Only 168

Table 8.38 Demographics of Direct-Selling Users: 65+ vs. <65 168

Table 8.39 Demographics of Party Plan Users vs. Nonusers: 65+ Only 169

Table 8.40 Demographics of Party Plan Users: 65+ vs. <65 169

Table 8.41 Demographics of In-Home Demonstration Users vs. Nonusers: 65+ Only 170

Table 8.42 Demographics of In-Home Demonstration Users: 65+ vs. <65 170

Table 8.43 Mean Shopping Orientation Scores: Total Sample 171

Table 8.44 Discriminant Analysis: Shopping Orientations across Three Age Groups 172

Table 8.45 Mean Shopping Orientation Scores across Four User Groups: 65+ Only 173

Table 8.46 Mean Shopping Orientation Scores across Four User Groups: 50-64 174

Table 8.47 Mean Shopping Orientation Scores across Four User Groups: ≤49 175

Table 9.1 Information Source Typology 198

Figure A.1 Demographic Profile of Sample 199

Figure A.2 Customer and Job Orientation Scales for Salespeople 202

Acknowledgments

This book could not have been written without the cooperation of the over 2,500 individuals who took the time to supply us with information. They deserve the credit for their patience in providing us with a wealth of insight into direct marketing and direct selling. Market Facts, Inc. graciously allowed us to work with these members of their consumer panel.

One person, in particular, deserves special recognition. Donna Randall worked many hours to type, edit, and search for facts. She took our early scribblings and molded them into something that looked like a book. She kept us on deadline and organized. She criticized, worked with our writing styles, and even coped with our tendency to be redundant and our seemingly endless quantity of tables.

Finally, we thank the American Association of Retired Persons (AARP) Andrus Foundation for providing the funding that made this research possible. Their commitment to research aimed at producing information of a practical and usable nature to assist older people was a constant source of inspiration.

Preface

This study investigated the shopping behavior of the mature consumer. The study compared shopping behaviors and attitudes of the mature market (65 and older) to that of consumers in both the 50-64 age group and the under-50 age group. We sought to identify the various shopping needs of the mature and their perceptions of how direct marketers and direct sellers are meeting those needs. Purchase behavior and attitudes toward seven direct marketing and selling modes—catalogues, direct mail, media ads, telephone solicitation, door-to-door salespeople, party plan, and in-home demonstrations—were evaluated. In addition, various demographic and psychological variables were measured.

A national sample was obtained from Market Facts, Inc. Questionnaires were sent to 4,000 households, 2,400 of which had at least one household member 65 years of age or older. The sample was stratified by population density and by a combination of sex of respondent and marital status to insure representation of rural and urban, male and female, and married and unmarried respondents.

The eight-page questionnaire yielded data on:

1. respondents' willingness to purchase from various direct sources,
2. respondents' actual six-month purchase behavior from various direct sources,
3. respondents' preferences for purchasing from various direct sources,
4. respondents' likes and dislikes about direct marketing and selling,
5. characteristics that respondents feel are important in their purchase decisions, and
6. the degree to which various direct-marketing and direct-selling sources are perceived to have these characteristics.

Data were analyzed in a series of univariate and multivariate analysis techniques. A wide range of interesting and useful findings were obtained. For example, mature users of direct marketers' and sellers' products and services like the convenience of direct marketing and direct selling and the ability to see and discuss many of the products available. However, many of our mature respondents reported that they liked nothing about direct marketing and selling. They disliked high-pressure sales tactics and the uncertainty associated with shopping from pictures.

No one demographic factor or combination of demographic factors was useful in profiling users across direct modes. However, demographic differences between users and nonusers for each direct-marketing and -selling mode were observed.

Similarly, no one psychological variable, or set of psychological variables, universally differentiated users from nonusers. However, users tended to be positive toward the convenience of in-home shopping, associated less risk with in-home shopping, and were more positive toward price and quality of products purchased through direct modes than were nonusers. The mature tended to be more loyal to local merchants, less price conscious, more personalizing, and to have greater service needs than did younger consumers.

Mature purchasers of products through direct modes felt that catalogues were as good as or better on nine shopping-mode characteristics than traditional retail outlets. However, the same could not be said for other direct modes.

Overall, direct marketers and direct sellers still have a long way to go to develop trust relationships with the mature consumer. Since this market is growing, direct marketers and direct sellers are well advised to recognize opportunities here and tailor their programs accordingly.

Direct Marketing, Direct Selling, and the Mature Consumer

CHAPTER 1

Direct Marketing and Direct Selling

The direct-marketing and direct-selling industries have been growing in size and prestige over the past two decades. In those twenty years, many push-pull changes have altered ways of selling and buying. These changes have combined to make both direct marketing and direct selling multi-billion dollar industries.

The success of direct marketing and direct selling depends on acquiring knowledge about customers—old and new. Many firms have implemented this concept through what is called "data base marketing." That is, they develop and maintain a data base of customers. Such data bases are critical to measuring purchase behavior and the results of advertising as well as for designing future communications with customers.

Advertisers, in particular, have become increasingly aware of the tremendous sales potential associated with data base strategies and direct media. Both direct approaches have some distinct advantages over other marketing approaches. One of those advantages is the ability to target specific markets and market segments, the mature market being of particular interest in this study. Each year, the American Association of Retired Persons enlists about 1 million new members. It has been estimated that by the year 2000 the number of U.S. citizens over 50 years of age will be 82 million. A substantial portion of these mature consumers will be 65 or older. It is the latter group that is the focus of this book. This chapter will introduce some pertinent vocabulary and definitions used with direct marketing and direct selling and will discuss some of the basic characteristics of the industries. It will conclude with a brief review of what is known about the mature market.

DEFINITIONS

"*Direct marketing* is an interactive system of marketing which uses one or more advertising media to effect a measurable response and/or transaction at any location" (*Direct Marketing* 1987, 24). Just as *marketing* is the total of activities of moving goods and services from seller to buyer, so *direct marketing* requires the existence and maintenance of data bases. The data base has four functions: (1) to record names of customers, expires, and prospects; (2) to provide a vehicle for storing, then measuring results of direct response advertising; (3) to provide a vehicle for storing, then measuring, purchasing performance; and (4) to provide a vehicle for continuing direct communication by mail and/or phone. Unfortunately, direct marketing, which is a broad, umbrella concept, is often confused with several other terms. The following definitions (Bovée and Arens 1986, 469-470) will clarify these relationships.

Media advertisements use mass media such as television, radio, newspaper, or magazines to ask the recipient for an immediate response. A broadcast commercial may ask the audience to write or to call a toll-free number. A newspaper ad may provide a coupon to be filled out and returned to the advertiser as a request for additional product information.

Catalogues are used to reach a variety of prospects including consumers, salespeople, dealers, or any specifically targeted market segment. Users can order through the mail or often via a toll-free telephone number.

Direct mail is any form of direct advertising that is sent through the mail and which, as an advertising medium, has the advantages of selectivity, intensive coverage, flexibility, personalization, uniform production quality, fewer immediate distractions, and response measurement. Although catalogues are most often distributed through the mail, they are separated into a distinct category.

Direct selling is also a form of direct-to-consumer marketing through personal explanation and demonstration of products and services to consumers, primarily in homes. Direct selling takes the form of party plans, telephone solicitation, in-home demonstrations, and door-to-door selling. Direct marketing is a term that represents any type of direct-to-consumer marketing. However, the Direct Marketing Association's (DMA) Industry Statistics Task Force, for the purpose of data gathering within their industry, used the following definition: "Direct Marketing Sales . . . are sales resulting from a transaction that *both* (1) originated when the individual responded to a direct response advertisement and (2) was concluded by telephone or mail." Although it is clear that direct selling is a subset of direct marketing, two separate trade associations exist for the two areas, and practitioners generally differentiate the two. Therefore, direct marketing and direct selling will be referred to as separate entities. The umbrella term *in-home shopping* will be used as a collective version of these various marketing approaches.

INDUSTRY SIZE

Mayer (1982) estimated that mail order sales alone would exceed $40 billion in the United States in 1980. Mayer also estimated that mail order marketing had been growing at an annual rate of 15 percent—twice the rate of retail stores sales growth. Schneiderman predicted a continuation of growth in nonstore sales and has estimated that by 1990 "American consumers will be buying fully one-half of their general merchandise without setting foot in a retail store" (1980, 60).

By 1986 mail order/phone sales had risen to $135 billion with consumer mail order at $62 billion, business mail order at $38 billion, and charitable mail order at $35 billion. Consumer mail order was comprised of $40 billion for products and $22 billion for services. Consumer product mail order can be further subdivided into $29 billion for specialty merchandisers and $11 billion for general merchandisers (Fishman 1987, 40).

Growth in consumer mail order for 1986 was estimated to be in the 8 to 12 percent range in current dollars or 5 to 9 percent when adjusted for inflation. These figures reflect growth rates that are somewhat higher than those for overall retail or department store chain sales. Although these are impressive growth figures, they are much more moderate than the 15 percent growth rates of the past.

In terms of specific direct-marketing modes, direct mail in 1984 accounted for $13.8 billion of the more than $88 billion spent on advertising media—15.7 percent of total media dollars. In 1986, direct mail advertising was estimated at $17.2 billion or only about 12 percent of the $143.29 billion total media spending. Nevertheless *Direct Marketing* magazine (July 1987, 24) believes that 65 percent of the volume is direct response advertising.

CHARACTERISTICS OF DIRECT MARKETING AND DIRECT SELLING

Although the cost per person reached is higher for direct mail than for most other advertising media, direct mail does offer some distinctive advantages. First, the audience can be carefully selected to avoid wasted coverage. It is possible to limit contact only to those who qualify as real prospects. Since a mailing list is used, each piece can be personalized with the name and address of the recipient and even with other information such as birth date. Multiple mailings enable the advertiser to achieve high frequency with direct mail. Further, serial mailings can be employed to maintain a high level of interest as the advertiser reveals the message through a series of attention-getting mailings.

Direct mail commands the immediate attention of the recipient and is less likely to be diluted by environmental distractions than are other media. Direct mail lends itself well to response measurement, unlike many other advertising media. Sales volume, number of orders, average order size, repeat orders, returned inquiry cards, new memberships, and information requests are only a few of the ways in which direct mail effectiveness can be assessed.

Nowhere is the maturation of mail order more evident than in cataloguing. Cataloguers have responded to industry maturation and the glut of catalogues on the market by reducing the frequency (by as much as one half) with which they mail and the number of catalogues mailed.

The turnover rate in mail order also continues to be very high with as many as 30 percent of new companies not surviving a year in business. The solution has been to concentrate on higher impact mailings and more targeted audiences. While some cataloguers, notably Sears and Fingerhut, continue to appeal to middle- and lower-income households with their catalogues, more and more direct mailers are focusing on the upper-income market.

A realistic estimate of the number of catalogues mailed each year would be approximately 10 billion. This translates to more than 100 per U.S. household. However, upper-income households may find two or more a day in their mailboxes while lower-income households may receive fewer than a dozen a year.

Since the universe of mail-order buyers is not growing at the rate catalogue mailers would like to see, it is imperative that direct mail marketers sell potential customers on the ease, practicality, and benefits of buying by mail.

Direct selling is a form of product distribution that involves direct-to-consumer marketing through personal presentation and demonstration of goods and services, primarily in homes. In 1983, direct selling represented a contribution of $8.5 billion to the U.S. economy and provided employment for 4.9 million independent direct salespeople across the country. By 1986 direct selling to consumers amounted to approximately $9 billion in sales, representing a plateauing of the industry.

Personal service is one benefit offered by direct selling that is often lacking in traditional retail service. Customers like to feel that they are being given individualized attention; they also appreciate a relaxed atmosphere in which to ask questions and learn more about the product. Direct selling offers customers the convenience of shopping at home without the annoyance of traffic, crowded parking, lack of sales assistance, and waiting in check-out lines.

From the seller's perspective, the opportunity is available to fully explain product features. Obligation is another advantage of direct selling from the seller's perspective; many prospects buy on the basis of friendship.

TARGETING THE CUSTOMER

The firms in the direct-marketing and direct-selling fields realize that the mass market is increasingly splitting apart. To succeed today marketers must offer multiple options to meet the varied tastes and circumstances of a fragmented population. Fortunately for direct marketers and direct sellers many of their techniques enable them to identify those targets and to speak to them directly. Special promotions may be independently targeted at women, regional markets, or college students. Further, these methods are being used by traditional retailers. For example, Bloomingdale's, which has spent millions building a high-fashion image, is able to use catalogues to exploit its established reputation. Catalogues are more cost-effective than building a national network of stores.

The key to successful direct marketing and direct selling in these many markets is the element of *trust*. Companies that have built a respected image with their prospects have a real advantage when they market direct. One of the best ways to build a trust relationship with customers is to know who they are and to target their needs specifically. For example, most consumer marketers plan their media strategies based on fairly broad demographic statistics: "women, 25-49, $25,000 + household income, AB counties" is a standard formula. Direct marketers and direct sellers approach the problem from a different viewpoint. Marketing dog food? How about a list of the owners of large dogs versus small dogs? It is possible to target a special message to owners of poodles or show dogs. If the product is medical care, one might obtain lists of people who suffer from various ailments or have other particular medical needs. These detailed direct marketing plans identify target audiences and set specific communications goals for each.

Even traditional marketers are using a variety of direct-marketing techniques to develop lists of customers and key prospects. For example, Procter & Gamble includes a toll-free, 800 service number on its packages. Millions of its customers use the number every year. P&G believes that these calls act as a valuable source of marketing information while simultaneously expanding the firm's data base. Similarly, Clairol offers an 800 number to call for instant advice should a woman run into unexpected problems while coloring or bleaching her hair.

Additionally, retailers are increasingly developing house lists and promoting to them. Radio Shack has mastered this technique; it is hard to get out of one of their stores without the cashier capturing your name and address. Once on the list, you can be sure of receiving a series of direct mail promotions.

For these reasons, direct response advertising is growing faster than general advertising, and the costs of managing and using data are declining. Such conditions open up new profit-making opportunities for many companies.

However, although in-home shopping has become an important and integral part of the American retailing scene, very little published research exists regarding these new methods of retailing (Korgaonkar 1982) and even less that focuses on how the mature consumers view in-home shopping.

RESEARCH FINDINGS

Scholars within the marketing academic community have also predicted that in-home shopping will increase in importance as a shopping alternative (Doody and Davidson 1967; McNair and May 1978). Technological advances have contributed to the development of in-home shopping by making it easier for consumers to procure goods through this mode. For example, Sears has initiated the distribution of its catalogues on video discs (Weiner 1981), and other novel in-home distribution experiments have been documented by McQuade (1980). He reported that in 1980 consumers were purchasing cameras, furniture, appliances, and other products by submitting orders through in-home computers that were connected (over telephone lines) to the information bank of the seller located in Virginia, and that consumers in Canada were ordering catalogue items from Simpson-Sears by using Touch-Tone telephones to communicate with a talking computer.

The few studies of in-home shoppers that exist suggest that these consumers tend to be younger (Berkowitz, Walton, and Walker 1979; Reynolds 1974), have higher income (Cunningham and Cunningham 1972; Gillett 1970; Reynolds 1974), have more education (Berkowitz, Walton, and Walker 1979; Cunningham and Cunningham 1972), and are generally of a higher social status (Berkowitz, Walton, and Walker 1979; Cunningham and Cunningham 1972; Gillett 1970); they have characteristics that closely match Lumpkin's (1985c) active shopper group. Conversely, Lumpkin and McConkey (1984) found that in-home shoppers use credit less, have lower incomes, and represent smaller households than shoppers who use specialty stores and department stores. In-home shoppers were not found to be price-oriented and were seen as self-confident shoppers.

Lumpkin and Hawes (1985) report several demographic variables associated with catalogue usage. Married homeowners with children tended to be more frequent purchasers. The association of catalogue shopping with higher education and higher income was reconfirmed by their research. Women were more likely to purchase from catalogues, and contrary to previous studies, older respondents reported more frequent shopping by catalogue. The other demographic variable found to be statistically associated with catalogue usage was the employment status of the female head of the household. Nonusers were more likely to be employed full-time outside the home.

Lumpkin and Greenberg (1982) confirmed earlier findings (Mason and Smith 1974; Mason and Bearden 1978a) that mature consumers do not use in-home shopping to a greater extent than do younger consumers. While in-home shopping is the shopping mode used least by all age groups, the mature consumer's use of mail or phone orders is significantly less than that of other groups.

At this juncture it appears that direct marketers are failing to meet the needs of the mature consumer through in-home shopping. The discrepancy exists despite evidence of a close match between the characteristics of at least one significant segment of the mature market—the active mature consumer—and the profile of younger in-home shoppers. Further, several researchers have recognized the seemingly good fit between shopping needs of the mature consumer and the benefits provided by direct marketing and direct selling. Yet the evidence suggests that fewer mature consumers participate in direct purchase than is the case among younger consumers.

Not only is there a need to discover the range of attributes and services desired by the mature consumer from direct marketers, but it is essential to discover areas of satisfaction and, more importantly, dissatisfaction with current products, services, and methods.

As can be seen from a review of the literature, the information pertaining to direct marketing and direct selling to the elderly is scant indeed. Although some evidence exists to suggest that the mature consumers are not heavy users of in-home buying, other evidence suggests that they ought to be. Research was needed to clarify these issues so that direct marketers and direct sellers can develop and administer programs that the mature consumers find satisfying and beneficial.

Figure 1.1
Direct Marketing . . . An Aspect of Total Marketing

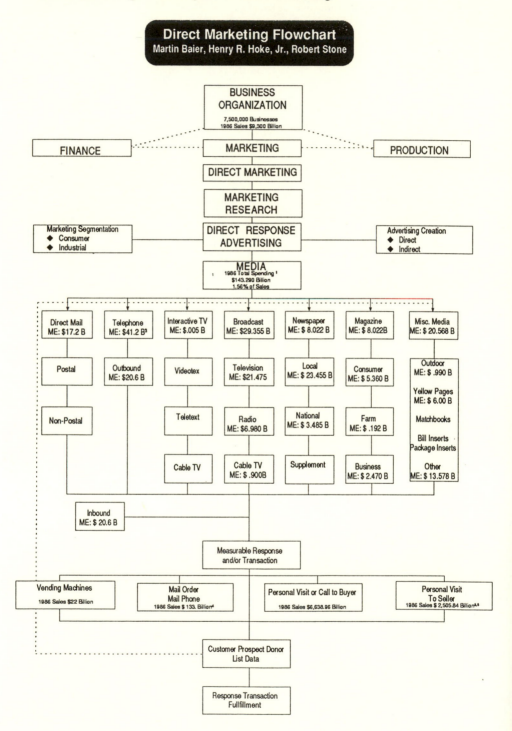

Direct Marketing Flowchart
Martin Baier, Henry R. Hoke, Jr., Robert Stone

8

Figure 1.1 (continued)

[1]Source: Arnold Fishman, U.S. Census, Robert Coen, McCann Erikson (Media Figures)..

[2]Personal visit to seller includes $1.204 billion of Consumer Products Sales at retail plus 90% of Consumer Services Sales. 10% of Consumer Services Sales are conducted by salespeople visiting the buyer.

[3]Rudy Oetting, Telephone Marketing Resources, New York City, working with AT&T figures, says that roughly half of Telemarketing Expenditures are for Outbound Calls; 50% for Inbound.

[4]The Mail Order Sales Figure includes roughly $33 billion of charitable contributions which are not included in the $9,300 billion of U.S. Aggregate Sales

[5]This total does not include $870 billion in nivestment spending minus $75 billion in Net Exports.

*Dollars in Billions

ME: Media Expenditures

Source: Direct Marketing Magazine, 224 Seventh Street, Garden City, New York 11530-5771.

Figure 1.2
Mail Order Growth Rate Estimation Indicators

The growth rate of consumer mail order based on available cost and sales growth indicators was in the range of 8 percent to 12 percent in money terms (current dollars). Assuming a 3 percent inflation rate, a growth rate of from 5 percent to 9 percent in real terms is estimated. Although these estimates are substantially lower than more extravagant estimates ascribed by other sources to consumer mail order sales, they reflect economic evidence and are still several points higher than estimates of general economic growth in 1986.

I. Economic Environment				
Gross national product-nominal	5.2%			
Gross national product-real	2.5%			
Personal consumption expenditures:				
Overall	6.3%			
Durable goods	8.1%			
Non-durable goods	3.0%			
Services	7.9%			
Consumer price index	2.6%			
Real rate of growth of personal consumption expenditures	4.1%			

III. Media		1986	1985
Third class unit volume		6%	8%
Third class dollar volume		15%	15%
Direct mail		11%	13%
Direct mail coupon distribution		10%	10%
Direct response ad agency billings		23%	26%
Advertising expenditures excluding direct mail		7.1%	7.1%

II. Related Marketing Sectors	
Retail	5.2%
Catalog showrooms	1.1%
Department stores (including mass merchandisers and discount stores)	8.4%

IV. Sales Performace

Publicly Held Mail Order vs. Retail Companies

	Mail Order	Retail
Sales	29.2%	8.1%
Profits	6.0%	2.7%

Direct mail expenditure growth in excess of the rest of advertising (11 percent versus 7.1 percent) and sales growth of a publicly held mail order versus publicly held retail companies (29.2 percent versus 6 percent) reinforced by enhanced sales performance readings by leading mail order marketers in 1986 compared to 1985 suggest a growth rate for mail order about twice that for overall retail (10 percent versus 5 percent).

9

CHAPTER 2

Classification of the Aging Population

The older age group as a percentage of total population has increased far more rapidly than any other age group during the most recent part of this century. In the last two decades alone the 65 + population grew by 54 percent while the under-65 population increased by less than half that. This clearly indicates the aging of the American population, a trend that is expected to continue well into the twenty-first century.

The U.S. census specifically cites four age groups in the aging population, but there are no standardized labels that are used exclusively with any particular group. The four segments and their census titles include:

	Ages	Size	Percentage of Total Population
Older	55-64	22 million	9
Elderly	65-74	17 million	7
Aged	75-84	9 million	4
Very Old	85 +	2.7 million	1

Further, the general make-up of the over-55 group continues to change. While the distribution of this group is presently weighted toward the younger end of the range, in the next few decades the "aged" and "very old" age groups will grow from representing 40 percent of the over-55 group to being almost one-half of all those in the 55 + group (see Table 2.1).

DEMOGRAPHICS FOR THE 65 + POPULATION

Income

Table 2.2 shows the aggregate distribution of income sources for mature persons. Tables 2.3, 2.4, and 2.5 shed more light on the sources of income by various age groups. As indicated in Table 2.3, from age 55 on total income for the average person decreases approximately 20 percent for each incremental five years. On the other hand, the average income from earnings (Table 2.4) makes a dramatic decrease at age 65, showing that most people over age 65 have become fairly dependent on social security as a major source of income.

Nevertheless, approximately half of the 65 + age group's total income still comes from earnings, having a median income from earnings of $5,600 and the remainder coming from social security benefits. Older Americans depend more heavily on social security for their income than they do on any other single source. The next largest contributors are (in order): assets, earnings, and pensions (Table 2.2).

Married couples' incomes do not fall prey to the rapid decline. Instead of the 20 percent incremental decline, married incomes only suffer a 11-12 percent decrease for every five years. Consequently, for most older age groups, the majority of people have total incomes over $10,000 per year. It is not until after age 75 that the majority of incomes fall below the $10,000 mark.

Although older persons are slightly more likely than other adults to be poor, when other family members are considered, elderly poverty rates are somewhat below poverty rates for the rest of the population. The elderly are much more likely to have incomes just above the poverty level (Table 2.6).

Although older workers are less likely to become unemployed, once they become unemployed they are far less likely than younger persons to find a job, and spend a much longer amount of time between jobs. Just over one out of every ten people over 65 still work. The percentage of mature males still in the work force is over twice that of the mature female population. The ratio of older females to older males in the work force decreases slowly as age increases, and then drops off dramatically upon reaching the 65 and 70 year range.

Geographical Distribution

Older persons tend to move far less often than younger persons, causing a graying of some areas of the country where older persons have remained and younger persons have moved away. For example, in 1984, almost half the older population was living in eight states, all of which (see Table 2.7) experienced substantial increases in their mature population from 1970 to 1980. Although the highest quantities of older persons are typically in the largest states (Texas, California, New York) and in the sunbelt areas, the states with the largest percentages of their total population consisting of persons 65 and older are located in the midwest.

Migration of the mature is essentially a mirror of a national trend where state-to-state movers are leaving the Northwest and Midwest and moving into the sunbelt states of the South and West. In the 1970s 50 percent more older persons migrated than during the 1960s, and they tended to migrate to the sunbelt. As a result, the largest percentage increases in the mature populations occurred in the South and West. Of the 1,662,520 Americans over the age of 60 who moved out-of-state during the 1970s, nearly half went to five states: Florida, California, Arizona, Texas, and New Jersey. Some 60 + persons who migrated to the sunbelt in their early retirement years eventually returned to their home states or to states outside the sunbelt to be near their children. This trend, called countermigration, is relatively small in absolute numbers, but is important.

Health

As individuals age, acute conditions become less frequent and chronic conditions become more prevalent. More than four out of five persons 65 and over have at least one chronic condition and multiple conditions are commonplace in the mature (Table 2.8).

As shown in Table 2.8, heart conditions are the fourth most frequently occurring chronic condition. Even if cancer were eliminated as a cause of death, the average life span would be extended by only two to three years because of the prevalence of heart disease. Eliminating deaths due to cardiovascular diseases would add an average 11.4 years to life at age 65, and would lead to a sharp increase in the proportion of older persons in the total population (see Table 2.9).

Although more than half of the Very Old (85 +) are not disabled, the probability of becoming at least mildly disabled increases for the oldest age groups. Males and females 85 and older are four times more likely to be physically disabled than those age 75 to 84. Females are more likely than males to have activity limitations when they live beyond age 65, and they are increasingly more likely to have limitations as they grow older (Table 2.10).

Family Composition

Largely due to contrasting mortality rates, a sizable majority of men are married, while half of the mature women have been widowed (Table 2.11), leading to a larger portion of the older male population living in "family settings." The great majority of men live in family settings as opposed to just over half of the women living in those circumstances.

Although older women are more likely to be widowed than their male counterparts, there is no distinct disparity between the sexes as to where they will live once their partners pass on. Men and women are equally likely to live alone (or with non-relatives), and male and female widows are more than twice as likely to live alone or with non-relatives than to live with other relatives. It should be noted that these figures apply only to non-institutionalized persons over 65 (see Table 2.12).

After age 75 there is a great reduction in the percentage of women living in a "family setting," but there is a lesser reduction in the number of men living in that manner. Once again this is probably due to the earlier mortality of men as opposed to women. By the time they reach 75 many women have been widowed and must change styles of living. Conversely, men who reach 75 are usually still married so they remain in the "family setting."

Expenditures

Mature households on average tend to consume more of their before-tax income than households in most other age groups. The 65 + age group consume an average of 98 percent of their before-tax income, but other age groups consume only an average of 71 to 85 percent of their before-tax income. The high rate of before-tax consumption may be a function of lower rates of savings among the elderly or a result of having reduced income in old age to meet living expenses. Higher consumption may also result from the fact that older persons pay less of their income in taxes than younger persons. The tax burden tends to be lighter since most 65 + persons no longer pay social security taxes (and their income tax payments tend to be based on a lower marginal tax rate).

Mature households devote more of their expenditures to necessities than do younger households. Approximately 80 percent of the spending by mature households is for food, housing, transportation, and health care, as opposed to 71 to 73 percent for younger households. Health care spending is particularly significant for the mature consumer. Mature households spend twice as much of their income as the average younger group, and while health care comprises only 1 percent of the 55-64 age group's expenditures, it makes up 10 percent of the 65 + group's expenses (Tables 2.13 and 2.14).

In the last thirty years the percentage of national health care for drugs and drug sundries has decreased by approximately 50 percent, largely due to the increase in the use of nursing homes during that period. Yet there is little difference between income levels for the dollar amount spent on nonprescription drugs. Each older income group (with the exception of the lowest income group) spends roughly the same dollar amount on drugs. The lowest income group spends approximately one-third of what the average older person spends.

CONCLUSIONS

Although the youngest groups of the mature population (ages 55-70) are well off, those persons over 70 are susceptible to financial strain. They typically have a lower total income, and, at the same time, have a much higher probability of being severely disabled. The individuals who are in need of extra medical care do not have the ability to pay for that care. They are over the poverty level, but a catastrophe could send them into financial straits.

A second conclusion from this review has to do with the manner in which the mature population is grouped. It would be questionable to group all people from 1 to 30 years of age into one marketing segment; yet most research, and the majority of information from the U.S. Census, is presented with reference only to the "65 and over" group. In many ways the 65 + population is just as diverse as those in the 1-30 year old range. They have many different life-styles, incomes, and expenses. With the amount of discretionary income that the mature sector has in its control, it is surprising that there has not been much research aimed at dissecting the older population.

Table 2.1
Population Growth Trends of the Mature Market

Projected Growth of the Older Population (1000s)

Year	55-64 years		65-74 years		75-84 years		85+		65+	
	Number	%	Number	%	Number	%	Number	%	Number	%
1990	21051	8.4	18035	7.2	10349	4.1	3313	1.3	31697	12.7
2000	23767	8.9	17677	6.6	12318	4.6	4926	1.8	34921	13.0
2010	34848	12.3	20318	7.2	12326	4.4	6551	2.3	39195	13.8
2020	40298	13.6	29855	10.1	14486	4.9	7081	2.4	51422	17.3
2030	34025	11.2	34535	11.3	21434	7.0	8621	2.8	64581	21.2
2040	34717	11.3	29272	9.5	24882	8.1	12834	4.2	66988	21.7
2050	37327	12.1	30114	9.7	21263	6.9	16034	5.2	67411	21.8

Projected Percentage of Elderly Persons
Who Are Age 75 and Over: 1980-2000

Year	Percentage of Elderly 75+
1980	39
1990	43
2000	49

Source: U.S. Bureau of the Census, _Current Population Reports_, Series P-25, No. 952.

Table 2.2
Income Sources of the Mature

Source	Income Percentage
Social Security	40%
Assets	25%
Earnings	18%
Pensions	14%
Other	3%

Source: U.S. Bureau of the Census, Current Population Reports, Series P-25, No. 952.

Table 2.3
Total Money Income of Aged Units by Age

All Units

Income	Age 55-61	Age 62-64	Total	65-69	Age 65+ 70-74	75-79	80+
<$ 1000- 4,999	13.3	13.3	19.4	14.9	16.3	20.1	29.2
$ 5,000- 9,999	12.5	18.7	30.0	23.5	29.6	33.4	36.2
$10,000-14,999	11.7	14.2	16.9	16.9	19.3	17.7	14.8
$15,000-50,000	62.5	53.8	33.7	44.7	35.8	28.8	19.8
Median $ Income	20,830	16,530	10,170	13,390	11,050	9,130	6,990

Married Couples

Income	Age 55-61	Age 62-64	Total	65-69	Age 65+ 70-74	75-79	80+
<$ 1000- 4,999	4.1	4.0	2.7	2.9	2.1	2.9	4.7
$ 5,000- 9,999	6.6	9.7	16.8	11.3	17.4	20.2	27.2
$10,000-14,999	8.5	12.5	22.1	18.7	21.4	26.9	27.3
$15,000-50,000	80.8	73.8	58.4	67.1	59.1	50.0	40.8
Median $ Income	29,780	23,580	17,250	19,500	17,480	15,100	13,190

Source: Income of the Population 55+, 1984 U.S. Dept. of Health & Human Services, SSA Publication No. 13-11871.

Table 2.4
Income from Earnings by Age

Income	Age 55-61	Age 62-64	Age 65+ Total	65-69	70-74	75-79	80+
<$1,000- 4,999	10.8	17.5	44.9	36.7	53.2	54.5	62.9
$ 5,000- 9,999	10.4	14.1	21.0	20.3	22.3	21.8	16.2
$10,000-14,999	12.5	12.4	9.3	11.0	8.1	6.2	6.9
$15,000-39,999	47.2	41.8	18.6	23.8	12.4	14.5	8.9
> 40,000	19.1	14.2	6.2	8.2	4.0	3.0	5.1
Median $ Income	21,450	17,120	5,660	7,120	4,330	4,030	2,630

Table 2.5
Income from Social Security Benefits by Levels of Total Money Income and Marital Status: 65+

	All Units					Married Couple				
	Total	5000	5000-9999	10000-19999	> 20000	Total	< 5000	5000-9999	10000-19999	> 20000
$ 1-2499	7.9	24.8	4.2	3.7	4.8	3.9	28.6	3.3	2.6	4.0
$ 2500-4999	30.3	74.9	32.6	14.4	12.3	11.3	67.1	20.2	6.4	9.7
$ 5000-9999	48.7	0.4	63.2	62.1	49.2	53.7	3.3	76.8	57.1	43.2
$10,000--->	13.1	0.0	0.0	19.8	33.7	30.9	1.0	0.0	33.9	43.1
Median $ Income	5,740	3,420	5,390	7,200	8,310	8,470	3,450	6,590	9,030	9,340

Table 2.6
Poverty and the Mature

Total Income Below Poverty Line

	Ages 55-61	Ages 62-64 All Units	Ages 65+
Below poverty level	12%	14%	15%
Below 125% poverty level	16%	19%	25%

Live with Other Family Members

	Ages 55-61	Ages 62-64 All Units	Ages 65+
Below poverty level	9%	12%	10%
Below 125% poverty level	14%	16%	17%

Live with No Family Members

	Ages 55-61	Ages 62-64 All Units	Ages 65+
Below poverty level	15%	15%	16%
Below 125% poverty level	19%	21%	27%

Table 2.7
Top Ten States According to Percentage of Population 65+

Rank	% of Population 65+ 1980	% Increase 1980-1984	% of Population 65+ 1984
1. Florida	17.3	14.4	17.6
2. Arkansas	13.7	7.4	14.3
3. Rhode Island	13.4	8.7	14.3
4. Iowa	13.3	5.9	14.1
5. Missouri	13.2	5.3	13.6
6. South Dakota	13.2	5.8	13.6
7. Nebraska	13.1	4.8	13.4
8. Kansas	13.0	5.6	13.3
9. Pennsylvania	12.9	9.5	14.1
10. Massachusetts	12.7	6.9	13.4

Source: U.S. Bureau of the Census, Decennial Census of the Population, "Estimates of Population of States, by Age: July 1, 1981-83," Current Population Reports, Series P-25, No. 95. "State Population Estimates by Age and Components of Change: 1980-1984," Current Population Reports, Series P-25, No. 970.

18

Table 2.8
Top Ten Chronic Conditions for Mature Persons (Rates Per 1000 Persons)

	Condition	Ages 45-64	Ages 65+
1.	Arthritis	276.2	495.8
2.	Hypertension	245.7	390.4
3.	Hearing	142.7	299.7
4.	Heart Conditions	136.8	256.8
5.	Orthopedic Impairment	139.0	168.5
6.	Sinusitis	179.1	151.7
7.	Visual Impairment	53.4	101.1
8.	Diabetes	57.6	88.9
9.	Varicose Veins	64.1	77.7
10.	Arteriosclerosis	21.5	73.6

Source: National Center for Health Statistics. 1981 National Ambulatory Medical Care Survey. Reported in U.S. Senate Special Committee on Aging. Aging America. 1984, p. 88.35

Table 2.9
Ten Leading Causes of Death by Older Age Groups (Rates Per 100,000 Population in Specific Groups)

Causes of Death	55-64	65-74	75-84	85+
All Causes	1298	2885	6330	15048
Diseases of the Heart	469	1156	2801	7342
Malignant Neoplasms	440	825	1239	1599
Cardiovascular Diseases	59	194	675	2001
Accidents and Adverse Effects	37	51	104	256
Chronic Obstructive Pulmonary	42	131	236	278
Pneumonia and Influenza	16	48	183	748
Diabetes	26	60	125	212
Suicide	17	17	20	18
Chronic Liver Disease and Cirrhosis	37	40	31	18
Arteriosclerosis	5	21	103	563

Source: National Center for Health Statistics, Advance Report of Final Mortality Statistics, 1982, vol. 33, no. 9; December 20, 1984.

19

Table 2.10

Percent of the 65+ Population in the Community with ADL* Limitations

Age/Sex	Mildly Disabled	Disabled	Severely Disabled	**Instrumentally Disabled	Total
65-74	4.2	1.8	2.1	4.5	12.6
Male	3.4	1.7	2.4	4.2	11.7
Female	4.7	1.9	1.9	4.8	13.3
75-84	9.0	3.6	4.5	7.9	25.0
Male	6.5	2.5	4.6	7.1	20.9
Female	10.3	4.3	4.4	8.5	27.6
85+	17.4	7.8	10.4	10.2	45.8
Male	15.7	7.7	7.5	9.9	40.8
Female	18.2	7.9	11.8	10.3	48.2
All 65+	6.6	2.8	3.5	6.0	18.9
Male	5.1	2.3	3.3	5.4	16.0
Female	7.7	3.2	3.6	6.4	20.9

* ADL - Activity of Daily Living Limitation Score
** Needs assistance with the instrumental activities of daily living.

Source: Tabulations from the 1982 "Long-Term Care Survey" prepared by the Center for Demographic Studies, Duke University. Reported by Soldo, Beth J. and Manton, Kenneth G., "Health Service Needs of the Oldest Old, Health and Society," Mibank Memorial Fund, Quarterly (Spring 1983), 55-60.

Table 2.11

Marital Status of Persons 65+

	Men	Women
Married	78%	40%
Widowed	14%	50%
Single (never married)	5%	6%
Divorced	3%	4%

Source: AARP, A Profile of Older Americans 1985.

20

Table 2.12
Living Arrangements of Persons 65+ (Noninstitutionalized)

	Men	Women	Men	Women
	Family Setting			
Living with Spouse	76%	38% --	83%	57%
Living with other Relatives	7%	.19% --		
	Nonfamily Setting			
Living Alone or with Non Relatives	17%	43%		

Source: AARP, <u>A Profile of Older Americans 1985</u>.

Table 2.13
Average Annual Expenditures: 1980-1981

Expenditure	Ages 55-64		Ages 65+	
	Dollars	%	Dollars	%
Food	3,375	19	2,215	21
Housing	4,678	27	3,577	33
Transportation	3,575	20	1,706	16
Health Care	874	1	1,048	10
Personal Insurance/Pensions	1,460	8	322	3
Other	<u>3,515</u>	25	<u>1,886</u>	17
Total	17,477		10,754	

Source: <u>Aging America, Trends and Projections, 1985-86</u>, p. 63.

21

Table 2.14
Weekly Expenditures of Urban Consumer Units by Age and Income before Taxes: 1982-1983

			Income Level					
Ages 55-64	Total	<5000	5000-9999	10000-14999	15000-19999	20000-29999	30000-39999	40000-Over
Personal Care Product/ Services	$ 5.46	1.98	2.52	3.80	3.41	5.27	8.87	10.69
Non-Prescription Drugs/Supplies	2.46	.84	1.20	.99	2.33	3.77	3.36	3.55
Ages 65+								
Personal Care Products/ Services	$ 4.01	2.06	3.19	4.74	4.19	6.58	6.58	8.93
Non-Prescription Drugs/Supplies	2.26	.76	2.40	2.80	2.80	3.72	1.02	2.36

Source: Consumer Expenditure Survey: Diary Survey, 1982-83, U.S. Dept. of Labor, Bureau of Statistics, February 1986, p. 30

CHAPTER 3

The Study

INTRODUCTION AND STATEMENT OF THE PROBLEM

The number of people 65 years old and older in the United States is currently 24.6 million or 11.2% of the population (U.S. Department of Commerce 1980). This 65 + group has been growing at twice the rate of the population as a whole (Brotman 1977) and is projected to reach 230.6 million by the year 2000 (Fowles 1975). Furthermore, it is evident that the discretionary income of this group is substantial. While the potential of the mature consumer segment is obvious, only recently has significant research been conducted on this group of consumers.

Articles in the marketing literature by Bartos (1980), Gelb (1978), Lambert (1979), Lumpkin and Greenberg (1982), Mason and Bearden (1978a; 1978b), Reinecke (1964), Schiffman (1971), and Tongren (1976; 1981), as well as by many others, have been extensively cited, analyzed, and criticized. The findings are for the most part based on samples of limited size, restricted geographic area, or an ill-defined definition of "the elderly." Nonetheless, these studies have responded selectively to interests among marketers with respect to the older members of the population and to that group's potential as a viable market segment. A number of issues raised by previous research remain unresolved but retain many implications for marketing strategy.

Some of the issues are:

1. Who constitutes the "elderly" group in the population? The conventional onset of old age appears to be 65, probably because, beginning in the 1930s, one could retire with full benefits at that age. Do those 65 and older differ in needs, attitudes, perceptions, and behaviors from those under 65?

2. Do mature consumers constitute a homogeneous group with similar wants, needs, attitudes, perceptions, and behaviors? Or do mature consumers consti-

tute a heterogeneous group depending on whether they are a member of the "young" old or "old" old, the poor old or the affluent old, the ill old or the well old? Do these criteria distinguish across groups with respect to differentiating wants, needs, attitudes, perceptions, and behaviors?

3. What does this group (or these groups) seek from retailers during their shopping activities? What are their expectations with respect to attributes such as location, service, price, merchandise quality, and selection?

Given such issues, a pressing need becomes apparent for comprehensive research on the behavior of the mature consumer in the marketplace, on the problems particular to this group, and on which needs should form the basis for consumer programs targeted to the mature consumer (Schneider 1976).

The attitude held by mature consumers toward various retail institutions, as well as practices by these retailers, may indicate the need for educational programs and/or additional protective regulations. For example, Waddell (1975) reported the most frequent complaint received at the National Consumer Assistance Center in 1974 dealt with mail order companies' failure to provide goods or services as promised. Waddell also points out that the NRTA-AARP survey indicated that the most prevalent problems encountered by mature consumers are often associated with deceptive sales practices and mail order selling. A recent book by Ostroff (*Capturing the Mature [Age 50+] Market: How to Prosper in an Aging America*, Prentice-Hall, 1988) does an excellent job of characterizing the mature market and providing guidelines for successfully marketing to the mature consumer segment. Accordingly, the most important research topics on older consumers revolve around "wise buymanship," including comparative shopping, sales resistance, and mail order purchasing.

Bearden and Mason (1979) offer evidence that mature consumers experience widespread dissatisfaction in their buying experiences, and that most of the people who are dissatisfied never complain. Mason and Bearden (1981) further report mature consumers tend to be less assertive with respect to complaining behavior and that people such as consumer educators, public policy formulators and business executives should be wary of reported incidents of dissatisfaction as representative of the total amount of dissatisfaction among older consumers. They call for the development of a representative information base from which policies can be designed to address this important issue.

The research reported here investigated the shopping behavior of the mature consumer with respect to direct marketing and direct selling, two major subsets of in-home shopping. The focus included the various physical, economic, social, and psychological needs of the mature consumer when shopping. This research will help determine how well the needs of the mature consumer are being met by in-home shopping. Perceptions held by mature consumers concerning various in-home shopping vehicles are used to provide an assessment of the strengths and weaknesses of direct marketers in meeting the mature consumer's needs and can be used as the basis for establishing consumer programs for the mature consumer.

In general, the behavior of consumers in the marketplace is dependent upon the type of product being purchased. For example, the mature consumer (or any consumer segment) will have differing needs when shopping for clothing vis-à-vis food. Thus, research should be conducted in light of specific product categories. For this research project, product categories were defined by level of financial risk and were represented by selected product category items that are frequently purchased via in-home shopping.

METHODOLOGY

The purpose of this section is to describe the process that was used to collect the data for the study. First, a section on the sample will be presented, followed by information on the questionnaire.

Sample

The research reported here was based on a cross-sectional, self-administered mail survey. The incidence of purchase through direct marketing for any individual over a reasonable time period would be expected to be relatively low. That is, during any given three-month period, most mature consumers would have shopped frequently at grocery and drug stores as well as department and discount stores. They were less likely to have exposure to or to have shopped via direct marketing or direct selling. Consequently, to obtain a sample that would contain sufficient numbers of those who had shopped in-home to compare with those who had not shopped in-home, a large initial sample was required.

A perhaps more important issue regarding sample size is the ability to generalize the findings to the mature population as a whole. The scope of previous research on the mature consumer has been rather limited. Relatively small (generally 100 or less) samples from one city or one rest home or retirement home within a city have, in the main, been used. Lambert (1979) did use four Standard Metropolitan Statistical Areas (SMSAs) as a sample frame, but he limited his study to Florida. To date, the only attempts to develop a sample that could be generalized to mature consumers throughout the nation have been Lumpkin and Greenberg (1982), Lumpkin, Greenberg, and Goldstucker (1985), Lumpkin (1984), Lumpkin (1985a), Lumpkin (1985b), and Lumpkin and Caballero (1985).

Another limitation of prior research is the exclusive focus on the mature consumer. Studies that are limited to profiling mature consumers' attitudes without comparison to other age groups are of questionable value at best. Martin (1975), Bernhardt and Kinnear (1975), and the research cited above by Lumpkin and his colleagues, are exceptions. The comparison of the mature consumer to other age groups to determine *when* and *why* changes occur is required to increase existing knowledge in any meaningful way with respect to the mature consumer. As Phillips and Sternthal (1977) reported: marketers know much about the purchasing power of the mature consumer and the products that they purchase, but little is known about how older persons develop different strategies to influence their consumption behavior.

This study utilized a representative national probability sample which, consequently, did not concentrate on one small "captive" mature consumer group. Rather, the population was defined to include all "active" mature consumers and other, younger, consumers. This population definition is deliberately biased to exclude members of the general population who are not active shoppers and consumers.

A disproportionate, stratified sample design was used to reach a national sample of 4,000 consumers which included both men and women. By *not* concentrating on one "captive" mature consumer group, the sample allows regional comparisons. The sample was not representative in that the mature consumer (65 and older) was disproportionately sampled. The 21-54 and 55-64 age groups were also sampled for comparison purposes. Of particular interest is the 55-64 age group because of its relative affluence and because it is often lumped together with the 65 + group as the "Gray Market." A ratio of 60 percent (the mature consumer group), 20 percent, and 20 percent for these three groups was used in specifying the sample. This stratification scheme was selected to provide adequate representation of the younger and preretirement groups.

A major problem in conducting consumer research on the mature consumer is finding an appropriate and *representative* sample frame. Membership lists of organizations to which the mature belong cannot necessarily be construed as containing representative consumers nor are they generally available on a national basis. A more viable method was to sample one of the national consumer mail panels available commercially. These panels maintain a nationally representative (based on census data) pool of over 200,000 households who have agreed to respond to questionnaires periodically. Consequently, the response rate and response quality is much higher than that available from other methods of sample development. Researchers can specify various demographic, socioeconomic, and geographic characteristics. The sample is then randomly drawn from those who meet the established criteria.

Since consumer panels are typically recruited through a female household head, provisions were made to include male members of panel households through a request on the cover letter. The strata were to be as representative of the national population as possible, given the limitations of total sample size and the nature of panel membership.

Most mail surveys with consumer panels are subject to some biases. Lower-income and poorly educated members of the general population tend to be underrepresented. This bias also leads to relatively poor participation among underprivileged groups in society, such as certain ethnic minorities. Although there is no evidence to suggest that an age bias exists in terms of willingness to participate on panels, reduced activity in the consumer role appears to result in little representation of the severely handicapped and the "frail" elderly. The foregoing biases are problematic for general population studies, but the sample frame that remains is quite appropriate for consumer studies of the type attempted in this project. The one bias that does lead to some potential frame error in this study is overrepresentation of single-family dwellings and married households. Both of these factors result from recruiting strategies employed by the panel companies. When alternative sample frames are considered, however, these potential biases are quite acceptable.

Mail panels for research on the mature consumer have been used with excellent results in three separate projects cited above by Lumpkin. The mature consumer respondents obtained were generally representative of the national mature population with the exception of the low-income elderly, the institutionalized elderly, and, for the most part, the old-old or frail elderly. The nature of the consumer mail panel requires a relatively active and economically viable individual; an appropriate response group when conducting research on the marketplace behaviors and needs of the mature consumer. The poor elderly or those in institutions are, of course, not viable candidates for direct marketing anyway. Thus, this research cannot be generalized to the *total* mature population but is representative of a large and important subgroup—those who must and do interact in the marketplace.

The sample, drawn from the Market Facts Consumer Mail Panel, was specified as follows:

Age	Percentage of Sample
21-54	20
55-64	20
65 and older	60

Then with each age group:

Population Density	
Rural/Urban (2,500-50,000)	37
SMSA (50,000-500,000)	37
SMSA (500,000 and larger)	26

Sex/Marital Status

Single Male	11
Single Female	11
Married Female	50
Married Male	28

All other sociodemographic variables including geographic region were balanced to national norms. The specifications provide a disproportionate random sample that specifically includes both male and female, married and unmarried, urban and rural, and all age groups. Such sociodemographic specifications allow cross-group comparisons that have largely been unavailable in previous research.

Of the 4,000 questionnaires sent, responses were obtained from 2,699 consumers; 2,527 (63 percent) were usable. This response rate compares favorably with previous research of this type. This demographic composition of respondents can be found in Appendix A, Figure A.1. Other than the frame biases discussed earlier, no particular bias is attributed to nonresponse.

Purchase Behavior

As will be discussed in Chapter 4, a wide variety of products were purchased through direct marketing modes by our sample of respondents. The table below indicates that the average number of orders and the percent of our sample who ordered varied consistently by direct-marketing mode. The average price per order was highest for in-home demonstrations. However this mode received only a small percentage of total orders.

	Average Number of Orders Per Respondent (Last 6 Months)	Percentage Respondents Who Ordered	Average Price Per Order
Department Store Catalogue	.78	34.5	$ 66
Specialty Catalogue	.80	35	$ 48
Direct Mail	.26	15	$ 58
Media Ad	.14	8	$ 60
Telephone Solicitation	.04	3	$ 34
Door-to-Door	.13	6	$ 61
Party Plan	.21	14	$ 30
In-Home Demonstration	.09	6	$211

Focus Groups

Six focus groups consisting of mature consumers were conducted as exploratory work for the development of the questionnaire. To obtain some diverse geographic representation, two each were conducted in Waco, Texas; Portland, Oregon; and Chapel Hill, North Carolina. At each location, separate focus groups were conducted for those who had purchased via direct marketing or direct selling during the previous six months and for those who had not. Both men and women were included in each of the six focus groups.

These focus groups were deemed quite successful in providing direction for the questions that were ultimately used in the questionnaire. They also suggested additional areas worth investigating that fall under the general rationale guiding this project. As a result of using three geographic regions coupled with the fact that as we progressed through the focus groups the same comments began to recur, we believe that we have obtained both representative and valid information.

Pretest

After the focus groups were conducted and analyzed, an initial questionnaire was developed for a pretest. The pretest, administered during August, 1986, randomly sampled 1,000 consumers. The sample was obtained from R. L. Donnelly and incorporated an equal number of respondents from eight major urban areas—Atlanta, Boston, Chicago, Dallas, Los Angeles, New York, Phoenix, and San Francisco. While not representative of the total population, the pretest sample provided some geographic representation on a national basis. Because the major objective of the pretest was to evaluate the survey instrument, the sample was judged adequate.

The pretest instrument was administered on Baylor University letterhead and without incentive or follow-up. Of the 1,000 sent, 365 responses were received. Given that such mailing lists generally have an estimated annual attrition rate of 20 percent, the actual response appears to be quite good.

Based on the evaluation of the pretest results as well as on the focus groups, the final questionnaire was developed. Among the major changes were a new slate of products to test specific willingness to purchase, the expansion of the psychographic inventory to include other relevant dimensions, the addition of a perceptual comparison of all shopping modes, and the deletion of the isolation and disengagement scales.

Survey Instrument

The Market Facts Consumer Mail Panel supplied information concerning location, residence type and ownership, income, and household size and composition for households in the sample. They also provided education, occupation, age, sex, and marital status information on each respondent.

The questionnaire obtained actual purchase behavior with respect to various direct-marketing and direct-selling sources. In addition, three products ranging from low price, low involvement to high price, high involvement were suggested to determine relative willingness to purchase these representative products from direct marketing vis-à-vis the "usual" *retail* outlets. Preferred sources for these products were also assessed. The questions allow the categorization of respondents into behavior/attitude groups for correlation with other attitudinal measures. Comparisons between exhaustive paired combinations of purchasing sources were included to help determine consumers' perceptual placing of each source vis-à-vis other sources. Questions were also asked pertaining to likes and dislikes associated with in-home shopping.

The instrument addresses various characteristics of direct marketing as to desirability and importance. These were developed both from experience and previous research. To date, no research has been conducted that asks mature consumers directly what they like or do not like about direct marketing nor what aspects are most desirable and important to them. Respondents were asked to evaluate in-home purchasing sources and to indicate the degree to which these sources are associated with certain positive benefits that consumers desire with respect to the shopping experience. Subjects were asked not only what their actual experiences have been, but also how they perceive the purchasing sources. These questions will give insight into the perceived advantages and disadvantages of various in-home shopping sources.

Respondent attitudes toward in-home shopping and toward salespeople who come into the home were obtained. Additional questions measured risk, ability to be satisfied, credibility, general satisfaction, selection, quality, and time convenience. Also included were questions measuring various psychographic constructs that deal with attitudes toward shopping as well as correlates that likely impact direct-marketing purchasing and attitudes. These include activity, mobility, health, and locus of control of the elderly.

CHAPTER 4

Buying Patterns of the Mature Consumer

In this chapter patronage behavior of the mature consumer will be examined by measuring the number of different purchases, typical price per purchase, and the types of products purchased for each of the direct-selling and direct-marketing modes. This will allow comparisons between alternatives and provide insight as to the number and types of products that are being purchased in-home. Such information will help direct sellers and direct marketers establish or fine tune their product offerings.

PREVIOUS FINDINGS

Martin (1975) found the mature consumer generally shops less and enjoys shopping less than other age groups, although the elderly tend to shop around more to get the best price (Mason and Bearden 1978a). Other research suggests that mature consumers shop for recreation and exercise (Mason and Smith 1974).

This study found that mature consumers rely on in-home shopping services to only a limited extent in purchasing. The primary sources of product information utilized were personal observation in terms of physical search and the newspapers. Clothing and household-furnishing purchases were primarily made in the central business district. For respondents in this study shopping appeared to be a major part of their lifestyle and provided more of a pleasure than a burden (Mason and Smith 1974).

Lumpkin and Greenberg (1982) reported the results of a study examining the apparel-shopping patterns of the mature consumer. Overall, older people tend to shop less frequently than their younger counterparts. The mature consumers, like all other age groups, shop most often at department stores and, consequently, more often at department stores than discount stores, as found by Bernhardt and Kinnear (1975). The mature consumers were also found to shop more often at specialty stores than at discount stores, as is *not* the case for the other age groups. These findings also substantiate the assumption that mature consumers do not use in-home shopping to a greater extent than younger consumers (Mason and Smith 1974; Mason and Bearden 1978a). While in-home shopping is used least by all age groups, mature consumers' use of mail or phone orders is significantly less than other age groups.

Thus, the role that shopping plays in the lives of the mature consumer is not yet clear. It does seem that shopping itself is a major source of purchase information. If the information search and the recreational aspects of shopping are borne out by research, there will be many opportunities for retailers, individually and collectively (i.e., malls, downtown shopping areas), to provide for the elderly through such inducements as special events and special shopping days, transportation to central shopping areas, information booths, and rest areas, as well as to provide a mix of products or stores that are needed by the mature consumer (Bellenger, Robertson, and Greenberg 1977).

USER CATEGORIES

In this study user categories are created by cross-tabulating those respondents who have made at least one direct-marketing purchase in the past six months with those who have made at least one direct-selling purchase in the past six months. These categories include all of the direct-marketing and direct-selling modes mentioned in the study (see Table 4.1).

Only 34 percent (n = 863) made *no* purchases via direct selling or direct marketing, while 61 percent made at least one purchase via direct marketing. However, users were much less likely to have purchased via direct selling—only 21 percent. Further, 75 percent of the users of direct selling are also direct-marketing users. Another way of looking at these user categories is that although only 5 percent used only direct selling, 45 percent used direct marketing only. This shows that consumers are far more likely to use direct-marketing modes for in-home shopping than they are to incorporate direct-selling modes into their buying behavior. The implications for direct-selling organizations are clear: Resistance to direct selling as a shopping vehicle must be addressed in order to expand market share and to continue to grow as an industry. The implications for direct marketers are less compelling. While direct marketers have done well in gaining acceptance for their industry among shoppers, there is still a large segment of the population (39 percent) who do not use direct-marketing modes. Reaching these consumers would add considerably to potential markets for industry firms.

AGE VERSUS USER CATEGORIES

In order to evaluate differences in user modes with respect to age—mature consumers versus younger consumers—a cross-tabulation was performed for those aged 65 and above versus those below age 65. The importance of investigating the mature consumer market with respect to direct selling/marketing is graphically portrayed by the findings. Although 66 percent of respondents were 65 +, of those making at least one direct-selling purchase, only 53 percent were 65 +. Therefore, fewer mature consumers are making purchases from direct sellers than are their younger counterparts. Further analysis also shows that actually only 17 percent of mature consumers are currently purchasing from direct sellers while 29 percent of younger consumers are making such purchases. Consequently, the data suggests a willingness to buy on the part of the mature consumer that is proportionately lower than would be expected compared to the general population, and the percentage of mature consumers that is actually being reached is rather small. However, these 17 percent represent heavy users of direct selling and should be studied carefully to gain insights into reaching other members of their age group.

With respect to direct marketing, 61 percent of those making at least one direct-marketing purchase were in the 65 + group. This finding is in the same direction as that of direct selling (i.e., smaller than the sample representation). However, 56 percent of mature consumers have purchased using direct marketing (compared to 17 percent for direct selling). This finding indicates direct-marketing modes have achieved far more acceptance among mature consumers than have direct-selling modes. It will be the purpose of this study to unfold some of the reasons for the differences in acceptance and usage of direct marketing and direct selling. It is hoped that further insights into how the mature consumer differs from the younger consumer will enable both direct marketers and direct sellers to better serve the mature consumer market. In many cases, the 50-64 age segment will also be examined, since this group is frequently lumped together with the 65+ age group as the mature market.

Table 4.2 shows a breakdown of the five categories of items most frequently purchased through direct marketing and direct selling. The most frequently purchased category is clothing followed by household items/ hardware, entertainment/electronics/business items, miscellaneous, and finally, personal items.

As can be seen from Table 4.3, different product categories are more popular depending on which shopping mode one is considering. Not too surprisingly women's apparel is the product most frequently purchased through department store catalogues, and Tupperware is the most frequently purchased product through party plans and the second most frequently purchased product category overall.

Women's apparel followed by Tupperware dominates direct marketing sales as has already been seen in Table 4.2 and Table 4.3. Other categories of frequently purchased products include men's apparel, shoes, cosmetics/toiletries, and interior decoration. The ten categories shown in Table 4.4 represent only about 37 percent of total purchases, leaving a huge variety of item categories unaccounted for. It is becoming apparent that almost any conceivable product can be sold through direct marketing or direct selling if the proper product design, packaging, pricing, and promotional tools are used.

FREQUENCY OF PURCHASE BY AGE AND MODE

In this section products representative of various modes of in-home shopping are further broken down by the ages of the purchasers. The top product categories in each mode are generally reflective of the reality of that type of mode. For example, that clothing is most often sold through catalogues reflects the historic precedent for selling clothing through catalogues. Also, the characteristics of the mode enhance presentation of certain product characteristics; for example, high-quality color reproduction enhances the presentation of clothing in catalogues.

A comparison of Tables 4.5, 4.6, and 4.7 indicates that the Clothing/Accessories category remained relatively constant across age groups. The Household Items/Hardware category was roughly comparable in both catalogue categories across age groups. However, the ≤ 49 age group was less likely to purchase these items from direct mail than were either of the older age groups.

Further, in the direct mail mode as well as the advertisement and telephone solicitation mode, the ≤ 49 age group was more likely to purchase Entertainment/Electronic/Business Items than any other item category.

Household Items/Hardware and Personal Items are the most frequently purchased categories. For all age groups, personal items are the category most frequently purchased door-to-door. Personal Items and Household/Hardware tie in the 50-64 age group in the In-Home Demonstration category. Otherwise, Household/Hardware are most frequently purchased by all age groups in the Party Plan and In-Home Demonstration categories.

The data reported in Table 4.11 show a consistent decrease in the percentage of respondents who made direct-marketing purchases as the eye moves from department store catalogues to telephone solicitation. For direct-selling modes, the party plan generated the most overall orders, and door-to-door generated the fewest on 1-2 orders across all age groups. For 3 + orders, in-home demonstrations generated the fewest orders in the ≤ 49 and 50-64 age groups, while party plans generated the fewest for the 65 + age group.

WILLINGNESS TO PURCHASE

Barnes and Peters (1982) examined buyer behavior relative to four retail modes: mail, door-to-door, telephone, and retail stores. The highest use was expressed in purchasing selected products in a retail store. Following this mode of distribution in popularity was mail, door-to-door, and telephone. Thus, telephone buying was apparently perceived as the least desirable by the mature consumer sample. In an earlier study (Cox and Rich 1964), the purchase of goods by telephone was found to have high perceived risk. The results of the study indicated that older consumers generally have low buying-rates for any products or services sold over the telephone, even if telephone solicitation is a convenient mode of distribution for this segment.

Bernhardt and Kinnear (1975) found older shoppers used department stores more and discount stores less and used credit cards less than other age groups. However, these findings were not related to any specific product category which reduces their usefulness. In the case of apparel, Lumpkin and Greenberg (1982) also found the mature consumer to use credit less and shop discount stores less, but found no difference between age groups with respect to department store patronage. They report mature consumers tend to shop less frequently than their younger counterparts. On the other hand, Barnes and Peters (1982) note mature consumers tend to shop at retail outlets less frequently for a variety of product categories, and they utilized telephone shopping the least of any age group. Convenience was found to be a significant factor in choosing a method of purchase.

It was also found by Lumpkin and Greenberg (1982) that the mature consumer tended not to use in-home shopping for apparel via mail or phone ordering more or less than other age groups. This result was reported earlier by others (Mason and Smith 1974; Mason and Bearden 1978b) and is especially significant as the results do not seem to support the notion that as mobility decreases with age and transportation becomes an important problem (Sherman and Brittan 1973; Gelb 1978; Lambert 1979) the mature consumer would use mail or phone ordering more. The use or lack of use of this shopping method would seem a fruitful area of inquiry. It has been suggested that in-home shopping is related to perceived risk (Cox and Rich 1964; Spence, Engel, and Blackwell 1970). Thus, determining the amount and type of risk perceived by mature consumers and the most promising types of risk reduction strategies for this group would be beneficial in helping direct marketers develop in-home shopping programs specifically for the mature consumer.

While actual purchase is a more desirable measurement than intentions to purchase, using recall over long time periods to measure purchase (i.e., twelve months) may create accuracy problems. Likewise, too short a period (i.e., last month) may not be representative of "usual" behavior.

Consequently, a six-month time reference was used in this research. Even so, the purchase incidence of a random sample for direct selling and direct marketing may or may not be typical. Therefore, this analysis will couple the actual purchase with stated "willingness" to purchase from each of the direct-selling and direct-marketing alternatives as well as from a retail outlet.

General willingness, however, can be misleading. For comparison, willingness must be associated with specific product(s). The problem is, which product(s)? This study used three different types of products: Hand tools or kitchen utensils ($8-$10), cosmetics and fragrances ($25-$50), and a set of luggage ($200-$350). These were chosen as typical products available from direct sellers, direct marketers, and retailers that both men and women would purchase. Further, the products range from low price/low involvement to high price/high involvement.

Tables 4.12 through 4.15 compare willingness to purchase across the four "user" categories for each shopping mode by age group and by product category. In general, it can be seen that willingness to purchase from traditional retail outlets was higher across all age groups and product categories than willingness to purchase via any of the in-home buying modes. This finding held for all user categories. While these findings are not surprising, they do indicate that direct marketers and direct sellers have a long way to go before their distribution systems will be as widely accepted as the traditional retail store.

Another question to consider is whether willingness and actual purchasing behavior are related. If so, one would expect that those who purchased by direct selling only, for example, would be *more* willing than other groups to purchase products from direct-selling modes. In general, this hypothesis was upheld. Users of direct selling were more willing to purchase again via direct selling than were direct-marketing purchasers or those who had done no in-home purchasing. Again, this finding held across age groups and product categories. As might be expected the willingness of those who had purchased from *both* direct-marketing and direct-selling modes was most closely identified with direct-selling purchasers. In some cases, purchasers from the "Both" user category were the most willing of all four user categories to purchase again via direct selling.

Similar findings held for willingness to purchase from direct-marketing modes. In general, those who had purchased from both modes were the most willing to buy via direct marketing again. Although there were some exceptions to this finding among the ≤ 64 age groups, there were no exceptions in the $65 +$ age group.

The same findings occurred among those who had made purchases from direct marketing only. Their willingness to buy was second only to users of both, and none of the exceptions occurred among the $65+$ age group. Those who had made no purchases via either direct marketing or direct selling were, as expected, the least likely to buy, although it must be pointed out they were also the *least* favorable toward traditional retailers.

It should also be mentioned that all groups tended to score on the less willing end of the scale for all product categories and age groups. The only mode that showed consistent acceptance was the department store catalogue in the Hand Tool/Kitchen Utensil category. Other modes showed limited acceptance among certain product categories and user groups. For example, specialty catalogues fared better among "Both" purchasers and among direct-marketing purchasers in the Hand Tool/Kitchen Utensil category. Party plans were reasonably well-accepted for the same product category among "Both" users and direct-selling users. Telephone solicitation as a direct marketing mode received extremely poor scores across product categories, age groups, and user categories, which is certainly in keeping with previous research.

Table 4.1
Cross-tabulations of Direct-Marketing and Direct-Selling Purchases

		Direct-Marketing Modes		
		Purchased	No Purchase	Total
Direct-Selling	Purchased	397	135	532
Modes	No Purchase	1120	863	1983
	Total	1517	998	2515

User Mode	Category Total	Category Percentage
Direct Marketing	1120	45%
Direct Selling	135	5%
Both Modes	397	16%
Neither Mode	863	34%
Total Direct Marketing	1517	61%
Total Direct Selling	532	21%

Table 4.2
Percent of Sales of Five Product Categories
Direct Marketers/Sellers

Product Category	Percent of Sales
Clothing	35%
Household Items/Hardware	31%
Entertainment/Electronics/ Business	13%
Miscellaneous	13%
Personal Items	8%

Table 4.3
Top Product Categories in Each Shopping Mode

Direct Mode	Product	% Sigma Purchases in Mode
Department Store Catalogue	Women's Apparel	33%
Specialty Catalogue	Women's Apparel	25%
Direct Mail	Women's Apparel	11%
Media Ad	Records/Tapes	17%
Telephone Solicitation	Magazines	25%
Door-to-Door	Food	13%
Party Plan	Tupperware	37%
In-Home Demonstration	Cosmetics/Toiletries	31%

Table 4.4
Overall Top Ten Product Categories with Shopping Modes

1.	Womens' Apparel: Department Store Cataglogue	9.7%
2.	Women's Apparel: Specialty Catalogue	7.2%
3.	Tupperware: Party Plan	4.3%
4.	Men's Apparel: Department Store Catalogue	3.7%
5.	Shoes: Department Store Catalogue	2.2%
6.	Cosmetics/Toiletries: Door-to-Door	2.1%
7.	Interior Decorations: Department Store Catalogue	2.0%
8.	Shoes: Specialty Catalogue	1.9%
9.	Other: Specialty Catalogue	1.9%
10.	Men's Apparel: Specialty Catalogue	1.8%

Table 4.5
Direct-Marketing Purchasers Aged ≤49* and the Product Percentages[1]

	Department Store Catalogue	Specialty Catalogue	Direct Mail	Advertisements	Phone Solicitation
Clothing/Accessories	64**	44	30	7	0
Household Items/Hardware	27	21	16	19	5
Personal Items	1	4	3	9	0
Entertainment/Electronic/ Business	4	15	38	53	55
Miscellaneous	4	16	13	12	40
Number of Purchases Reported	177	151	67	43	20
Top Two Product Categories					
Women's Apparel	39	28	9		
Men's Apparel	12	7			
Books			19		25
Magazines				19	25
Records/Cassette/ Tapes/Disks				16	

*
Only those who had made one or more purchases from direct-marketing mode.

**
Read: Of the age ≤49 respondents who purchased from any direct-marketing mode, 177 purchased from department store catalogues and 64 percent of this 177 bought Clothing/Accessories.

***
Does not equal number of orders because reflects typical product and not all respondents completed this section even though they reported purchases.

---

[1]All numbers in table are percentages except those following number of purchases reported.

39

Table 4.6
Direct-Marketing Purchasers Aged 50-64* and the Product Percentages[1]

	Department Store Catalogue	Specialty Catalogue	Direct Mail	Advertisements	Phone Solicitation
Clothing/Accessories	59**	42	30	8	0
Household Items/Hardware	31	22	32	10	0
Personal Items	2	6	3	3	0
Entertainment/Electronic/ Business	3	7	20	55	67
Miscellaneous	5	23	15	24	33
Number of Purchases*** Reported	172	164	60	38	3
Top Two Product Categories					
Women's Apparel	38	26	8		
Men's Apparel	10		8		
Tools/Auto Parts		9			
Records/Cassette/ Tapes/Disks			8	24	
Magazines				21	33
Books					33
Tickets					33

*Only those who had made one or more purchases from direct-marketing mode.

**Read: Of the age 50-64 respondents who purchased from any direct-marketing mode, 172 purchased from department store catalogues and 59 percent of this 172 bought Clothing/Accessories.

***Does not equal number of orders because reflects typical product and not all respondents completed this section even though they reported purchases.

[1]All numbers in table are percentages except those following number of purchases reported.

40

Table 4.7
Direct-Marketing Purchasers Aged 65 + and the Product Percentages[1]

	Department Store Catalogue	Specialty Catalogue	Direct Mail	Advertisements	Phone Solicitation
Clothing/Accessories	58[**]	45	35	11	7
Household Items/Hardware	33	19	25	20	25
Personal Items	2	4	6	10	6
Entertainment/Electronic/ Business	4	12	23	44	29
Miscellaneous	3	20	11	15	33
Number of Purchases Reported	457	489	204	116	31
Top Two Product Categories					
Women's Apparel	30	24	12		
Men's Apparel	14				
Shoes		8			
Jewelry/Watches			8		
Records/Cassette/ Tapes/Disks				16	
Magazines				11	23
Food					13

[*] Only those who had made one or more purchases from direct-marketing mode.

[**] Read: Of the age 65+ respondents who purchased from any direct-marketing mode, 457 purchased from department store catalogues and 58 percent of this 457 bought Clothing/Accessories.

[***] Does not equal number of orders because reflects typical product and not all respondents completed this section even though they reported purchases.

[1] All numbers in table are percentages except those following number of purchases reported.

41

Table 4.8
Direct-Selling Purchasers Aged $\leq 49^*$ and the Product Percentages[1]

	Door-to-Door	Party Plan	In-Home Demonstration
Clothing/Accessories	3**	8	0
Household Items/Hardware	28	68	61
Personal Items	35	13	31
Entertainment/Electronic/ Business	15	7	6
Miscellaneous	19	10	2
Number of Purchases*** Reported	29	107	36
Top Two Product Categories			
Cosmetics/Toiletries	35		31
Sweeper/Vacuum Cleaners	14		14
Tupperware		35	
Interior Decorations		20	14

* Only those who had made one or more purchases from direct-selling mode.

** Read: Of the age ≤ 49 respondents who purchased from any direct-marketing mode, 29 purchased from door-to-door and 3 percent of this 29 bought Clothing/Accessories.

*** Does not equal number of orders because reflects typical product and not all respondents completed this section even though they reported purchases.

[1] All numbers in table are percentages except those following number of purchases reported.

Table 4.9
Direct-Selling Purchasers Aged 50-64* and the Product Percentages[1]

	Door-to-Door	Party Plan	In-Home Demonstration
Clothing/Accessories	8 **	3	0
Household Items/Hardware	21	75	44
Personal Items	42	3	44
Entertainment/Electronic/ Business	16	2	4
Miscellaneous	13	17	8
Number of Purchases*** Reported	26	67	27
Top Two Product Categories			
Cosmetics/Toiletries	42		44
Food	15		
Tupperware		43	
Interior Decorations		9	15
Glassware/Dishes/Silverware		9	
Seasonal/Holiday Decorations		9	
Sweeper/Vacuum Cleaner			15

*
Only those who had made one or more purchases from direct-selling mode.

**
Read: Of the age 50-64 respondents who purchased from any direct-marketing mode, 26 purchased from door-to-door and 8 percent of this 26 bought Clothing/Accessories.

***
Does not equal number of orders because reflects typical product and not all respondents completed this section even though they reported purchases.

[1]All numbers in table are percentages except those following numbers of purchases reported.

43

Table 4.10
Direct-Selling Purchasers Aged 65+* and the Product Percentages[1]

	Door-to-Door	Party Plan	In-Home Demonstration
Clothing/Accessories	1**	7	3
Household Items/Hardware	20	68	60
Personal Items	48	9	27
Entertainment/Electronic/ Business	11	1	0
Miscellaneous	20	15	10
Number of Purchases*** Reported	75	151	60
Top Two Product Categories			
Cosmetics/Toiletries	47		27
Food	12		
Tupperware		36	
Interior Decorations		13	
Sweeper/Vacuum Cleaner			22

*Only those who had made one or more purchases from direct-selling mode.

**Read: Of the age 65+ respondents who purchased from any direct-marketing mode, 75 purchased from door-to-door and 1 percent of this 75 bought Clothing/Accessories.

***Does not equal number of orders because reflects typical product and not all respondents completed this section even though they reported purchases.

[1]All numbers in table are percentages except those following number of purchases reported.

44

Table 4.11
Direct-Marketing and -Selling Purchase Profiles by Age Group

	<49				50-64				65+			
	Number of Orders			Average	Number of Orders			Average	Number of Orders			Average
	0	1-2	3-	Price	0	1-2	3+	Price	0	1-2	3+	Price
Department Store Catalogue	37%	38%	25%	$76	42%	33%	25%	$64	48%	37	15	$63
Specialty Catalogue	44	38	18	58	43	37	20	54	41	41	18	42
Direct Mail	74	20	6	41	77	17	6	78	76	20	4	58
Advertisement	83	14	3	24	86	12	2	77	86	11	3	69
Phone Solicitation	92	8	0	24	97	2	1	17	96	3	1	46
Number (Base)*	289				306				922			
Door-to-Door	78%	15	7	84	71	19	10	44	70	28	7	62
Party Plan	25	59	16	37	28	64	8	26	40	57	3	28
In-Home Demonstration	74	25	1	175	70	24	6	185	74	22	4	254
Number (Base)*	151				100				281			

*Those in each age category who had made one or more purchases from a direct-marketing or direct-selling mode.

Table 4.12
Mean[1] Willingness to Purchase across Mode and Age Groups for Three Product Categories: *Direct-Selling* User Category[2]

	Hand Tools or Kitchen Utensils			Cosmetics and Fragrances			Luggage		
	<49	50-64	65+	<49	50-64	65+	<49	50-64	65+
Department Store Catalogues	2.41	2.42	2.41	3.25	3.57	3.44	3.00	3.00	3.58
Specialty Catalogues	3.16	3.61	3.27	3.95	4.05	3.87	3.66	3.90	4.01
Direct Mail	3.79	3.80	4.16	4.08	4.33	4.34	4.37	4.33	4.48
Advertisements	3.70	4.04	4.26	4.20	4.38	4.43	4.33	4.38	4.50
Phone Solicitation	4.54	4.71	4.93	4.62	4.71	4.89	4.70	4.66	4.90
Door-to-Door	4.04	3.95	4.20	4.12	3.71	4.03	4.54	4.14	4.44
Party Plan	2.20	2.57	2.81	2.41	2.71	2.98	3.75	3.28	3.78
In-Home Demonstration	3.37	3.19	3.08	3.25	3.33	3.03	4.00	3.61	3.62
Retail	1.25	1.23	1.55	1.68	1.33	1.84	2.00	1.42	2.05

[1]Based on a five point scale from Very Willing (1) to Very Unwilling (5).

[2]Those who have made purchases from direct-selling modes only.

Table 4.13
Mean[1] Willingness to Purchase across Mode and Age Groups for Three Product Categories: *Direct-Marketing* User Category[2]

	Hand Tools or Kitchen Utensils			Cosmetics and Fragrances			Luggage		
	<49	50-64	65+	<49	50-64	65+	<49	50-64	65+
Department Store Catalogues	2.07	1.97	2.11	3.05	3.30	3.26	2.98	3.32	3.21
Specialty Catalogues	2.56	2.73	2.97	3.43	3.70	3.83	3.22	3.75	3.80
Direct Mail	3.56	3.62	3.75	4.19	4.15	4.18	4.26	4.19	4.24
Advertisements	3.68	3.97	3.95	4.21	4.32	4.33	4.33	4.35	4.41
Phone Solicitation	4.68	4.86	4.83	4.76	4.90	4.88	4.75	4.92	4.90
Door-to-Door	4.36	4.56	4.49	4.39	4.57	4.55	4.58	4.76	4.71
Party Plan	3.16	3.61	3.68	3.29	3.82	3.82	3.93	4.22	4.21
In-Home Demonstration	3.83	3.82	3.75	3.83	3.94	3.89	4.09	4.17	4.15
Retail	1.43	1.39	1.52	1.74	1.72	1.92	1.93	1.92	2.13

[1]Based on a five-point Scale from Very Willing (1) to Very Unwilling (5).

[2]Those who have made purchases from direct-marketing modes only.

Table 4.14
Mean[1] Willingness to Purchase across Mode and Age Groups for Three Product Categories: *Both* User Categories[2]

	Hand Tools or Kitchen Utensils			Cosmetics and Fragrances			Luggage		
	<49	50-64	65+	<49	50-64	65+	<49	50-64	65+
Department Store Catalogues	2.04	1.93	1.73	3.08	3.24	3.15	2.82	3.12	3.07
Specialty Catalogues	3.07	2.94	2.81	3.60	4.05	3.76	3.53	3.83	3.61
Direct Mail	3.65	3.38	3.63	4.01	4.16	4.12	4.15	4.18	4.19
Advertisements	3.85	3.68	3.72	4.25	4.28	4.24	4.30	4.39	4.30
Phone Solicitation	4.71	4.81	4.72	4.75	4.89	4.76	4.82	4.90	4.81
Door-to-Door	4.42	4.18	4.07	4.34	3.94	3.96	4.63	4.51	4.54
Party Plan	2.36	2.57	2.82	2.45	2.84	3.06	3.47	3.83	3.83
In-Home Demonstration	3.38	3.38	3.20	3.31	3.40	3.27	3.88	3.90	3.78
Retail	1.44	1.28	1.37	1.60	1.79	1.85	1.99	2.11	2.05

[1]Based on a five-point scale from Very Willing (1) to Very Unwilling (5).

[2]Those who have purchased from both direct-marketing and direct-selling modes.

Table 4.15
Mean[1] Willingness to Purchase across Mode and Age Groups for Three Product Categories: *Neither* **User Category[2]**

	Hand Tools or Kitchen Utensils			Cosmetics and Fragrances			Luggage		
	<49	50-64	65+	<49	50-64	65+	<49	50-64	65+
Department Store Catalogues	2.60	2.43	2.62	3.30	3.48	3.67	3.05	3.54	3.65
Specialty Catalogues	3.37	3.40	3.50	3.86	4.02	4.12	3.63	4.01	4.12
Direct Mail	4.05	4.07	4.17	4.32	4.37	4.48	4.41	4.46	4.50
Advertisements	4.14	4.05	4.28	4.42	4.37	4.50	4.50	4.40	4.59
Phone Solicitation	4.78	4.75	4.78	4.88	4.84	4.86	4.84	4.84	4.88
Door-to-Door	4.46	4.40	4.49	4.55	4.52	4.54	4.71	4.68	4.67
Party Plan	3.37	3.58	3.73	3.82	3.84	3.92	4.00	4.19	4.24
In-Home Demonstration	3.69	3.83	3.81	3.83	3.99	3.96	3.98	4.18	4.15
Retail	1.65	1.50	1.74	2.01	1.99	2.18	2.01	2.10	2.29

[1]Based on a five-point scale from Very Willing (1) to Very Unwilling (5).

[2]Those who made no purchases from direct-marketing or direct-selling modes.

47

CHAPTER 5

Determinants of the Patronage Decision: In-Home vs. In-Store

The analysis will determine the importance of various attributes as mature consumers decide how and where to purchase and whether direct-selling modes (i.e., door-to-door, party plan, in-home demonstration), direct-marketing modes (i.e., catalogues, direct mail, telephone solicitation, media ads), or in-store shopping provides the desired attributes. However, establishing only the perceptions of these potentially desirable attributes will yield inconclusive results. That is, although direct selling may be perceived to have a particularly desirable attribute, if all alternative modes of purchase *also* have that attribute, then direct selling will not have an advantage, and the attribute will not be *determinant* in the patronage decision.

Consequently, the analysis will evaluate direct-selling modes as well as direct-marketing modes and retail outlets on twenty-two attributes. How each mode is perceived vis-à-vis the alternatives will be determined for both *users* and *nonusers*.

Because the twenty-two attributes may not encompass all possible factors considered, open-ended questions dealing with specific likes and dislikes will provide additional insight from those who use each mode compared to those who do not.

IMPORTANCE OF TRAITS BY AGE

We first look at the importance of various purchasing characteristics across three age groups (≤ 49, 50-64, 65 +). Each of five broad characteristics—convenience, selection, economics, knowledge of store/product, and risk reducers—is further broken down into specific items that relate to particular dimensions of that characteristic (see Table 5.1). Results pertaining to the characteristic "Selection" indicate no significant differences were found between the three age groups with respect to the importance of any of the three "Selection" items. All dimensions were seen to be of relatively high importance with "wide selection" the single most important for all three age groups.

"Convenience" encompasses eight scale items. The most significant difference was found with respect to the ability to charge a purchase, which was less important for the 65 + age group than for the other two groups. For the ≤ 49 age group, "convenience of access" ($p < .01$) and "access to a salesperson" were less important than for the other two groups.

For the 65 + group, the ability to charge is probably less important for a couple of reasons. First, this group formed their shopping patterns before the use of credit was as widespread as it is today. Second, they also generally do not anticipate an increase in income and thus may be less likely to commit tomorrow's income for today's purchases.

It is understandable that convenient access would be of less concern to younger age groups (≤ 49), since they have more mobility than older individuals. The younger age group has also grown up with more self-service shopping outlets than did the older age groups and is consequently less likely to feel the need for sales assistance.

For the characteristic "risk reducers," only two dimensions elicited differences on the basis of age. In both cases, it was the 65 + group who attached more significance ($p < .001$) to well-known companies and their brands. As mentioned in Chapter 4, the mature consumers appear to be risk avoiders, but they only differ from other groups on these two dimensions with respect to the importance of risk reducers that can be attached to a given buying mode. However, it should be noted that, with the exceptions of the "no obligation trial period" dimension, all of the risk reducers scored fairly high in importance for all groups.

For "knowledge of store product," all five dimensions are of some importance to all three age groups. However, the 65 + age group attached significantly ($p < .001$) more importance to previous experience with the brand, the product, and the company with which they are doing business.

No differences between groups were found for the two dimensions related to the purchase characteristic "economics." It should be noted that the means for each group on both dimensions indicate that these dimensions fall between somewhat important and very important to respondents.

Across all the purchase dimensions, the highest means for all three groups were associated with "getting what I ordered without substitution," "money-back guarantee," "availability of information about the product," and "wide selection" in that order.

IMPORTANCE OF TRAITS BY USER GROUPS

The four user groups examined in this section are as follows: direct-selling users only, direct-marketing users only, users of both direct marketing and direct selling, users of neither direct marketing nor direct selling.

"Selection" dimensions are again examined. Not surprisingly, users of neither mode were significantly ($p < .001$) less interested in the ability to get products not readily available in stores. Yet this same group ranked wide selection as a very important characteristic. It seems that they only associate a wide selection of products with traditional retailing outlets.

Additionally, direct-selling users were more likely ($p < .01$) to value availability of first and second choice. This dimension was of least interest to direct-marketing users. Such a finding is not too surprising since the products sold through direct-selling channels are practically always available, while direct marketers frequently suffer out-of-stock conditions.

The importance of various "Convenience" dimensions varied across the four groups. It is surprising that direct-selling users found delivery direct to the home or workplace less important ($p < .01$) than did other groups. The convenience of in-home delivery has been a prominent selling point for many direct-selling companies. It may be that this aspect of shopping is of less consequence to direct-selling users than was previously thought. Direct-marketing users and users of both feel that ability to decide in-home was more important ($p < .001$) than did the other two groups. Again, while this tendency is not surprising, it is notable that the in-home convenience aspect is of significantly less consequence to direct-selling users.

The "availability of cash on delivery (C.O.D.)" was of much less importance to all four groups than were some of the other convenience dimensions, such as "delivery direct to home/workplace" and "access to a salesperson." However, direct-selling users and users of neither found this benefit to be more important than did the other two groups. The option of not paying for the merchandise until it arrives (and, presumably, is inspected) may explain the lack of usage of direct marketing as a shopping vehicle for these two groups.

Finally, "having the product right away" was less important ($p < .01$) for direct-marketing users than for other groups. This dimension was most important for users of neither, which would help explain their reluctance to use nontraditional shopping modes. It is also worth noting that the least important dimension over all groups is the repeated solicitation at home. Apparently regular in-home service is not a particularly desirable shopping benefit for most consumers.

Purchasing a well-known brand from a well-known company was less important ($p < .001$) for users of both and more important for nonusers. This result makes sense given few direct-selling and direct-marketing brands and companies receive the widespread media exposure that brands and companies receive who are marketed through traditional distribution channels. While such companies as Avon and Tupperware have done some television and magazine advertising in recent years, these companies do not represent the norm for the direct-selling industry. Similarly, most of the large cataloguers and direct-marketing houses rarely, if ever, employ the major mass media for advertising. (The few exceptions deal mainly in television direct response.)

The "ability to examine the product before purchasing" was more important ($p < .001$) for both nonusers and direct-selling users. Since not being able to examine the product at the time of purchase is a characteristic of direct marketing, it is not surprising that this dimension is of less importance to the direct-marketing users and to users of both. This would also help explain why samples are of less importance ($p < .001$) to direct-marketing users.

Among "risk reducers," the "no obligation trial period" was of much less importance than the other dimensions for all groups. While this benefit is often stressed by direct sellers and direct marketers, its value to the customer is of far less magnitude than the value of the other risk reducers.

No significant differences occurred between user groups for either "knowledge" or "economics" dimensions. However, all of these dimensions scored "somewhat important" or higher on the rating scale, indicating their relative importance to shoppers of all groups.

IMPORTANCE OF SHOPPING CHARACTERISTICS BY USER AND AGE

Table 5.1 summarizes the findings that pertain to the importance of the five shopping characteristics (and their individual items) by user and age groups. This table provides more detail on the significant differences reported earlier in this chapter. For this analysis the sample was divided into twelve user groups, described at the top of Table 5.1.

With respect to the "convenience" characteristic, the 65+ direct-marketing users rated the "ability to decide on a purchase in my home" to be of more importance than did the 65+ nonuser group. However, the 65+ and 50-64 nonuser groups felt that C.O.D. was more important than did any of the direct-marketing user age groups. These findings with respect to convenience reinforce what appears to be a critical difference between the user and nonuser groups. Users like the convenience of purchasing in-home, while nonusers see it as an inconvenience because of the inability to examine the merchandise before committing to buy.

The only "selection" dimension with a significant difference has to do with the "ability to get products not readily available in the stores." This dimension was more important to 65+ direct-marketing users than to 65+ nonusers, a finding that one must recognize as intuitively obvious. However, it is interesting that these results are confined to the 65+ age group. This benefit may be one that has special appeal for 65+ users.

No differences between groups were observed for the "economics" characteristic. However, several differences are shown for the "knowledge" characteristics. Previous experience with the product was more important for 65+ users of both than for ≤49 users of both. This result may actually have to do with the mature consumer's aversion to risk, if one can consider previous experience as a factor in reducing the chances of disappointment. Previous experience with a company was less important for ≤49 direct-selling users than for many of the other groups, including all of the 65+ age groups and all of the users of both. This group may be among the most innovative of all the groups identified in the study. Certainly a lack of experience with a company implies some willingness to try a new experience.

Under the characteristic "risk reducers," it can be seen that the ≤49 users of both differ from several groups with respect "to well-known name brand," including all of the 65+ age groups. This dimension was of less importance to the ≤49 users. The same finding held for "well-known company," although fewer groups saw this dimension as more important than did the ≤49 user group. It is not surprising that the younger age group would assign less importance to some risk-reducing dimensions. Nor is it surprising that this group would also be representative of users of both methods of nontraditional shopping.

With respect to the ability to examine the product before purchasing, the ≤49 direct-marketing users assigned less importance than did the 65+ nonusers. Additionally, all three age groups of direct-marketing users saw this dimension as less important than did the 50-64 group of nonusers. Given the inherent nature of this dimension to direct marketing, it is reasonable that such a finding should be observed.

DEGREE TO WHICH DIRECT MODE HAS TRAITS

Age Group By User Group

Tables 5.2 through 5.10 show which traits are associated with a given shopping mode according to a respondent's age and usage category. For example, in Table 5.2, department store catalogues are the shopping mode of interest. Many of the traits—numbered 1 through 22 in the table—show no differences between groups. Item number ten is such a trait: "Order delivered when promised." No one age and/or user group was more apt than another to associate this trait with department store catalogues.

However, with respect to some of the other traits, differences between groups were observed. Older users of direct marketing and of both were more likely than elderly nonusers to believe that specialty store catalogues make "credible product claims" and that they make "accurate portrayals of products." They were also more likely to believe in "consistent order quality." These two older groups were also more likely than the ≤49 nonusers to believe that department store catalogues have "credible product claims" and that they "provide sufficient information about products." Generally, as expected, the older nonuser was the least likely to ascribe positive traits to department store catalogues. The 65+ user was more likely than the 65+ nonuser to associate money-back guarantees with the catalogues as well as the traits "delivery direct to home/workplace," "ability to charge purchase," and "capability of buying several things at same time." In each of these cases, it appears that there is a need for educating the 65+ nonusers as to some of the more beneficial characteristics of department store catalogue shopping.

Other groups were also more favorable such as the ≤49 groups on "ability to charge purchase" and the ≤49 user of both on "order filled in a timely manner" and "capability of buying several things at same time."

Table 5.3 shows the association of the 22 traits with specialty catalogues. The 65+ direct-marketing users show significantly more inclination than the 65+ nonusers to assign traits 1, 6, 8, 9, 15, 17, 19, and 22 to specialty catalogues. These traits cover a variety of shopping characteristics—from "order filled in a timely manner" to "ability to get products not readily available." Such a finding suggests a reluctance to use specialty catalogues may stem not from a disadvantage to the mature consumer that is inherent in the shopping mode itself, but rather a lack of experience with specialty catalogues on the part of this particular group.

The only other group that showed up with some consistency was the 65+ direct-selling users who were less likely than most of the other groups to associate the "ability to make exchanges" with specialty catalogues. They were also less likely than the ≤49 direct-marketing users and ≥49 users of both to believe that specialty catalogues provide a "number to call with complaints and questions." Finally, they were less likely than the 65+ direct-marketing users, the ≤49 users, and the 65+ nonusers to attribute "money-back guarantees" to specialty catalogues.

Table 5.4 deals with direct mail, and few differences between groups were found. The 65+ nonuser was less likely than the 65+ direct-marketing user to believe that direct mail has "delivery direct to home/workplace." The only other significant differences were observed with respect to item 19, "ability to charge purchase." Age 65+ direct-selling users were less convinced of this trait than almost every other group. Age 65+ nonusers were less convinced than any of the direct-marketing users, the 50-64 and the ≤49 users of both, and the ≤49 direct-selling users and the ≤49 nonusers. It can be seen that, in general, the 65+ age group is less convinced of the ability to charge purchases than the other groups. The ability to charge purchases is a benefit that direct mail marketers should emphasize to the mature market.

In Table 5.5 the traits associated with purchasing through media ads are considered. As in direct mail, differences between groups are apparent for only a few of the traits. The only truly significant findings are again associated with trait 19, "ability to charge purchases." All four 65+ groups were less likely to associate this trait with media ad purchases than were some of the other groups.

Telephone solicitation, another direct-marketing mode, is examined in Table 5.6. Age 65+ direct-marketing users were less likely than the 50-64 nonusers to attribute "provide sufficient information about product" and "company pays for call/postage when ordering" to telephone solicitation. Similarly, the 65+ direct-marketing users differed from 65+ nonusers with respect to "quality consistent from one order to next." The ≤ 49 group was more likely than several groups to attribute "company pays for call/postage when ordering" to telephone solicitation, but there was no discernible pattern to the groups involved. As with direct mail and media ads, the elderly were less likely to associate charge purchases with telephone solicitation.

Table 5.7 deals with door-to-door solicitation, a direct-selling mode. The most striking finding here was the consistency with which 65+ direct-marketing users were less likely than some other groups to associate the traits with door-to-door. The following traits showed significant differences between the 65+ direct-marketing users and at least some other groups: traits 1, 2, 3, 5, 7, 9, 10, 13, 14, 16, 19, 20, and 21. Additionally, respondents—particularly the older consumers—again failed to associate "ability to charge purchase" with the shopping mode.

Table 5.8 deals with party plans as a shopping mode. The 65+ direct-marketing users again showed a reluctance to assign positive traits to this shopping mode. Significant differences occurred with respect to *all* of the traits except numbers 15, 16, and 19.

Ages 50-64 and ≤ 49 users of both were more apt to recognize "credible product claims" associated with party plans. They were also in agreement concerning "wide selection," "good quality products," and a variety of other traits. In general, all of the users of both categories were fairly positive toward party plans. Users of neither, particularly the 65+ group, were less favorable on a number of traits such as "accurate portrayal of products" and "fills order requests accurately."

In-home demonstrations are the subject of Table 5.9. The 65+ direct-marketing users are less likely to associate many of these traits with in-home demonstrations. As might be expected, direct-selling users tend to be the most positive. However, as we have already seen, the 65+ direct-marketing users seem to be a particularly critical group of direct-selling modes.

Table 5.10 addresses retail selling which, for the purposes of this study, is used as a comparison base for all the other shopping modes. However, it may be surprising that agreement between groups is not as consistent here as it was with some of the other shopping modes. Younger (≤ 49) nonusers are less likely than most of the other groups to associate "credible product claims" with retail shopping. These shoppers may be more sophisticated retail shoppers, or they may be less easily satisfied regardless of shopping mode.

It may be seen that the "ability to charge purchase" (trait 19) was again viewed as less likely by the 65+ group (except for the 65+ direct-marketing users) even for retail shopping.

LIKES AND DISLIKES

Catalogue Users versus Nonusers

Table 5.11 shows a summary of the ranking of characteristics of in-home shopping that are liked by the mature consumer. The four most liked characteristics are "convenience," the option of "seeing and discussing the product" with sellers, "nothing" (that is, these respondents liked nothing about in-home shopping), and the ability to shop at "leisure." These rankings hold across the nonuser, light-user, and heavy-user categories with exception of the reversal of 3 and 4 in the heavy-user category.

The characteristics that were least often cited as being what respondents liked about in-home shopping were "guarantees" and "benefits of being a hostess" for nonusers, "low prices" and "benefits of being a hostess" for light users of catalogues, and "party plans" and "benefits of being a hostess" for heavy users of catalogues. Such findings suggest that in-home shoppers do not necessarily enjoy all forms of in-home shopping. Certainly the heavy catalogue user appears to be a poor target for party-plan selling. It is also interesting, since this is a selling point that in-home sellers generally stress, that nonusers have little interest in guarantees (see Table 5.11).

From Table 5.12 we find that the three 65+ user groups generally agree on what they dislike most about in-home shopping: "high pressure sales" and "risk from shopping by picture." The latter dislike was true even of heavy catalogue shoppers. Interestingly, the third most important dislike for heavy users was "waiting for delivery." Nonusers and light users were less likely to see waiting time as a negative. This finding suggests that expedited shipments may be an important selling point with heavy catalogue users. It further verifies something that direct mail marketers have long known about mail order shoppers—that products that are ordered by mail are highly anticipated by purchasers.

The least disliked characteristics of in-home shopping were similar for all three categories. All groups feel little "pressure to have parties," fear of "damaged goods," or "lack of personal contact," and few object to the fact that they "tend to buy more than they need." While there is a slight tendency for nonusers and heavy users to miss shopping, no such tendency exists for light users.

Nonusers are less likely to dislike "postage/handling costs" than are either of the user groups, while nonusers and light users are more likely to object to "higher prices." Generally, however, there is a high degree of correspondence between nonusers and the two user groups as well as between the three groups and the 65+ age group.

All catalogue user age groups rank the "convenience" of in-home shopping as their most-liked in-home shopping characteristic. The two younger groups like the "leisure" of in-home shopping next best, and the two older groups ranked the opportunity of "seeing/discussing the product" as their second most-liked characteristic. Interestingly, shopping at "leisure." These rankings hold across the nonuser, light-user, and heavy-due to a high number of retired persons in this group there is less time-pressurized shopping, and so the need for leisure shopping is less pronounced (Table 5.13).

"Hostess benefits" was the least liked characteristic among all catalogue users. Again, this signifies that although this group does engage in one form of in-home shopping (i.e., catalogue shopping), they are not necessarily favorably disposed toward other forms (e.g., party plans). Note that party plans generally ranked low among all groups. The youngest age group was the most favorable toward party plans.

For all age categories of catalogue users (Table 5.14) "high pressure sales" and the "uncertainty of shopping from pictures" ranked highest among respondents' dislikes.

There were a few other notable differences across the age groups with respect to what they disliked about in-home shopping. The 35-49 age group was far less likely than the other groups to feel obligated to buy, but they were more likely than any other group (more than twice as likely as all users) to object to "nonstandard clothing sizes and fit" as a characteristic of in-home shopping. However, as a whole this group has fewer objections.

Only the 65+ age group made any note of missing out on the shopping experience by using in-home shopping. Apparently, the social and/or recreational aspects of shopping are important to some members of this group.

Direct Mail Users versus Nonusers

All the mature shoppers ranked "convenience" as the aspect of in-home shopping that they liked best. However direct mail users, interestingly enough, felt that "seeing the product" was what they liked most about in-home shopping, although convenience ran a close second. However many users also claimed to like "nothing" (ranked number three) about in-home shopping, an opinion that is obviously at variance with their stated behavior (Table 5.15). As with catalogue shoppers, direct mail users ranked hostess benefits very low as did the nonusers and all older groups.

As might be expected, direct mail users saw a "lack of variety" in in-home shopping as less of a problem (ranked fifth) than did all the 65+ group or the 65+ nonuser group (ranked third). However, all three groups agreed in ranking "high pressure sales" as the most disliked characteristic and "not being sure of what you will get" as second most disliked. In general, direct mail users disliked in-home shopping less than did the other two groups but were in agreement with respect to ranking "pressure to have parties," "damaged products," and "no personal contact" among the least disliked attributes.

As might be expected, none of the direct mail users disliked "missing the shopping experience" which was mentioned by a few in the other two groups. One of the biggest discrepancies between groups was that direct mail users found in-home shopping to be far more inconvenient (ranked sixth) than did either the nonuser group (ranked sixteenth) or the 65+ group (ranked fifteenth). Perhaps 65+ users are more sensitive to inconvenience because through use of direct mail shopping they have been exposed to it more often than nonusers. However, users were also nearly twice as likely to say they disliked nothing about in-home shopping than were nonusers.

Older users of direct mail differed from younger users in that they ranked "seeing the product" as what they liked most about in-home shopping. Younger users ranked "convenience" first, and older users ranked it second. Younger users ranked the ability to shop at "leisure" second (Table 5.17). Older users (12.37%) were more likely than the younger users (8.59%) to say that there was "nothing" about in-home shopping that they liked. However, younger consumers were also more likely than the older consumers not to mention "party plans," "guarantees," and "hostess benefits" as characteristics that they liked in in-home shopping.

With respect to dislikes, all groups ranked "high-pressure sales" as their number one dislike. Being "not sure of what you will get" ranked second, and "delivery time" ranked third in terms of most disliked. Least disliked for mature consumers were "pressure to have parties" and "unfamiliar companies." Younger consumers cited "boring sales pitches" and "junk mail" less frequently (in fact, not at all) as what they dislike.

"Higher prices" were cited twice as often by the younger group as by the older group, and the older groups were far less likely (3.02%) than either the younger (9.52%) or the all users groups (5.54%) to dislike "return hassles" connected with in-home buying (Table 5.18).

Media Ads Users versus Nonusers

As can be seen from Table 5.19, users and nonusers of media ads were very much in agreement with respect to what they liked and did not like about in-home shopping. Ranking in first, second, and third place respectively for all three groups were "convenience," the opportunity to "see the product," and "nothing." As usual, "hostess benefits" ranked at the bottom for all three groups with "guarantees," "seeing new products," and "low prices" also ranking low for all three groups. Additionally, none of the users saw party plans as a positive benefit associated with in-home shopping.

The two attributes that were most disliked about in-home shopping were the same for all mature shoppers and nonusers and users of direct response media advertising. These were "high pressure sales" (ranked first) and "not being sure of what you would get" (ranked second). More users (9.48%) cited "interruptions" as something that they disliked than did nonusers (6.42%) or the all-elderly group (6.69%). With this exception, other high-ranking dislikes were much the same across the three groups (Table 5.20).

Users failed to cite a number of attributes as being disliked. These include "pressure to have parties," "damaged products," "lack of personal contact," missing shopping," "sales representative missed the appointment," and "unfamiliar companies." All of these objections were cited by small percentages from the mature shoppers and from the nonuser groups. It would seem then that users of direct response media advertising generally have fewer objections to in-home shopping, but the objections that they do have are cited as often by the user group as by the other two groups.

All three groups, as shown by Table 5.21 mentioned "convenience" and "home demonstrations" as the attributes they most liked about in-home shopping. However, older consumers were far more likely (13.51%) to say they liked "nothing" about in-home shopping than were the younger groups (4.82%) or the all user group as a whole (9.79%). More of the younger group valued "shopping at leisure" (12.05%) than did older consumers (8.11%). Again this is probably a reflection of the fact that the older consumers have a great deal of leisure, perhaps more than they want.

There were several attributes that very few users cited as an aspect of in-home shopping that they liked. These include "party plans," "low prices," "delivery," "name brands/familiar companies," and a "personal touch." Although these characteristics also ranked low with older consumers, the "personal touch" was mentioned more often by them (5.41%) than by the younger group (1.20%).

While all age groups disliked "high pressure sales" (Table 5.22), the older group was more likely to dislike being "unsure of what they were getting" (19.83%) than was the younger group (13.10%). The older group was more likely to dislike "interruptions" (9.48%) than was the younger group (4.76%), and less likely to dislike "delivery time" (older 7.76%; younger 13.10%). The mature were also more likely to dislike "feeling obliged to buy" (6.90%) than were the younger shoppers (1.19%) who presumably found it easier to say "no."

The characteristics that older consumers failed to mention that they disliked include "no personal contact," "damaged goods," and "missing shopping activity." By contrast, those dislikes not cited by the younger consumers were "boring sales pitches," "junk mail," and "buying more than is needed."

Telephone Users versus Nonusers

Table 5.23 shows what users of telephone solicitation purchasing like most about in-home shopping. Both the younger (26.67%) and the older group (46.63%) specified "convenience" more than other attributes. Nonusers were equally enthusiastic about the opportunity to "see the product" as they were about convenience. However, the older group was less likely to cite seeing the product as a likeable characteristic (17.86%). Far more older consumers (14.29%) found "nothing" to like about in-home shopping than did the younger group (3.33%), but the younger consumers were more than twice as likely to mention "leisure" (16.67%) than were the mature (7.14%). Although 10 percent of the younger group mentioned that in-home shopping "saves travel time and expense," none of the older group mentioned this advantage of in-home shopping. Other attributes mentioned by the younger group but totally ignored by the older group include "party plans" and "variety." The only attribute that was of no interest to any of the younger telephone solicitation users was the opportunity to purchase "name brands from familiar companies."

There was also less agreement between the two groups of telephone solicitation users with respect to disliked attributes than there was for other direct modes. Although "high pressure sales" and "not being sure of what you are buying" ranked high for the younger group (20.69%) and the older group (19.35%), the older group was far more likely to object to "no variety" (19.35% vs. 3.45%). Conversely, the younger group was more likely to object to in-home shopping on the basis of "higher prices" (10.34% vs. 3.23%).

The older group (9.68%) disliked "solicitation" more than did the younger group (3.45%), but the younger group mentioned "postage/handling costs" (6.90%), "return hassles" (6.90%), and "feeling obliged to buy" (6.90%) while the older group did not. A few of the older groups (3.23%) also mentioned "interruptions," "strangers," and "inconveniences" (Table 5.24).

Table 5.25 shows that there are a number of in-home shopping attributes that telephone solicitation users failed to like. These include "saving travel time and expense," "product variety," "party plans," "delivery," "guarantees," "seeing new products," "low prices," and "hostess benefits." However, for users, "convenience" was high on their list of likes (46.43%)—even more than for nonusers (28.02%) who also ranked convenience first. Both nonusers and users liked "seeing the product" (21.53% and 17.86%, respectively) but, predictably, this was of less interest to the users.

Such findings square well with the nature of shopping by telephone. Certainly convenience would have to be of top priority, since many of the other benefits of in-home shopping would necessarily be lacking in this case.

Users disliked "high pressure sales," "not being sure of what they would get," and "no variety" equally. Nonusers were more likely than users to dislike "high pressure sales" (26.48%) but were less likely to dislike "not being sure of what they would get" (16.03%) and "no variety" (6.62%). Further "interruptions" were cited (6.78%) more often than "no variety" by nonusers, and "feeling obliged to buy" was mentioned by 6.30 percent.

Conversely, users were far more likely to object to "solicitation" and "invasion of privacy" (4.68% each) than were nonusers (2.87% and 2.31%, respectively). Additionally, users failed to mention disliking a number of attributes including "feeling obliged to buy," "return hassles," "boring sales pitches," "postage/handling costs," "nothing," "unfamiliar companies," "rep missed appointment", "junk mail", "tend to buy more than need," "miss shopping," "no personal contact," "damaged products," and "pressure to have parties" (Table 5.26).

Door-to-Door Users versus Nonusers

Both groups liked "convenience," "seeing the product," "nothing," and "leisure shopping" in that order. Nonusers (4.60%) were more likely than users (2.78%) to like "seeing what they got," but users (8.33%) were more likely than nonusers (4.01%) to value the "personal touch," a finding that was not too unexpected for users of direct selling. Users (8.33%) were also far more likely than nonusers (1.79%) to view "name brands/ familiar companies" as a plus. Users failed to mention "guarantees," "seeing new products," "low prices," and "hostess benefits," although there was at least a small mention of each of these among nonusers (Table 5.27).

With few exceptions, users and nonusers were in agreement concerning what they disliked about in-home shopping. "High pressure sales," "not sure of what they would get," "no variety," and "interruptions" ranked one through four, respectively. Nonusers were slightly more likely to object to "strangers" and "interruptions" than were users but, interestingly, users (5.63%) were more likely to dislike the "inconvenience" than were nonusers (1.40%). Additionally, a number of attributes were never cited negatively by the user group, including "solicitation," "invasion of privacy," "unfamiliar companies," "junk mail," "tendency to buy more than one needs," "missing shopping," "lack of personal contact," and "damaged products." However, users (1.41%) were more likely than nonusers (.16%) to dislike the "pressure to have parties" (Table 5.28).

The younger groups (39.34%) liked the "convenience" of in-home shopping even more than did the mature (26.39%), although both groups ranked this first. "Seeing the product" (25.00%) ranked second for the older shoppers, while "shopping at leisure" (21.31%) ranked second for the younger shoppers. The mature ranked all of the following equally (8.33%) and in a tie for third place: "shopping at leisure," "personal touch," "name brands/familiar companies," and "nothing." None of the younger respondents mentioned liking "nothing" or "delivery." None of the older mentioned liking to "see new products" (Table 5.29).

When comparing older users against younger users, some differences in ranking attributes emerged. "High pressure sales" was still disliked most by both groups, although the older group (26.76%) disliked it more than did the younger user (19.67%). The younger group (18.03%) ranked "delivery time" as the next most-disliked attribute; however the older group mentioned delivery time far less frequently (4.23%) and ranked it only seventh (Table 5.30).

Older users cited "no variety" (9.86%) as a disliked attribute with "interruptions" (8.45%) following closely on its heels.

The younger group made no mention of disliking "boring sales pitches," "postage/handling costs," "rep missed the appointment," or "pressure to have parties." However, the older group only failed to mention three attributes: "damaged products," "solicitation," and a "tendency to buy more than they needed."

The younger group (11.48%) was more likely to dislike "higher prices" than the older group (2.82%), but the mature (8.45% vs. 1.64%) expressed more dislike for "interruptions." Here again, the older group (7.04%) "felt obliged to buy" more often than the younger group (1.64%). Such pressure on those with lower incomes could easily have the effect of driving the older group away from in-home shopping.

Party Plan Users versus Nonusers

For users, "seeing the product" was the most liked attribute of in-home shopping. This is not too surprising since one of the great benefits of party plan shopping is the opportunity to examine products in great detail. Users also ranked "convenience" second and "leisure shopping" third in terms of what attributes they like most (Table 5.31).

Nonusers cited "convenience" as the most liked attribute, while "seeing the product" was cited next most often. Additionally, nonusers mentioned liking "nothing" about in-home shopping as their third-ranked attribute, while party plan users were only half as likely as nonusers to say they liked "nothing" about in-home shopping.

Interestingly, users failed to mention "hostess benefits" as a liked attribute, suggesting that such incentives hold little allure for the mature party plan user.

Table 5.32 shows that older users and nonusers were very much in agreement with respect to what they dislike about in-home shopping. "High pressure sales," "not being sure of what one will get," and "no variety" ranked one, two, and three, respectively, for both groups. Users also ranked "delivery time" and "feeling obliged to buy" along with "no variety." Apparently users may feel some ambivalence about some of the characteristics of in-home shopping even though they do choose to participate in party plans.

There were a few disliked attributes that were not mentioned at all by users. These include "rep missed the appointment," "junk mail," "missing shopping," "lack of personal contact," and "damaged products." Consequently, as expected, users tend to be generally more positive about in-home shopping than nonusers.

From Table 5.33 we note that the younger group is far more interested in "convenience" (33.91%) than is the older group (23.81%), but both groups ranked convenience high in terms of what they like about in-home shopping. For the older group, the most liked attribute is "seeing the product" with "convenience" ranking second and "leisure shopping" (13.61%) ranking third.

Table 5.34 shows the rankings of attributes of in-home shopping that are disliked. Both the groups agree that "high pressure sales," "not sure of what you get," and "delivery" are their highest-ranked dislikes.

The older group failed to mention either "damaged products" or "no personal contact" as disliked attributes; the younger group failed to mention "boring sales pitches" and "pressure to have parties."

In-Home Demonstration Users versus Nonusers

From Table 5.35, we note that both users and nonusers of in-home demonstrations rank "convenience" as the most-liked characteristic of in-home shopping. While nonusers ranked "seeing the product" as the second most-liked attribute (21.87%), the users ranked it equally with "convenience" (28.57%). Nonusers (16.07%) were more likely to like nothing about in-home shopping than were users (9.52%), but users and nonusers mentioned "leisure shopping" in roughly equal percentages (12.70% and 12.18%, respectively). None of the users mentioned "party plans," "delivery," "low prices," or "hostess benefits" as attributes that they liked about in-home shopping. On the other hand, all of the attributes were mentioned by at least some nonusers.

From Table 5.36 it can be seen that, as usual, "high pressure sales" and "not being sure of what they would get" ranked first and second for both users and nonusers. However, users (36.07%) mentioned "high pressure sales" far more often than did nonusers (25.82%), while nonusers (16.34%) mentioned "not being sure of what they would get" more often than users (11.48%) did. Nonusers disliked "no variety" (7.03%) and "interruptions" (6.86%) more than users (4.92% and 3.28%, respectively). However, both groups were close on the number of times "delivery time" and "feeling obliged to buy" were cited. It should be noted that nonusers had far more dislikes than users including such attributes as "unfamiliar companies" and "missed appointments."

Table 5.37 shows that both groups like "home demonstrations" almost equally, and this, not surprisingly, was the attribute of in-home selling liked most by both groups. Users of in-home demonstrations were the only group who ranked a specific characteristic of the in-home shopping mode that they use at the top of their list of liked attributes. "Convenience" ranked second for both groups (actually tied with first for the mature), but then some divergence can be noted.

The younger group (17.74%) was more likely to be interested in shopping at "leisure" than was the older group (12.70%). They (11.29%) were also far more likely to cite "personal touch" than the older group (1.59%). This is surprising given previous research findings (Lumpkin, Greenberg, and Goldstucker 1985) suggesting that the older consumers desire personal interaction with sales personnel.

The younger group (9.68%) was also more likely to mention "seeing what you buy" as a liked attribute than were the older consumers (3.17%).

In contrast, the mature were more likely to like "nothing" (9.52%) and "seeing new products" (4.76%) than were the younger consumers (1.61% for each attribute). The only in-home shopping attribute that was not mentioned by the mature was "delivery."

Table 5.38 provides information on various aspects of in-home shopping that are disliked by various groups. Both the younger respondents (46.03%) and the elderly (36.07%) mentioned "high pressure sales" first. Such high percentages on this attribute among in-home demonstration users may reflect past negative experiences with such salespersons.

The second most negative attribute was "not being sure of what they bought," "higher prices," and "delivery time." Although the two groups were fairly close on their rankings of most attributes, the mature (6.56%) mentioned "feeling obliged to buy" more often than the younger group (1.59%). The mature also mentioned "boring sales pitches" (4.92%), whereas the younger group failed to cite this attribute at all.

Table 5.1
Importance of Shopping Characteristics by User/Age Groups

Groups

1	+65	DM User		7	+65	Both
2	50-64	DM User		8	50-64	Both
3	$\leq$49	DM User		9	$\leq$49	Both
4	+65	DS User		10	+65	Neither
5	50-64	DS User		11	50-64	Neither
6	$\leq$49	DS User		12	$\leq$49	Neither

CONVENIENCE	Groups That Differ	How Groups Differ
Delivery direct to home/workplace	No difference	
Ability to decide on purchase in my home	1 differs from 10[a]	1 more important[b]
Availability of cash on delivery (C.O.D.)	1, 2, 3 vs. 10, 11	10, 11 more important
Ability to charge purchase	No difference	
Convenience of access (parking/traffic)	No difference	
Repeated solicitation at home	No difference	
Having product right away	No difference	
Access to a salesperson	No difference	

SELECTION		
Ability to get products not readily available in stores	1 differs from 10	1 more important
Wide selection	No difference	
Availability of first and second choice	No difference	

ECONOMICS		
Company pays for call/postage when you order	No difference	
Company pays for postage for returned goods	No difference	

KNOWLEDGE OF STORE/PRODUCT		
Previous experience with brand	No difference	
Previous experience with product	7 differs from 9	7 more important
Company recommended by friends/family	No difference	
Availability of information about the product	No difference	
Previous experience with company	6 differs from 1, 2, 4, 7, 8, 9, 10, 11	6 less important

RISK REDUCERS		
Money-back guarantee	No difference	
Well-known name brand	9 differs from 1, 4, 7, 10, 11	9 less important
Well-known company	9 differs from 1, 10, 11	9 less important
No obligation trial period	No difference	
Ability to examine product before purchasing	3 differs from 10; 1, 2, 3, vs. 11	10, 11 more important
Samples for evaluation of color, quantity, etc.	No difference	
Number to call with complaints/ questions	No difference	
Getting what I ordered without substitution	No difference	

---

[a] Group 1 differs from Group 10; all other groups are the same.

[b] For Group 1, ability to decide on purchase in my home is more important.

Table 5.2

Perception of Department Store Catalogues by User/Age Groups

Groups

1	+65	DM User	7	+65	Both
2	50-64	DM User	8	50-64	Both
3	$\leq$49	DM User	9	$\leq$49	Both
4	+65	DS User	10	+65	Neither
5	50-64	DS User	11	50-64	Neither
6	$\leq$49	DS User	12	$\leq$49	Neither

Trait	Groups That Differ	How Groups Differ
1. Credible product claims	(1, 2, 7, 9 vs. 12); (1, 7 vs. 10)[a]	12 less[b]; 10 less
2. Provides wide selection	(1, 9 vs. 10)	10 less
3. Good quality products	(1 vs. 10)	10 less
4. Price matches quality	(1 vs. 10)	10 less
5. Provides sufficient info. about products	(1, 7 vs 12)	12 less
6. Accurate portrayal of products	(1, 7 vs. 10)	10 less
7. Fills order requests accurately	(1, 7 vs. 6); (1 vs. 10, 12)	1 more; 7 more
8. Quality consistent from one order to next	(1 vs. 4, 10); (7 vs. 10)	1 more; 7 more
9. Order filled in timely manner	(6 vs. 1, 9); (10 vs. 1)	6 less; 10 less
10. Order delivered when promised	No difference	
11. Competitive prices	No difference	
12. Money-back guarantee	(1 vs. 10)	1 more
13. Well-known brand name	No difference	
14. Company pays for call/ postage when ordering	No difference	
15. Delivery direct to home/ workplace	(1 vs. 4, 10)	1 more
16. Company pays postage for returned goods	No difference	
17. Ability to get products not readily available	(1, 10 vs. 12)	12 less
18. Number to call with complaints/questions	No difference	
19. Ability to charge purchase	(1, 3 vs. 4); (1, 3, 9, 12 vs. 10)	4 less; .10 less
20. Availability of alteration and repair	No difference	
21. Ability to make exchanges	No difference	
22. Capability of buying several things at same time	(1, 9 vs. 10)	10 less

[a] Group 12 differs from groups 1, 2, 7 and 9; Group 10 differs from groups 1 and 7.

[b] Group 12 feels that department store catalogues have less credible product claims than do groups 1, 2, 7 and 9.

66

Table 5.3
Perception of Specialty Catalogues by User/Age Groups

Groups

1	+65	DM User		7	+65	Both
2	50-64	DM User		8	50-64	Both
3	$\leq$49	DM User		9	$\leq$49	Both
4	+65	DS User		10	+65	Neither
5	50-64	DS User		11	50-64	Neither
6	$\leq$49	DS User		12	$\leq$49	Neither

	Trait	Groups That Differ	How Groups Differ
1.	Credible product claims	(1 vs. 10)	10 less
2.	Provides wide selection	No difference	
3.	Good quality products	(3 vs. 10, 11)	3 more
4.	Price matches quality	No difference	
5.	Provides sufficient info. about products	No difference	
6.	Accurate portrayal of products	(10 vs. 1, 7)	10 more
7.	Fills order requests accurately	No difference	
8.	Quality consistent from one order to next	(1 vs. 10)	10 less
9.	Order filled in timely manner	(1 vs. 10)	10 less
10.	Order delivered when promised	No difference	
11.	Competitive prices	No difference	
12.	Money-back guarantee	(4 vs. 1, 3, 10)	4 less
13.	Well-known brand name	No difference	
14.	Company pays for call/ postage when ordering	(9 vs. 1, 4, 10)	9 more
15.	Delivery direct to home/ workplace	(1, 11 vs. 10)	10 less
16.	Company pays postage for returned goods	(2 vs. 9)	2 less
17.	Ability to get products not readily available	(1, 8, 9 vs. 10)	10 less
18.	Number to call with complaints/questions	(3, 9 vs. 4)	4 less
19.	Ability to charge purchase	(4 vs. all but 5); (10 vs. 1, 2, 3, 8, 9, 12)	4 less; 10 less
20.	Availability of alteration and repair	(1, 7, 11 vs. 3, 9, 12); (2 vs. 3, 12); (12 vs. 1, 4, 10)	1, 7, 11 less; 2 less; 12 more
21.	Ability to make exchanges	(4 vs. 1, 2, 3, 7, 8, 9, 10, 11, 12);	4 less;
22.	Capability of buying several things at same time	(1 vs. 10)	10 less

67

Table 5.4
Perception of Direct Mail by User/Age Groups

Groups

1	+65	DM User		7	+65	Both
2	50-64	DM User		8	50-64	Both
3	≤49	DM User		9	≤49	Both
4	+65	DS User		10	+65	Neither
5	50-64	DS User		11	50-64	Neither
6	≤49	DS User		12	≤49	Neither

Trait	Groups That Differ	How They Differ
1. Credible product claims	No difference	
2. Provides wide selection	No difference	
3. Good quality products	No difference	
4. Price matches quality	No difference	
5. Provides sufficient info. about products	No difference	
6. Accurate portrayal of products	No difference	
7. Fills order requests accurately	No difference	
8. Quality consistent from one order to next	No difference	
9. Order filled in timely manner	No difference	
10. Order delivered when promised	No difference	
11. Competitive prices	No difference	
12. Money-back guarantee	No difference	
13. Well-known brand name	No difference	
14. Company pays for call/ postage when ordering	No difference	
15. Delivery direct to home/ workplace	(1 vs. 10)	10 less
16 Company pays postage for returned goods	No difference	
17. Ability to get products not readily available	No difference	
18. Number to call with complaints/questions	No difference	
19. Ability to charge purchase	(4 vs. all but 5); (10 vs. 1, 2, 3, 6, 8, 9, 12); (7 vs. 3, 8, 9, 12); (1, 11 vs. 3, 9, 12)	4 less; 10 less; 7 less; 1, 11 less
20. Availability of alteration and repair	No difference	
21. Ability to make exchanges	No difference	
22. Capability of buying several things at same time	No difference	

Table 5.5
Perception of Media Ads by User/Age Groups

Groups

1	+65	DM User	7	+65	Both
2	50-64	DM User	8	50-64	Both
3	$\leq$49	DM User	9	$\leq$49	Both
4	+65	DS User	10	+65	Neither
5	50-64	DS User	11	50-64	Neither
6	$\leq$49	DS User	12	$\leq$49	Neither

Traits	Groups That Differ	How They Differ
1. Credible product claims	No difference	
2. Provides wide selection	No difference	
3. Good quality products	No difference	
4. Price matches qualtiy	No difference	
5. Provides sufficient info. about products	No difference	
6. Accurate portrayal of products	No difference	
7. Fills order requests accurately	No difference	
8. Quality consistent from one order to next	No difference	
9. Order filled in timely manner	No difference	
10. Order delivered when promised	No difference	
11. Competitive prices	No difference	
12. Money-back guarantee	No difference	
13. Well-known brand name	No difference	
14. Company pays for call/ postage when ordering	(2 vs. 9)	2 less
15. Delivery direct to home/ workplace	(3 vs. 10)	10 less
16. Company pays postage for returned goods	No difference	
17. Ability to get products not readily available	No difference	
18. Number to call with complaints/questions	No difference	
19. Ability to charge purchase	(4 vs. 1, 2, 3, 6, 8, 9, 12);	4 less;
	(7 vs. 3, 8, 9, 12);	7 less;
	(10 vs. 2, 3, 8, 9, 12);	10 less;
	(1 vs. 3, 8, 9, 12);	1 less;
	(11 vs. 3, 9, 12)	11 less
20 Availability of alteration and repair	No difference	
21. Ability to make exchanges	No difference	
22. Capability of buying several things at same time	No difference	

69

Table 5.6
Perception of Telephone Solicitation by User/Age Groups

Groups

1	+65	DM User		7	+65	Both
2	50-64	DM User		8	50-64	Both
3	$\leq$49	DM User		9	$\leq$49	Both
4	+65	DS User		10	+65	Neither
5	50-64	DS User		11	50-64	Neither
6	$\leq$49	DS User		12	$\leq$49	Neither

Trait	Groups That Differ	How They Differ
1. Credible product claims	No difference	
2. Provides wide selection	No difference	
3. Good quality products	No difference	
4. Price matches quality	No difference	
5. Provides sufficient info. about products	(1 vs. 11)	1 less
6. Accurate portrayal of products	No difference	
7. Fills order requests accurately	No difference	
8. Quality consistent from one order to next	(1 vs. 10)	1 less
9. Order filled in timely manner	No difference	
10. Order delivered when promised	No difference	
11. Competitive prices	No difference	
12. Money-back guarantee	No difference	
13. Well-known brand name	No difference	
14. Company pays for call/ postage when ordering	(1 vs. 3, 9, 11, 12); (9 vs. 2, 4, 7, 10)	1 less; 9 more
15. Delivery direct to home/ workplace	No difference	
16. Company pays postage for returned goods	No difference	
17. Ability to get products not readily available	No difference	
18. Number to call with complaints/questions	No difference	
19. Ability to charge purchase	(1, 4, 10, vs. 2, 3, 6, 8, 9, 12); (7 vs. 1, 2, 3, 6, 8-12); (11 vs. 3, 9, 12); (11 vs. 3, 9, 12)	1, 4, 10 less; 7 less; 11 less
20. Availability of alteration and repair	No difference	
21. Ability to make exchanges	(7 vs. 11)	7 less
22. Capability of buying several things at same time	No difference	

70

Table 5.7
Perception of Door-to-Door by User/Age Groups

Groups

1	+65	DM User		7	+65	Both
2	50-64	DM User		8	50-64	Both
3	$\leq$49	DM User		9	$\leq$49	Both
4	+65	DS User		10	+65	Neither
5	50-64	DS User		11	50-64	Neither
6	$\leq$49	DS User		12	$\leq$49	Neither

	Trait	Groups That Differ	How They Differ
1.	Credible product claims	(9 vs. 1, 10)	9 more
2.	Provides wide selection	(5 vs. 1, 2, 11)	5 more
3.	Good quality products	(1 vs. 9)	1 less
4.	Price matches quality	No difference	
5.	Provides sufficient info. about products	(1 vs. 9, 11, 12)	1 less
6.	Accurate portrayal of products	No difference	
7.	Fills order requests accurately	(1 vs. 9, 10, 11)	1 less
8.	Quality consistent from one order to next	No difference	
9.	Order filled in timely manner	(1 vs. 9, 12)	1 less
10.	Order delivered when promised	(1 vs. 9, 10)	1 less
11.	Competitive prices	No difference	
12.	Money-back guarantee	No difference	
13.	Well-known brand name	(1 vs. 8, 9, 10, 11)	1 less
14.	Company pays for call/ postage when ordering	(1 vs. 9)	1 less
15.	Delivery direct to home/ workplace	(3 vs. 10)	10 less
16.	Company pays postage for returned goods	(1 vs. 9)	1 less
17.	Ability to get products not readily available	No difference	
18.	Number to call with complaints/questions	No difference	
19.	Ability to charge purchase	(4 vs. 2, 3, 6, 8, 9, 11, 12); (7 vs. 3, 6, 8, 9, 11, 12); (5 vs. 12); (10 vs. 3, 6, 9, 12); (1 vs. 3, 6, 8, 9, 12); (12 vs. 2, 11)	4 less; 7 less; 5 less; 10 less; 1 less; 12 more
20.	Availability of alteration and repair	(1 vs. 9, 11, 12)	1 less
21.	Ability to make exchanges	(1 vs. 11)	1 less
22.	Capability of buying several things at same time	No difference	

71

Table 5.8
Perception of Party Plan by User/Age Groups

Groups

1	+35	DM User		7	+65	Both
2	50-64	DM User		8	50-64	Both
3	$\leq$49	DM User		9	$\leq$49	Both
4	+65	DS User		10	+65	Neither
5	50-64	DS User		11	50-64	Neither
6	$\leq$49	DS User		12	$\leq$49	Neither

	Trait	Groups That Differ	How They Differ
1.	Credible product claims	(9 vs. 1, 2, 10, 11); (8 vs. 1, 2, 3, 10,11)	9 more; 8 more
2.	Provides wide selection	(1, 10 vs. 4, 5, 7, 8, 9); (11 vs. 4, 5, 8); (2, 3, vs. 8, 5); (5 vs. 12)	1, 10 less; 11 less; 2, 3 less; 12 less
3.	Good quality products	(2, 11 vs. 4, 5, 8, 9); (1, 10 vs. 4, 5, 7, 8, 9)	2, 11 less; 1, 10 less
4.	Price matches quality	(2, 10 vs. 4, 5, 8); (1 vs. 4, 5, 7, 8); (3, 11, vs. 4, 5); (5 vs. 12)	2, 10 less; 1 less; 3, 11 less; 12 less
5.	Provides sufficient info. about products	(1 vs. 4, 7, 8, 9); (8 vs. 10)	1 less; 10 less
6.	Accurate portrayal of products	(1 vs. 4, 7, 8); (8 vs. 10)	1 less; 10 less
7.	Fills order requests accurately	(1 vs. 7, 9); (9 vs. 10)	1 less; 10 less
8.	Quality consistent from one order to next	(1 vs. 4, 5, 7, 8, 9); (11 vs. 7, 8, 9); (8 vs. 2, 3, 12); (10 vs. 4, 7, 8, 9)	1 less; 11 less; 8 more; 10 less
9.	Order filled in timely manner	(1 vs. 4, 7, 8, 9); (8 vs. 2, 3, 10, 11)	1 less; 8 more
10.	Order delivered when promised	(1 vs. 4, 7, 8, 9); (4, 8 vs. 10, 11)	1 less; 10, 11 less
11.	Competitive prices	(3 vs. 5, 8); (5 vs. 1, 2, 12);	3 less; 5 more
12.	Money-back guarantee	(5, 8 vs. 2, 3, 11, 12); (1 vs. 5, 7, 8, 9); (10 vs. 5, 8, 9); (7 vs. 8)	5, 8 more; 1 less; 10 less; 7 less
13.	Well-known brand name	(8, 9 vs. 1, 12); (9 vs. 10)	1, 12 less; 10 less
14.	Company pays for call/ postage when ordering	(1 vs. 10)	1 less
15.	Delivery direct to home/ workplace	No difference	
16.	Company pays postage for returned goods	No difference	
17.	Ability to get products not readily available	(1 vs. 9)	1 less
18.	Number to call with complaints/questions	(1 vs. 8)	1 less
19.	Ability to charge purchase	(4 vs. 8, 9, 11, 12); (10 vs. 9, 12)	4 less; 10 less
20.	Availability of alteration and repair	(1 vs. 8, 9); (9 vs. 10)	1 less; 10 less
21.	Ability to make exchanges	(8 vs. 1, 10)	8 more
22.	Capability of buying several things at same time	(4 vs. 1, 10)	4 more

72

Table 5.9
Perception of In-Home Demonstration by User/Age Groups

Groups

1	+65	DM User		7	+65	Both
2	50-64	DM User		8	50-64	Both
3	$\leq$49	DM User		9	$\leq$49	Both
4	+65	DS User		10	+65	Neither
5	50-64	DS User		11	50-64	Neither
6	$\leq$49	DS User		12	$\leq$49	Neither

	Trait	Groups That Differ	How They Differ
1.	Credible product claims	(7 vs. 1, 2, 10); (9 vs. 10)	7 more; 10 less
2.	Provides wide selection	No difference	
3.	Good quality products	(2 vs. 4)	2 less
4.	Price matches quality	(5 vs. 1, 2, 3, 10)	5 more
5.	Provides sufficient info. about products	(1 vs. 4, 7)	1 less
6.	Accurate portrayal of products	(1, 10 vs. 7)	7 more
7.	Fills order requests accurately	No difference	
8.	Quality consistent from one order to next	(1 vs. 7)	1 less
9.	Order filled in timely manner	(8 vs. 1, 3, 10)	8 more
10.	Order delivered when promised	(1 vs. 4, 7, 8, 9)	1 less
11.	Competitive prices	(3 vs. 5)	3 less
12.	Money-back guarantee	(9 vs. 1, 2, 10); (8 vs. 1, 10)	9 more; 8 more
13.	Well-known brand name	(1 vs. 4, 9)	1 less
14.	Company pays for call/ postage when ordering	(1 vs. 10)	1 less
15.	Delivery direct to home/ workplace	No difference	
16.	Company pays postage for returned goods	(9 vs. 1, 10)	9 more
17.	Ability to get products not readily available	(1 vs. 4)	1 less
18.	Number to call with complaints/questions	(1 vs. 8)	1 less
19.	Ability to charge purchase	(9 vs. 1, 4, 10); (12 vs. 4, 10)	9 more; 12 more
20.	Availability of alteration and repair	(1 vs. 9)	1 less
21.	Ability to make exchanges	(1 vs. 5, 8); (10 vs. 8)	1 less; 10 less
22.	Capability of buying several things at same time	(5 vs. 1, 2, 3, 10, 11)	5 more

73

Table 5.10
Perception of Retail by User/Age Groups

Groups

1	+65	DM User		7	+65	Both
2	50-64	DM User		8	50-64	Both
3	$\leq$49	DM User		9	$\leq$49	Both
4	+65	DS User		10	+65	Neither
5	50-64	DS User		11	50-64	Neither
6	$\leq$49	DS User		12	$\leq$49	Neither

Trait	Groups That Differ	How They Differ
1. Credible product claims	(12 vs. 1, 2, 3, 7, 8, 9, 10 11)	12 less
2. Provides wide selection	No difference	
3. Good quality products	No difference	
4. Price matches quality	No difference	
5. Provides sufficient info. about products	(11 vs. 1, 2, 7, 10, 12)	11 more
6. Accurate portrayal of products	No difference	
7. Fills order requests accurately	No difference	
8. Quality consistent from one order to next	No difference	
9. Order filled in timely manner	(9 vs. 10)	10 less
10. Order delivered when promised	No difference	
11. Competitive prices	No difference	
12. Money-back guarantee	No difference	
13. Well-known brand name	No difference	
14. Company pays for call/ postage when ordering	No difference	
15. Delivery direct to home/ workplace	(4 vs. 10)	4 less
16. Company pays postage for returned goods	No difference	
17. Ability to get products not readily available	No difference No difference	
18. Number to call with complaints/questions	No difference	
19. Ability to charge purchase	(4 vs. 1, 2, 3, 9, 11, 12); (7, 10 vs. 3, 9, 12)	4 less; 7, 10 less
20. Availability of alteration and repair	(3 vs. 4)	3 less
21. Ability to make exchanges	No difference	
22. Capability of buying several things at same time	No difference	

74

Table 5.11
In-Home Shopping Likes: 65+ Only

											CATALOGUE USE			
	ALL 65+			NONUSERS			LIGHT USERS			HEAVY USERS				
	Freq	$\%^1$	Rank^2	Freq	$\%^3$	Rank^2	Freq	$\%^3$	Rank^2	Freq	$\%^3$	Rank^2		
Convenient	354	28.4	1	175	30.3	1	98	25.3	1	81	28.8	1		
Seeing/discussing product	267	21.5	2	125	21.7	2	94	24.2	2	48	17.1	2		
Nothing	196	15.7	3	108	18.8	3	53	13.7	3	35	12.5	4		
Leisure	152	12.2	4	65	11.3	4	51	13.2	4	36	12.8	3		
Catalogues-product availability	56	4.5	5	23	4.0	6	21	5.4	5	12	4.3	8		
Personal touch	53	4.3	6	25	4.3	5	19	4.9	6	9	3.2	9		
Saves travel/time	50	4.0	7	17	3.0	7	18	4.7	7	15	5.3	6		
Variety	35	2.8	8	9	1.6	9	9	2.3	8	17	6.1	5		
Name brand/ familiar company	27	2.2	9	10	1.8	8	4	1.0	11	13	4.6	7		
Party plans	12	1.0	10	8	1.4	10	4	1.0	11	0	0.0	15		
Delivery	12	1.0	10	3	0.5	12	3	0.8	13	6	2.1	10		
Guarantees	11	0.9	12	1	0.2	14	6	1.6	9	4	1.4	11		
Seeing new products	10	0.8	13	3	0.5	12	5	1.3	10	2	0.7	12		
Low prices	8	0.6	14	4	0.7	11	2	0.5	14	2	0.7	12		
Benefits of being a hostess	2	0.2	15	1	0.2	14	0	0.0	15	1	0.4	14		

^{1}Percent of total sample

^{2}Across likes, within group

^{3}Percent within user category

75

Table 5.12
In-Home Shopping Dislikes: 65+ Only

							CATALOGUE USE					
	All 65+			NONUSERS			LIGHT USERS			HEAVY USERS		
	Freq	$\%^1$	Rank^2	Freq	$\%^3$	Rank^2	Freq	$\%^3$	Rank^2	Freq	$\%^3$	Rank^2
High pressure sales	338	26.3	1	170	28.2	1	105	26.7	1	63	21.8	1
Risk from shopping by picture	207	26.3	2	87	14.4	2	73	18.6	2	47	16.3	2
No variety/can't compare	89	6.9	3	44	7.3	4	27	6.9	5	18	6.2	4
Surprise interruptions/ being bothered	86	6.7	4	42	7.0	5	31	7.9	3	13	4.5	8
Waiting for delivery	83	6.5	5	31	5.1	7	22	5.6	6	30	10.4	3
Feeling obligated to buy	79	6.2	6	35	5.8	6	29	7.4	4	15	5.2	6
Strangers in home	74	5.8	7	45	7.5	3	18	4.6	7	11	3.8	9
Higher prices	51	4.0	8	25	4.2	8	18	4.6	7	8	2.8	13
Return hassles	47	3.7	9	21	3.5	10	11	2.8	9	15	5.2	6
Telephone/door-to-door solicitation	39	3.0	10	22	3.7	9	8	2.0	12	9	3.1	10
Invasion of privacy	32	2.5	11	15	2.5	11	9	2.3	11	8	2.8	13
Clothing sizes/fit	31	2.4	12	9	1.5	14	5	1.3	13	17	5.9	5
Boring/detailed sales pitches	27	2.1	13	15	2.5	11	5	1.3	13	7	2.4	15
Postage/handling costs	23	1.8	14	4	0.7	17	10	2.5	10	9	3.1	10
Inconvenient/ time consuming	21	1.6	15	11	1.8	13	5	1.3	13	5	1.7	16
Nothing	19	1.5	16	7	1.2	15	4	1.0	16	8	2.8	13
Unfamiliar companies	9	0.7	17	3	0.5	19	4	1.0	16	2	0.7	17
Junk mail	6	0.5	18	4	0.7	17	0	0.0	23	2	0.7	17
Missed appointment by sales rep	6	0.5	18	4	0.7	17	1	0.3	20	1	0.4	19
Tend to buy more than need	5	0.4	20	2	0.3	21	3	0.8	18	0	0.0	21
Miss shopping	4	0.3	21	3	0.5	19	0	0.0	23	1	0.4	19
Lack of personal contact	3	0.2	22	2	0.3	21	1	0.3	20	0	0.0	21
Damaged goods	3	0.2	22	2	0.3	21	1	0.3	20	0	0.0	21
Pressure to have parties	3	0.2	22	0	0.0	24	3	0.8	18	0	0.0	21

^{1}Percent of total sample

^{2}Across likes, within group

^{3}Percent within user category

76

Table 5.13
Shopping Likes of Catalogue Users across Age

	ALL USERS			AGE < 34			35-49			50-64			65+		
	Freq	$\%^1$	$Rank^2$	Freq	$\%^3$	$Rank^2$	Freq	$\%^3$	$Rank^2$	Freq	$\%^3$	$Rank^2$	Freq	$\%^3$	$Rank^2$
Convenient	331	29.1	1	37	30.1	1	29	26.6	1	86	36.4	1	179	26.8	1
Seeing/discussing the product	231	20.3	2	21	17.1	3	22	20.2	3	46	19.5	2	142	21.3	2
Leisure	171	15.1	3	29	23.6	2	23	21.1	2	32	13.6	3	87	13.0	4
Nothing	125	11.0	4	8	6.5	5	4	3.7	6	25	10.6	4	88	13.2	3
Product availability	55	4.8	5	6	4.9	6	6	5.5	5	10	4.2	5	33	4.9	5
Saves travel/time	55	4.8	5	9	7.3	4	3	2.8	8	10	4.2	5	33	4.9	5
Product variety	47	4.1	7	5	4.1	7	9	8.3	4	7	3.0	7	26	3.9	8
Personal Touch	39	3.4	8	3	2.4	8	4	3.7	6	4	1.7	8	28	4.2	7
Name brand/ familiar company	25	2.2	9	1	0.8	10	4	2.8	8	4	1.7	8	17	2.5	9
Delivery	18	1.6	10	2	1.6	9	3	2.8	8	4	1.7	8	9	1.4	11
Seeing new products	10	0.9	11	0	0.0	13	2	0.2	11	1	0.4	13	6	1.1	12
Guarantees	10	0.9	11	0	0.0	13	0	0.0	13	0	0.0	14	10	1.5	10
Party plans	9	0.8	13	1	0.8	10	1	0.8	12	3	1.3	12	4	0.6	13
Low prices	9	0.9	12	1	0.8	10	0	0.0	13	4	1.7	8	4	0.6	13
Hostess benefits	1	0.1	14	0	0.0	13	0	0.0	13	0	0.0	14	1	0.2	15

^{1}Percent of total sample

^{2}Across likes, within group

^{3}Percent within age category

77

Table 5.14
In-Home Shopping Dislikes: Catalogue Users across Age

	ALL USERS			AGE < 34			35-49			50-64			65+		
	Freq	%[1]	Rank[2]	Freq	%[3]	Rank[2]	Freq	%[3]	Rank[2]	Freq	%[3]	Rank[2]	Freq	%[3]	Rank[2]
High pressure sales	297	25.9	1	36	29.7	1	24	22.2	1	69	29.0	1	168	24.6	1
Uncertainty of shopping from pictures	208	18.1	2	22	18.2	2	19	17.6	2	47	19.8	2	120	17.6	2
Waiting for delivery	90	7.8	3	13	10.7	3	12	11.11	3	13	5.5	4	52	7.6	3
No variety/comparison	74	6.4	4	7	5.8	5	6	5.6	6	16	6.7	3	45	6.6	4
Surprise interruptions	66	5.7	5	3	2.5	8	6	5.6	6	13	5.5	4	44	6.5	5
Feel obligated to buy	59	5.1	6	3	2.5	8	1	0.9	14	11	4.6	6	44	6.5	5
Return hassles	54	4.7	7	9	7.4	4	9	8.3	4	10	4.2	8	26	3.8	8
Higher prices	49	4.3	8	7	5.8	5	6	5.6	6	10	4.2	8	26	3.8	8
Strangers in home	40	3.5	9	3	2.5	8	2	1.9	10	6	2.5	11	29	4.3	7
Non-standard clothing size/fit	36	3.1	10	3	2.5	8	7	6.5	5	4	1.7	13	22	3.2	9
Invasion of privacy	35	3.1	11	5	4.1	7	6	5.6	6	7	2.9	8	17	2.5	12
Postage/handling costs	31	2.7	12	2	1.7	13	0	0.0		10	4.2	7	19	2.8	11
Telephone/door-to-door solicitation	22	1.9	13	1	0.8	14	2	1.9	10	2	0.8	14	17	2.5	12
Nothing	16	1.4	14	3	2.5	8	0	0.0		1	0.4	19	12	1.8	15
Inconvenient/time consuming	16	1.4	14	0	0.0		2	1.9	10	4	1.7	13	10	1.5	16
Boring/detailed sales pitch	16	1.4	14	1	0.8	14	1	0.9	14	2	0.8	14	16	1.4	14
Unfamiliar companies	9	0.8	17	1	0.8	14	2	1.9	10	0	0.0		6	0.9	17
Lack of personal contact	7	0.6	18	0	0.0		1	0.9	14	5	2.1	12	1	0.2	22
Damaged products	5	0.4	19	1	0.8	14	1	0.9	14	2	0.8	14	1	0.2	22
Junk Mail	5	0.4	19	0	0.0		1	0.9	14	2	0.8	14	2	0.3	20
Buy more than need	5	0.4	19	0	0.0		0	0.0		2	0.8	14	3	0.4	18
Parties/pressure to have	5	0.4	19	1	0.8	14	0	0.0		1	0.4	19	3	0.4	18
Inconvenient/time consuming	3	0.3	23	0	0.0		0	0.0		1	0.4	19	2	0.4	20
Miss shopping	1	0.9	24	0	0.0		0	0.0		0	0.0		1	0.2	22

[1]Percent of total sample

[2]Across likes, within group

[3]Percent within age category

78

Table 5.15
Shopping Likes of Direct Mail Users vs. Nonusers: 65+ Only

DIRECT MAIL USE

ATTRIBUTE	All 65+			NONUSERS			USERS		
	Freq	$\%^1$	Rank^2	Freq	$\%^3$	Rank^2	Freq	$\%^3$	Rank^2
Convenient	354	28.43	1	303	28.61	1	51	27.42	2
Seeing the product	267	21.45	2	215	20.30	2	52	27.96	1
Nothing	196	15.74	3	173	16.34	3	23	12.37	3
Leisure	152	12.21	4	135	12.75	4	17	9.14	4
See what you get	56	4.50	5	46	4.34	5	10	5.38	5
Personal touch	53	4.26	6	44	4.15	6	9	4.84	6
Saves time/travel expense	50	4.02	7	41	3.87	7	9	4.84	6
Product variety	35	2.81	8	33	3.12	8	2	1.08	9
Name brand/familiar companies	27	2.17	9	25	2.36	9	2	1.08	9
Party plans	12	.96	10	10	.94	10	2	1.08	9
Delivery	12	.96	10	9	.85	12	3	1.61	8
Guarantees	11	.88	12	10	.94	10	1	.54	11
Seeing new products	10	.80	13	8	.76	13	2	1.08	9
Low prices	8	.64	14	6	.57	14	2	1.08	9
Hostess benefits	2	.16	15	1	.09	15	1	.54	11

^{1}Percent of total sample

^{2}Across likes, within groups

^{3}Percent within use category

Table 5.16
Shopping Dislikes of Direct Mail Users vs. Nonusers: 65+ Only

DIRECT MAIL USE

ATTRIBUTE	All 65+			NONUSERS			USERS		
	Freq	$\%^1$	Rank^2	Freq	$\%^3$	Rank^2	Freq	$\%^3$	Rank^2
High pressure sales	338	26.30	1	284	26.15	1	54	27.14	1
Not sure of what you get	207	16.11	2	172	15.84	2	35	17.59	2
No variety	89	6.93	3	76	7.00	3	13	6.53	5
Interruptions	86	6.69	4	72	6.63	5	14	7.04	4
Delivery time	83	6.46	5	68	6.26	7	15	7.54	3
Feeling obliged to buy	79	6.15	6	74	6.81	4	5	2.51	11
Strangers	74	5.76	7	69	6.35	6	5	2.51	11
Higher prices	51	3.97	8	46	4.24	8	5	2.51	11
Return hassles	47	3.66	9	41	3.78	9	6	3.02	9
Solicitation	39	3.04	10	32	2.95	10	7	3.52	7
Invasion of privacy	32	2.49	11	25	2.30	11	7	3.52	7
Unstandard sizes	31	2.41	12	25	2.30	11	6	3.02	9
Boring sales pitches	27	2.10	13	24	2.21	13	3	1.51	13
Postage/handling costs	23	1.79	14	22	2.03	14	1	.50	15
Inconvenient	21	1.63	15	10	.92	16	11	5.53	6
Nothing	19	1.48	16	14	1.29	15	5	2.51	11
Unfamiliar companies	9	.70	17	9	.83	17	0	0.00	17
Rep missed appointment	6	.47	18	5	.46	18	1	.50	15
Junk mail	6	.47	18	3	.28	21	3	1.51	13
Tend to buy more than need	5	.39	20	4	.37	19	1	.50	15
Miss shopping	4	.31	21	4	.37	19	0	0.00	17
No personal contact	3	.23	22	2	.18	23	1	.50	15
Damaged products	3	.23	22	2	.18	23	1	.50	15
Parties/pressure to have	3	.23	22	3	.28	21	0	0.00	17

^{1}Percent of total sample

^{2}Across likes, within groups

^{3}Percent within use category

79

Table 5.17
Shopping Likes of Direct Mail Users: 65+ vs. <65

| | | | | | DIRECT MAIL USE | | | | |
| | ALL USERS | | | <65 | | | 65+ | | |
ATTRIBUTE	Freq	$\%^1$	Rank^2	Freq	$\%^3$	Rank^2	Freq	$\%^3$	Rank^2
Convenient	92	29.30	1	41	32.03	1	51	27.42	2
Seeing the product	67	21.34	2	15	11.72	3	52	27.96	1
Leisure	49	13.61	3	32	25.00	2	17	9.14	4
Nothing	34	10.83	4	11	8.59	4	23	12.37	3
Saves time/travel expense	18	5.73	5	9	7.03	5	9	4.84	6
See what you get	17	5.41	6	7	5.47	6	10	5.38	5
Personal touch	13	4.14	7	4	3.13	7	9	4.84	6
Delivery	5	1.59	8	2	1.56	9	3	1.61	7
Low prices	5	1.59	8	3	2.34	8	2	1.08	8
Product variety	4	1.27	10	2	1.56	9	2	1.08	8
Seeing new products	3	.96	11	1	.78	11	2	1.08	8
Name brands/familiar companies	3	.96	11	1	.78	11	2	1.08	8
Party plans	2	.64	13	0	0.00	13	2	1.08	8
Guarantees	1	.32	14	0	0.00	13	1	.54	10
Hostess benefits	1	.32	14	0	0.00	13	1	.54	10

^{1}Percent of total sample

^{2}Across likes, within groups

^{3}Percent within category

Table 5.18
Shopping Dislikes of Direct Mail Users: 65+ vs. <65

| | | | | | DIRECT MAIL USE | | | | |
| | ALL USERS | | | <65 | | | 65+ | | |
ATTRIBUTE	Freq	$\%^1$	Rank^2	Freq	$\%^3$	Rank^2	Freq	$\%^3$	Rank^2
High pressure sales	82	25.23	1	28	22.22	1	54	27.14	1
Not sure of what you get	61	18.67	2	26	20.63	2	35	17.59	2
Delivery time	27	8.31	3	12	9.52	3	15	7.54	3
Interruptions	21	6.46	4	7	5.56	5	14	7.04	4
No variety	18	5.54	5	5	3.97	8	13	6.53	5
Return hassles	18	5.54	5	12	9.52	3	6	3.02	9
Invasion of privacy	13	4.00	7	6	4.76	7	7	3.52	7
Inconvenient	13	4.00	7	2	1.59	11	11	5.53	6
Higher prices	12	3.69	9	7	5.56	5	5	2.51	11
Solicitation	10	3.08	10	3	2.38	9	7	3.52	7
Unstandard sizes	8	2.46	11	2	1.59	11	6	3.02	9
Strangers	8	2.46	11	3	2.38	9	5	2.51	11
Feeling obliged to buy	7	2.15	13	2	1.59	11	5	2.51	11
Nothing	6	1.85	14	1	.79	13	5	2.51	11
Boring sales pitches	3	.92	15	0	.00	15	3	1.51	13
Junk mail	3	.92	15	0	.00	15	3	1.51	13
Tend to buy more than need	3	.92	15	2	1.59	11	1	.50	15
Postage/handling costs	2	.62	17	1	.79	13	1	.50	15
No personal contact	2	.62	17	1	.79	13	1	.50	15
Unfamiliar companies	2	.62	17	2	1.59	11	0	0.00	17
Rep missed appointment	2	.62	17	1	.79	13	1	.50	15
Damaged products	2	.62	17	1	.79	13	1	.50	15
Parties/pressure to have	2	.62	17	2	1.59	11	0	0.00	17

^{1}Percent of total sample

^{2}Across likes, within groups

^{3}Percent within category

Table 5.19
Shopping Likes of Media Ad Users vs. Nonusers: 65+ Only

MEDIA AD USE

ATTRIBUTE	ALL 65+			NONUSERS			USERS		
	Freq	$\%^1$	Rank^2	Freq	$\%^3$	Rank^2	Freq	$\%^3$	Rank^2
Convenient	354	28.43	1	326	28.75	1	28	25.23	1
Seeing the product	267	21.45	2	240	21.16	2	27	24.32	2
Nothing	196	15.74	3	181	15.96	3	15	13.51	3
Leisure	152	12.21	4	143	12.61	4	9	8.11	4
See what you get	56	4.50	5	50	4.41	5	6	5.41	6
Personal touch	53	4.26	6	47	4.14	6	6	5.41	6
Saves time/travel expense	50	4.02	7	44	3.88	7	6	5.41	6
Product variety	35	2.81	8	26	2.29	8	9	8.11	4
Name brand/familiar companies	27	2.17	9	24	2.12	9	3	2.70	8
Party plans	12	.96	10	12	1.06	10	0	0.00	11
Delivery	12	.96	10	11	.97	11	1	0.00	9
Guarantees	11	.88	12	11	.97	11	0	0.00	11
Seeing new products	10	.80	13	10	.88	13	0	0.00	11
Low prices	8	.64	14	7	.62	14	1	.90	9
Hostess benefits	2	.16	15	21	.18	15	0	0.00	11

^{1}Percent of total sample

^{2}Across likes, within groups

^{3}Percent within use category

Table 5.20
Shopping Dislikes of Media Ad Users vs. Nonusers: 65+ Only

MEDIA AD USE

ATTRIBUTE	ALL 65+			NONUSERS			USERS		
	Freq	$\%^1$	Rank^2	Freq	$\%^3$	Rank^2	Freq	$\%^3$	Rank^2
High pressure sales	338	26.30	1	314	26.86	1	24	20.69	1
Not sure of what you get	207	16.11	2	184	15.74	2	23	19.83	2
No variety	89	6.93	3	82	7.01	3	7	6.03	6
Interruptions	86	6.69	4	75	6.42	4	11	9.48	3
Delivery time	83	6.46	5	74	6.33	5	9	7.76	4
Feeling obliged to buy	79	6.15	6	71	6.07	6	8	6.90	5
Strangers	74	5.76	7	70	5.99	7	4	3.45	7
Higher prices	51	3.97	8	47	4.02	8	4	3.45	7
Return hassles	47	3.66	9	43	3.68	9	4	3.45	7
Solicitation	39	3.04	10	35	2.99	10	4	3.45	7
Invasion of privacy	32	2.49	11	30	2.57	11	2	1.72	9
Unstandard sizes	31	2.41	12	27	2.31	12	4	3.45	7
Boring sales pitches	27	2.10	13	25	2.14	13	2	1.72	9
Postage/handling costs	23	1.79	14	19	1.63	14	4	3.45	7
Inconvenient	21	1.63	15	19	1.63	14	2	1.72	9
Nothing	19	1.48	16	17	1.45	16	2	1.72	9
Unfamiliar companies	9	.70	17	9	.77	17	0	0.00	13
Rep missed appointment	6	.47	18	6	.51	18	0	0.00	13
Junk mail	6	.47	18	5	.43	19	1	.86	11
Tend to buy more than need	5	.39	20	4	.34	20	1	.86	11
Miss shopping	4	.31	21	4	.34	20	0	0.00	13
No personal contact	3	.23	22	3	.26	22	0	0.00	13
Damaged products	3	.23	22	3	.26	22	0	0.00	13
Parties/pressure to have	3	.23	22	3	.26	22	0	0.00	13

^{1}Percent of total sample

^{2}Across likes, within groups

^{3}Percent within use category

81

Table 5.21
Shopping Likes of Media Ad Users: 65+ vs. <65

MEDIA AD USE

	ALL USERS			<65			65+		
ATTRIBUTE	Freq	$\%^1$	Rank^2	Freq	$\%^3$	Rank^2	Freq	$\%^3$	Rank^2
Convenient	63	32.47	1	35	42.17	1	28	25.23	1
Home demonstration	43	22.16	2	16	19.28	2	27	34.32	2
Nothing	19	9.79	4	4	4.82	5	15	13.51	3
Leisure	19	9.79	4	10	12.05	3	9	8.11	4
Product variety	14	7.22	6	5	6.02	4	9	8.11	4
Saves time/travel expense	10	5.15	7	4	4.82	5	6	5.41	6
See what you want	10	5.15	7	4	4.82	5	6	5.41	6
Personal touch	7	3.61	8	1	1.20	7	6	5.41	6
Name brand/familiar companies	4	2.06	9	1	1.20	7	3	2.70	8
Delivery	2	1.03	10	1	1.20	7	1	.90	9
Low prices	2	1.03	10	1	1.20	7	1	.90	9
Party plans	1	.52	11	1	1.20	7	0	0.00	11

^{1}Percent of total sample

^{2}Across likes, within groups

^{3}Percent within category

Table 5.22
Shopping Dislikes of Media Ad Users: 65+ vs. <65

MEDIA AD USE

	ALL USERS			<65			65+		
ATTRIBUTE	Freq	$\%^1$	Rank^2	Freq	$\%^3$	Rank^2	Freq	$\%^3$	Rank^2
High pressure sales	44	22.00	1	20	23.81	1	24	20.69	1
Not sure of what you get	34	17.00	2	11	13.10	2	23	19.83	2
Delivery time	20	10.00	3	11	13.10	2	9	7.76	4
No variety	17	8.50	4	10	11.90	4	7	6.03	6
Interruptions	15	7.50	5	4	4.76	7	11	9.48	3
Higher prices	9	4.50	6	5	5.95	6	4	3.45	7
Feeling obliged to buy	9	4.50	6	1	1.19	12	8	6.90	5
Return hassles	8	4.00	8	8	4.76	5	4	3.45	7
Strangers	7	3.50	9	3	3.57	9	4	3.45	7
Unstandard sizes	6	3.00	10	2	2.38	10	4	3.45	7
Invasion of privacy	6	3.00	10	4	4.76	7	2	1.72	9
Solicitation	6	3.00	10	2	2.38	10	4	3.45	7
Postage/handling costs	5	2.50	12	1	1.19	12	4	3.45	7
Nothing	3	1.50	13	1	1.19	12	2	1.72	9
Inconvenient	3	1.50	13	1	1.19	12	2	1.72	9
No personal contact	2	1.00	15	2	2.38	10	0	0.00	12
Boring sales pitches	2	1.00	15	0	0.00	14	2	1.72	9
Damaged products	1	.50	17	1	1.19	12	0	0.00	12
Junk mail	1	.50	17	0	0.00	14	1	.86	11
Buy more than need	1	.50	17	0	0.00	14	1	.86	11
Miss shopping	1	.50	17	1	1.119	12	0	0.00	12

^{1}Percent of total sample

^{2}Across likes, within groups

^{3}Percent within category

82

Table 5.23
Shopping Likes of Users of Phone Solicitation: 65+ vs. <65

PHONE SOLICITATION USE

ATTRIBUTE	ALL USERS			<65			65+		
	Freq	$\%^1$	Rank^2	Freq	$\%^3$	Rank^2	Freq	$\%^3$	Rank^2
Convenient	21	36.21	1	8	26.67	1	13	46.63	1
Seeing the product	13	22.41	2	8	26.67	1	5	17.86	2
Leisure	7	12.07	3	5	16.67	3	2	7.14	4
Nothing	5	8.62	4	1	3.33	6	4	14.29	3
Saves time/travel expense	3	5.17	5	3	10.00	4	0	0.00	8
Personal touch	3	5.17	5	1	3.33	6	2	7.14	4
See what you get	3	5.17	5	2	6.67	5	1	3.57	6
Party plans	1	1.72	7	1	3.33	6	0	0.00	8
Name brand/familiar companies	1	1.72	7	0	0.00	8	1	3.57	6
Product variety	1	1.72	7	1	3.33	6	0	0.00	8

^{1}Percent of total sample

^{2}Across likes, within groups

^{3}Percent within category

Table 5.24
Shopping Dislikes of Users of Phone Solicitation: 65+ vs. <65

PHONE SOLICITATION USE

ATTRIBUTE	ALL USERS			<65			65+		
	Freq	$\%^1$	Rank^2	Freq	$\%^3$	Rank^2	Freq	$\%^3$	Rank^2
High pressure sales	12	20.00	1	6	20.69	1	6	19.35	1
Not sure of what you get	12	20.00	1	6	20.69	1	6	19.35	1
No variety	7	11.67	3	1	3.45	7	6	19.35	1
Invasion of privacy	6	10.00	4	3	10.34	3	3	9.68	3
Higher prices	4	6.67	5	3	10.34	3	1	9.68	3
Solicitation	4	6.67	5	1	3.45	7	3	9.68	3
Delivery time	2	3.33	7	0	0.00	9	2	6.45	5
Postage/handling costs	2	3.33	7	2	6.90	5	0	0.00	9
Return hassles	2	3.33	7	2	6.90	5	0	0.00	9
Unstandard sizes	2	3.33	7	1	3.45	7	1	3.23	7
Feeling obliged to buy	2	3.33	7	2	6.90	7	0	0.00	9
Interruptions	1	1.67	9	0	0.00	9	1	3.23	7
Strangers	1	1.67	9	0	0.00	9	1	3.23	7
Nothing	1	1.67	9	1	3.45	7	0	0.00	9
Tend to by more than need	1	1.67	9	1	3.45	7	0	0.00	9
Inconvenient	1	1.67	9	0	0.00	9	1	3.23	7

^{1}Percent of total sample

^{2}Across likes, within groups

^{3}Percent within category

83

Table 5.25

Shopping Likes of Users vs. Nonusers of Phone Solicitation: 65+

PHONE SOLICITATION USE

	ALL 65+			NONUSERS			USERS		
ATTRIBUTE	Freq	$\%^1$	Rank^2	Freq	$\%^3$	Rank^2	Freq	$\%^3$	Rank^2
Convenient	354	28.43	1	341	28.02	1	13	46.43	1
Seeing the product	267	21.45	2	262	21.53	2	5	17.86	2
Nothing	196	15.74	3	192	15.78	3	4	14.29	3
Leisure	152	12.21	4	150	12.33	4	2	7.14	4
See what you get	56	4.50	5	55	4.52	5	1	3.57	6
Personal touch	53	4.26	6	51	4.19	6	2	7.14	4
Saves time/travel expense	50	4.02	7	50	4.11	7	0	0.00	8
Product variety	35	2.81	8	35	2.88	8	0	0.00	8
Name brand/familiar company	27	2.17	9	26	2.14	9	1	3.57	6
Party plans	12	.96	10	12	.99	10	0	0.00	8
Delivery	12	.96	10	12	.99	10	0	0.00	8
Guarantees	11	.88	12	11	.90	12	0	0.00	8
Seeing new products	10	.80	13	10	.82	13	0	0.00	8
Low prices	8	.64	14	8	.66	14	0	0.00	8
Hostess benefits	2	.16	15	2	.16	15	0	0.00	8

^{1}Percent of total sample

^{2}Across likes, within groups

^{3}Percent within use category

Table 5.26

Shopping Dislikes of Users vs. Nonusers of Phone Solicitation: 65+

PHONE SOLICITATION USE

	ALL 65+			NONUSERS			USERS		
ATTRIBUTE	Freq	$\%^1$	Rank^2	Freq	$\%^3$	Rank^2	Freq	$\%^3$	Rank^2
High pressure sales	338	26.30	1	332	26.48	1	6	19.35	1
Not sure of what you get	207	16.11	2	201	16.03	2	6	19.35	1
No variety	89	6.93	3	83	6.62	4	6	19.35	1
Interruptions	86	6.69	4	85	6.78	3	1	3.23	7
Delivery time	83	6.46	5	81	6.46	5	2	6.45	5
Feeling obliged to buy	79	6.15	6	79	6.30	6	0	0.00	9
Strangers	74	5.76	7	73	5.82	7	1	3.23	7
Higher prices	51	3.97	8	50	3.99	8	1	3.23	7
Return hassles	47	3.66	9	47	3.75	9	0	0.00	9
Solicitation	39	3.04	10	36	2.87	10	3	9.68	3
Invasion of privacy	32	2.49	11	29	2.31	12	3	4.68	3
Unstandard sizes	31	2.41	12	30	2.39	11	1	3.23	7
Boring sales pitches	27	2.10	13	27	2.15	13	0	0.00	9
Postage/handling costs	23	1.79	14	23	1.83	14	0	0.00	9
Inconvenient	21	1.63	15	20	1.59	15	1	3.23	7
Nothing	19	1.48	16	19	1.52	16	0	0.00	9
Unfamiliar companies	9	.70	17	9	.72	17	0	0.00	9
Rep missed appointment	6	.47	18	6	.48	18	0	0.000	9
Junk mail	6	.47	18	6	.48	18	0	0.00	9
Tend to buy more than need	5	.39	20	5	.40	20	0	0.00	9
Miss shopping	4	.31	21	4	.32	21	0	0.00	9
No personal contact	3	.33	22	3	.24	22	0	0.00	9
Damaged products	3	.23	22	3	.24	22	0	0.00	9
Parties/pressure to have	3	.23	22	3	.24	22	0	0.00	9

^{1}Percent of total sample

^{2}Across likes, within groups

^{3}Percent within use category

Table 5.27
Shopping Likes of Users vs. Nonusers of Direct Selling: 65+

					DIRECT SELLING USE				
	ALL 65+			NONUSERS			USERS		
ATTRIBUTE	Freq	$\%^1$	Rank^2	Freq	$\%^3$	Rank^2	Freq	$\%^3$	Rank^2
Convenient	354	28.43	1	335	28.56	1	19	26.39	1
Seeing the product	267	21.45	2	249	21.23	2	18	25.00	2
Nothing	196	15.74	3	190	16.20	3	6	8.33	3
Leisure	152	12.21	4	146	12.45	4	6	8.33	3
See what you get	56	4.50	5	54	4.60	5	2	2.78	7
Personal touch	53	4.26	6	47	4.01	6	6	8.33	3
Saves time/travel expenses	50	4.02	7	47	4.01	6	3	4.17	5
Product variety	35	8.57	8	32	2.73	8	3	4.17	5
Name brands/familiar companies	27	2.17	9	21	1.79	9	6	8.33	3
Party plans	12	.96	10	11	.94	10	1	1.39	9
Delivery	12	.96	10	10	.85	12	2	2.78	7
Guarantees	11	.88	12	11	.94	10	0	0.00	10
Seeing new products	10	.80	13	10	.85	12	0	0.00	10
Low prices	8	.64	14	8	.68	14	0	0.00	10
Hostess benefits	2	.16	15	2	.17	15	0	0.00	10

^{1}Percent of total sample

^{2}Across likes, within groups

^{3}Percent within use category

Table 5.28
Shopping Dislikes of Users vs. Nonusers of Direct Selling: 65+

					DIRECT SELLING USE				
	ALL 65+			NONUSERS			USERS		
ATTRIBUTE	Freq	$\%^1$	Rank^2	Freq	$\%^3$	Rank^2	Freq	$\%^3$	Rank^2
High pressure sales	338	26.30	1	319	26.28	1	19	26.76	1
Not sure of what you get	207	16.11	2	196	16.14	2	11	15.49	2
No variety	89	6.93	3	82	6.75	3	7	9.86	3
Interruptions	86	6.69	4	80	6.59	4	6	8.45	4
Delivery time	83	6.46	5	80	6.59	4	3	4.23	7
Feeling obliged to buy	79	6.15	6	74	6.10	6	5	7.04	5
Strangers	74	5.76	7	72	5.93	7	2	2.82	9
Higher prices	51	3.97	8	49	4.04	8	2	2.82	9
Return hassles	47	3.66	9	44	3.62	9	3	4.23	7
Solicitation	39	3.04	10	39	3.21	10	0	0.00	13
Invasion of privacy	32	2.49	11	32	2.64	11	0	0.00	13
Unstandard sizes	31	2.41	12	29	2.39	12	2	2.82	9
Boring sales pitches	27	2.10	13	25	2.06	13	2	2.82	9
Postage/handling costs	23	1.79	14	22	1.81	14	1	1.41	11
Inconvenient	21	1.63	15	17	1.40	15	4	5.63	6
Nothing	19	1.48	16	17	1.40	15	2	2.82	8
Unfamiliar companies	9	.70	17	9	.74	17	0	0.00	13
Rep missed appointment	6	.47	18	5	.41	19	1	1.41	11
Junk mail	6	.47	18	6	.49	18	0	0.00	13
Tend to buy more than need	5	.39	20	5	.41	19	0	0.00	13
Miss shopping	4	.31	21	4	.33	21	0	0.00	13
No personal contact	3	.23	22	3	.25	22	0	0.00	13
Damaged products	3	.23	22	3	.25	22	0	0.00	13
Parties/pressure to have	3	.23	22	2	.16	24	1	1.41	11

^{1}Percent of total sample

^{2}Across likes, within groups

^{3}Percent within use category

85

Table 5.29
Shopping Likes of Users of Direct Selling: 65+ vs. <65

DIRECT SELLING USE

ATTRIBUTE	ALL USERS			<65			65+		
	Freq	$\%^1$	Rank^2	Freq	$\%^3$	Rank^2	Freq	$\%^3$	Rank^2
Convenient	43	32.33	1	24	39.34	1	19	26.39	1
Seeing the product	27	20.30	2	9	14.75	3	18	25.00	2
Leisure	19	14.29	3	13	21.31	2	6	8.33	3
Personal touch	9	6.77	4	3	4.92	5	6	8.33	3
Name brand/familiar companies	8	6.02	5	2	3.28	6	6	8.33	3
Saves time/travel expense	7	5.26	6	4	6.56	4	3	4.17	5
Nothing	6	4.51	7	0	0.00	10	6	8.33	3
Product variety	4	3.01	8	1	1.64	8	3	4.17	5
See what you want	4	3.01	8	2	3.28	6	2	2.78	7
Party plans	3	2.26	10	2	3.28	6	1	1.39	9
Delivery	2	1.50	11	0	0.00	10	2	2.78	7
Seeing new products	1	.75	12	1	1.64	8	0	0.00	10

^{1}Percent of total sample

^{2}Across likes, within groups

^{3}Percent within category

Table 5.30
Shopping Dislikes of Users of Direct Selling: 65+ vs. <65

DIRECT SELLING USE

ATTRIBUTE	ALL USERS			<65			65+		
	Freq	$\%^1$	Rank^2	Freq	$\%^3$	Rank^2	Freq	$\%^3$	Rank^2
High pressure of sales	31	23.48	1	12	19.67	1	19	26.76	1
Not sure of what you get	21	15.91	2	10	16.39	3	11	15.49	2
Delivery time	14	10.61	3	11	18.03	2	3	4.23	7
No variety	10	7.58	4	3	4.92	5	7	9.86	3
Higher prices	9	6.82	5	7	11.48	4	2	2.82	9
Interruptions	7	5.30	6	1	1.64	9	6	8.45	4
Inconvenient	7	5.30	6	3	4.92	5	4	5.63	6
Feeling obliged to buy	6	4.55	8	1	1.64	9	5	7.04	5
Return hassles	5	3.79	9	2	3.28	7	3	4.23	7
Unstandard sizes	4	3.03	10	2	3.28	7	2	2.82	9
Strangers	3	2.27	11	1	1.64	9	2	2.82	9
Nothing	3	2.27	11	1	1.64	9	2	2.82	9
Boring sales pitches	2	1.52	12	0	0.00	11	2	2.82	9
Damaged products	2	1.52	12	2	3.28	7	0	0.00	13
Postage/handling costs	1	.76	14	0	0.00	11	1	1.41	11
Rep missed appointment	1	.76	14	0	0.00	11	1	1.41	11
Solicitation	1	.76	14	1	1.64	9	0	0.00	13
Tend to buy more than need	1	.76	14	1	1.64	9	0	0.00	13
Parties/pressure to have	1	.76	14	0	0.00	11	1	1.41	11

^{1}Percent of total sample

^{2}Across likes, within groups

^{3}Percent within category

Table 5.31
Shopping Likes of Party Plan Users vs. Nonusers: 65+ Only

PARTY PLAN USE

	ALL 65+			NONUSERS			USERS		
ATTRIBUTE	Freq	$\%^1$	Rank^2	Freq	$\%^3$	Rank^2	Freq	$\%^3$	Rank^2
Convenient	354	28.43	1	319	29.05	1	35	23.81	2
Seeing the product	267	21.45	2	222	20.22	2	45	30.61	1
Nothing	196	15.74	3	184	16.76	3	12	8.16	4
Leisure	152	12.21	4	132	12.02	4	20	13.61	3
See what you get	56	4.50	5	51	4.64	5	5	3.40	7
Personal touch	53	4.26	6	44	4.01	7	9	6.12	5
Saves time/travel expense	50	4.02	7	46	4.19	6	4	2.72	8
Product variety	35	2.81	8	32	2.91	8	3	2.04	10
Name brand/familiar companies	27	2.17	9	21	1.91	9	6	4.08	6
Party plans	12	.96	10	8	.73	14	4	2.72	8
Delivery	12	.96	10	10	.91	10	2	1.36	11
Guarantees	11	.88	12	10	.91	10	1	.68	12
Seeing new products	10	.80	13	9	.82	12	1	.68	12
Low prices	8	.64	14	8	.73	14	0	0.00	14
Hostess benefits	2	.16	15	2	.18	16	0	0.00	14

^{1}Percent of total sample

^{2}Across likes, within groups

^{3}Percent within use category

Table 5.32
Shopping Dislikes of Party Plan Users vs. Nonusers: 65+ Only

PARTY PLAN USE

	ALL 65+			NONUSERS			USERS		
ATTRIBUTE	Freq	$\%^1$	Rank^2	Freq	$\%^3$	Rank^2	Freq	$\%^3$	Rank^2
High pressure sales	338	26.30	1	290	25.46	1	48	32.88	1
Not sure of what you get	207	16.11	2	185	16.24	2	22	15.07	2
No variety	89	6.93	3	80	7.02	3	9	6.16	3
Interruptions	86	6.69	4	78	6.85	4	8	5.48	5
Delivery time	83	6.46	5	74	6.50	5	9	6.16	3
Feel obliged to buy	79	6.15	6	70	6.15	6	9	6.16	3
Strangers	74	5.76	7	69	6.06	7	5	3.42	8
Higher prices	51	3.97	8	47	4.13	8	4	2.74	9
Return hassles	47	3.66	9	44	3.86	9	3	2.05	10
Solicitation	39	3.04	10	36	3.16	10	3	2.05	10
Invasion of privacy	37	2.49	11	26	2.28	11	6	4.11	6
Unstandard sizes	31	2.41	12	25	2.19	12	6	4.11	6
Boring sales pitches	27	2.10	13	24	2.11	13	3	2.05	10
Postage/handling costs	23	1.79	14	22	1.93	14	1	.68	12
Inconvenient	21	1.63	15	15	1.32	16	6	4.11	6
Nothing	19	1.48	16	18	1.58	15	1	.68	12
Unfamiliar companies	9	.70	17	8	.70	17	1	.68	12
Rep missed appointment	6	.47	18	6	.53	18	0	0.00	14
Junk mail	6	.47	18	6	.53	18	0	0.00	14
Tend to buy more than need	5	.38	20	4	.35	20	1	.68	12
Miss shopping	4	.31	21	4	.35	20	0	0.00	14
No personal contact	3	.23	22	3	.26	22	0	0.00	14
Damaged products	3	.23	22	3	.26	22	0	0.00	14
Parties/pressure to have	3	.23	22	2	.18	22	1	.68	12

^{1}Percent of total sample

^{2}Across likes, within groups

^{3}Percent within use category

Table 5.33
Shopping Likes of Party Plan Users: 65+ vs. <65

PARTY PLAN USE

	ALL USERS			<65			65+		
ATTRIBUTE	Freq	$\%^1$	Rank^2	Freq	$\%^3$	Rank^2	Freq	$\%^3$	Rank^2
Convenient	94	29.28	1	59	33.91	1	35	23.81	2
Seeing the product	83	25.86	2	38	21.84	2	45	30.61	1
Leisure	50	15.58	3	30	17.24	3	20	13.61	3
Nothing	21	6.54	4	9	5.17	4	12	8.16	4
Personal touch	16	4.98	5	7	4.02	7	9	6.12	5
Saves time/travel expense	12	3.74	6	8	4.60	5	4	2.72	8
Party plans	12	3.74	6	8	4.60	5	4	2.72	8
See what you want	10	3.12	8	5	2.87	8	5	3.40	7
Name brand/familiar companies	8	2.49	9	2	1.15	11	6	4.08	6
Product variety	6	1.87	10	3	1.72	9	3	2.04	10
Delivery	5	1.56	11	3	1.72	9	2	1.36	11
Seeing new products	3	.93	12	2	1.15	11	1	.68	12
Guarantees	1	.31	13	0	0.00	13	1	.68	12

^{1}Percent of total sample

^{2}Across likes, within groups

^{3}Percent within category

Table 5.34
Shopping Dislikes of Party Plan Users: 65+ vs. <65

PARTY PLAN USE

	ALL USERS			<65			65+		
ATTRIBUTE	Freq	$\%^1$	Rank^2	Freq	$\%^3$	Rank^2	Freq	$\%^3$	Rank^2
High pressure sales	94	29.84	1	46	27.22	1	48	32.88	
Not sure of what you get	30	15.87	2	28	16.57	2	22	15.07	
Delivery time	27	8.57	3	18	10.65	3	9	6.16	
No variety	18	5.71	4	9	5.33	6	9	6.16	
Higher prices	16	3.08	5	12	7.10	4	4	2.74	
Feeling obliged to buy	16	3.08	5	7	4.14	7	9	6.16	
Interruptions	12	3.81	7	4	2.37	11	8	5.48	
Invasion of privacy	12	3.81	7	6	3.55	9	6	4.11	
Inconvenient	11	3.49	9	5	2.96	10	6	4.11	
Return hassles	10	3.17	10	7	4.14	7	3	2.05	
Unstandard sizes	10	3.17	10	4	2.37	11	6	4.11	
Strangers	8	2.84	12	3	1.78	13	5	3.42	
Solicitation	7	2.22	13	4	2.37	11	3	2.05	
Nothing	5	1.59	14	4	2.37	11	1	.68	
Damaged products	4	1.27	15	4	2.37	11	0	0.00	
Postage/handling costs	3	.95	16	12	7.10	4	4	2.74	
No personal contact	3	.95	16	3	1.78	13	0	0.00	
Unfamiliar companies	3	.95	16	2	1.18	15	1	.69	
Boring sales pitches	3	.95	16	0	0.00	17	3	2.05	
Tend to buy more than need	2	.63	20	1	.59	16	1	.68	
Parties/pressure to have	1	.32	21	0	0.00	17	1	.68	

^{1}Percent of total sample

^{2}Across likes, within groups

^{3}Percent within category

88

Table 5.35
Shopping Likes of In-Home Demonstration Users vs. Nonusers: 65+ Only

				IN-HOME DEMONSTRATION USE					
	65+			NONUSERS			USERS		
ATTRIBUTE	Freq	$\%^1$	Rank^2	Freq	$\%^3$	Rank^2	Freq	$\%^3$	Rank^2
Convenient	354	28.43	1	336	28.43	1	18	28.57	1
Seeing the product	267	21.45	2	249	21.87	2	18	28.57	1
Nothing	196	15.74	3	190	16.07	3	6	9.52	4
Leisure	152	12.21	4	144	12.18	4	8	12.70	3
See what you get	56	4.50	5	54	4.57	5	2	3.17	6
Personal touch	53	4.26	6	52	4.40	6	1	1.59	8
Saves time/travel expense	50	4.02	7	49	4.15	7	1	1.59	8
Product variety	35	2.81	8	33	2.79	8	2	3.17	6
Name brand/familiar companies	27	2.17	9	25	2.12	9	2	3.17	6
Party plans	12	.96	10	12	1.02	10	0	0.00	10
Delivery	12	.96	10	12	1.02	10	0	0.00	10
Guarantees	11	.88	12	9	.76	12	2	3.17	6
Seeing new products	10	.80	13	7	.59	14	3	4.76	5
Low prices	8	.64	14	8	.68	13	0	0.00	10
Hostess benefits	2	.16	15	2	.17	15	0	0.00	10

^{1}Percent of total sample

^{2}Across likes, within groups

^{3}Percent within use category

Table 5.36
Shopping Dislikes of In-Home Demonstration Users vs. Nonusers: 65+ Only

				IN-HOME DEMONSTRATION USE					
	ALL 65+			NONUSERS			USERS		
ATTRIBUTE	Freq	$\%^1$	Rank^2	Freq	$\%^3$	Rank^2	Freq	$\%^3$	Rank^2
High pressure sales	338	26.30	1	316	25.82	1	22	36.07	1
Not sure of what you get	207	16.11	2	200	16.34	2	7	11.48	2
No variety	89	6.93	3	86	7.03	3	3	4.92	5
Interruptions	86	6.69	4	84	6.86	4	2	3.28	7
Delivery time	83	6.46	5	79	6.45	5	4	6.56	3
Feel obliged to buy	79	6.15	6	75	6.13	6	4	6.56	3
Strangers	74	5.76	7	73	5.96	7	1	1.64	9
Higher prices	51	3.97	8	47	3.84	8	4	6.56	3
Return hassles	47	3.66	9	44	3.59	9	3	4.92	5
Solicitation	39	3.01	10	37	3.02	10	2	3.28	7
Invasion of privacy	32	2.49	11	31	2.53	11	1	1.64	9
Unstandard sizes	31	2.41	12	28	2.29	12	3	4.92	5
Boring sales pitches	27	2.10	13	24	1.96	12	3	4.92	5
Postage/handling costs	23	1.79	14	23	1.88	14	0	0.00	11
Inconvenient	21	1.63	15	20	1.63	15	1	1.64	9
Nothing	19	1.48	16	18	1.47	16	1	1.64	9
Unfamiliar companies	9	.70	17	9	.74	17	0	0.00	11
Rep missed appointment	6	.47	18	6	.49	18	0	0.00	11
Junk mail	6	.47	18	6	.49	18	0	0.00	11
Tend to buy more than need	5	.34	20	5	.41	20	0	0.00	11
Miss shopping	4	.31	21	4	.33	21	0	0.00	11
No personal contact	3	.23	22	3	.25	22	0	0.00	11
Damaged products	3	.23	22	3	.25	22	0	0.00	11
Parties/pressure to have	3	.23	22	3	.25	22	0	0.00	11

^{1}Percent of total sample

^{2}Across likes, within groups

^{3}Percent within use category

Table 5.37
Shopping Likes of In-Home Demonstration Users: 65+ Only

IN-HOME DEMONSTRATION USE

ATTRIBUTE	ALL 65+			NONUSERS			USERS		
	Freq	$\%^1$	Rank^2	Freq	$\%^3$	Rank^2	Freq	$\%^3$	Rank^2
Home demonstrations	36	28.80	1	18	29.03	1	18	28.57	1
Convenient	33	26.40	2	15	24.19	2	18	28.57	1
Leisure	19	15.20	3	11	17.74	3	8	12.70	3
Personal touch	8	6.40	4	7	11.29	4	1	1.59	8
See what you get	8	6.40	4	6	9.68	5	2	3.17	6
Nothing	7	5.60	6	1	1.61	7	6	9.52	4
Seeing new products	4	3.20	7	1	1.61	7	3	4.76	5
Name brand/familiar companies	3	2.40	8	1	1.61	7	2	3.17	6
Delivery	2	1.60	9	2	3.23	6	0	0.00	10
Guarantees	2	1.60	9	0	0.00	9	2	3.17	6
Product variety	2	1.60	9	0	0.00	9	2	3.17	6
Saves time/travel expense	1	.80	11	0	0.00	9	1	1.59	8

^{1}Percent of total sample

^{2}Across likes, within groups

^{3}Percent within category

Table 5.38
Shopping Dislikes of In-Home Demonstration Users: 65+ Only

IN-HOME DEMONSTRATION USE

ATTRIBUTE	ALL 65+			NONUSERS			USERS		
	Freq	$\%^1$	Rank^2	Freq	$\%^3$	Rank^2	Freq	$\%^3$	Rank^2
High pressure sales	51	41.13	1	29	46.03	1	22	36.07	1
Not sure of what you get	15	12.10	2	8	12.70	2	7	11.48	2
Higher prices	10	8.06	3	6	9.52	3	4	6.56	3
Delivery time	7	5.65	4	3	4.76	4	4	6.56	3
No variety	6	4.84	5	3	4.76	4	3	4.92	5
Unstandard sizes	5	4.03	6	2	3.17	6	3	4.92	5
Feeling obliged to buy	5	4.03	6	1	1.59	8	4	6.56	3
Solicitation	5	4.03	6	3	4.76	4	2	3.28	7
Interruptions	4	3.23	8	2	3.17	6	2	3.28	7
Return hassles	4	3.23	8	1	1.59	8	3	4.92	5
Boring sales pitches	3	2.42	10	0	0.00	10	3	4.92	5
Strangers	2	1.61	11	1	1.59	8	1	1.64	9
Invasion of privacy	2	1.61	11	1	1.59	8	1	1.64	9
Nothing	2	1.61	11	1	1.59	8	1	1.64	9
Junk mail	1	.81	13	1	1.59	8	0	0.00	11
Parties/pressure to have	1	.81	13	1	1.59	8	0	0.00	11
Inconvenient	1	.81	13	0	0.00	10	1	1.64	9

^{1}Percent of total sample

^{2}Across likes, within groups

^{3}Percent within category

CHAPTER 6

The Mature Consumer and Direct Salespeople

This chapter highlights the direct-selling industry with a particular focus on consumer attitudes toward direct selling and direct sellers. Willingness to purchase via direct selling as well as consumer perceptions of various direct-selling modes will be examined. Predictors of direct-selling usage will be indicated along with perceptions of salesperson traits.

WILLINGNESS TO PURCHASE

Consumers in this study were questioned as to whether they would be willing to buy from three different direct-selling modes: door-to-door, party plans, and in-home demonstration. Because it was felt that the nature of the product and/or the financial risk involved might color the answers, three different product categories were used with each direct-selling mode. These included hand tools or kitchen utensils in the $8-$10 range, cosmetics and fragrances in the $25-$50 range, and a set of luggage in the $200-$350 range.

As can be seen in Table 6.1, users were generally more willing than nonusers to buy across all direct-selling modes and across the three product categories. Further, users of a specific age group (e.g., 65+) were in every case more willing to buy than nonusers of the same age group.

For door-to-door sales, the 50-64 user group was most willing to buy, and the 50-64 nonuser group was the least willing to buy. This finding held across all three product categories. For party plans, the most willing to buy were the ≤49 users, and the least willing were the 65+ nonusers. Finally, for in-home demonstrations, the most willing were the 65+ users, and the least willing were the 50-64 nonusers. Only for the party plan does age appear to be a factor in willingness to purchase; in this case younger consumers appear more likely to use party plans. It should be noted that only for party plans was a *real* willingness to purchase indicated (shown by means <30). In the other cases the means simply indicate a lesser or greater unwillingness to purchase.

PERCEPTION OF MODE TRAITS

Table 6.2 shows the extent to which users and nonusers of various age groups associate certain purchase characteristics with given direct-selling modes and with traditional retailing. In general, users of all age groups see retailers as possessing more of the various traits than any of the three direct-selling modes. The same finding holds true for nonusers. Also, nonusers of all age groups generally associate less of a trait with the direct-selling modes than do users. The differences observed in Table 6.2 appear to be based primarily on user/nonuser categories and the different selling modes rather than on age groups.

There were particular strengths associated with some of the direct-selling modes. For example, both party plans and in-home demonstrations were rated high on providing sufficient product information, filling order requests accurately, and delivery direct to home. Door-to-door tended to have low scores on many shopping characteristics, most notably providing wide selection, company pays for call/postage when ordering, and availability of alteration/repair. Scores among nonusers on these dimensions tended to be even lower.

SHOPPING ORIENTATIONS

In Table 6.3, various characteristics relating to shopping orientation are examined for users and nonusers of all three age groups. The 65+ user has lower mobility than other users and lower mobility than the two younger age groups among nonusers. These 65+ users tend to be more personalizing shoppers than other groups with more loyalty to local merchants, more positive toward convenience, and more likely to purchase a service than a product in-home.

Conversely, this group is less likely to profess self-confidence in shopping ability and less likely than younger groups to feel a great deal of time pressure associated with shopping behavior. They are less negative toward merchants and, at the same time, less positive toward the price/quality/ selection relationship for products sold in-home. In spite of the latter, however, they are also less distrustful concerning the risk elements of in-home purchasing.

The 65+ nonusers cite lower mobility than younger groups, but they are still less positive toward the convenience aspects of in-home shopping. Whether they have failed to carefully consider this aspect of in-home shopping or have simply experienced negative consequences of in-home shopping cannot be determined from this data. Nevertheless, since the convenience aspect is often cited by direct sellers as a reason for using this shopping mode, it would be well to uncover the precise cause for the perception of less convenience.

Some explanations *may* be related to other findings. For example, 65+ nonusers are more suspicious than 65+ users, they are less likely to be shopping innovators, and they are more loyal to local merchants than the younger groups. They are less negative toward merchants than the ≤ 49 age groups and are less positive toward the price/quality/convenience relationship associated with buying products in-home. They also are more likely to be shopping innovators, which may explain their willingness to situation. These nonusers prefer personalizing shopping more than younger groups, experience less time pressure than all age groups, and are more likely to prefer purchasing a service over a product in-home.

Finally, it was found that 65+ nonusers were lower in mobility and higher in their distrust and risk assessment for in-home shopping. Users in the 65+ group were less interested in shopping with friends, but were more likely to want to shop where they are known. They are also more likely to be shopping innovators which may explain their willingness to shop using direct-selling modes.

SOURCE TRAITS

Table 6.4 presents perceptions of the importance of source traits by users and nonusers of direct selling in each of the three age groups. Certain characteristics of the shopping process are more important to the 65+ group than to one or more of the younger age groups, regardless of user status. These characteristics include getting a well-known brand from a well-known company, having previous experience with the product and brand, having access to a salesperson, and having previous experience with the company.

However, the 65+ user also differs from the 65+ nonuser on some dimensions. Predictably, 65+ users consider a personalized demonstration of the product to be more desirable than do 65+ nonusers. Also having a salesperson come to "my" home, post-purchase follow-up by the salesperson, and post-purchase follow-up by the telephone were all seen as less desirable to the 65+ nonusers.

Direct-selling nonusers in the 65+ age group associate less importance with the ability to charge purchases than do other groups. But this group also considers several characteristics more important than do other groups, notably the availability of C.O.D., the ability to examine the product, having a salesperson come to "my" home, and follow-up by the sales representative.

PERCEPTIONS OF SALESPERSON'S TRAITS

This section highlights the perceptions of the six groups with respect to attributing particular sales traits to direct-selling salespeople. Included in the traits that were examined are the five power traits that salespeople may embody (Table 6.5). Since these power traits are believed to impact selling effectiveness, it would be well to first examine some of the conceptual background pertaining to interpersonal power.

The five sources, or bases, of power were identified in 1959 (French and Raven, 1959, p. 163) and can be defined as follows:

- B's perceptions that A has the ability to mediate rewards for him,
- B's perception that A has the ability to mediate punishments for him,
- B's perception that A has some special knowledge or expertise,
- B's identification with A, and
- B's perception that A has a legitimate right to prescribe behavior for him.

These are commonly referred to as reward, coercive, expert, referent, and legitimate power sources, respectively. It is not surprising that these power sources have received considerable conceptual and empirical attention from marketers, since nothing could be more useful to a business than the ability to get relevant others—suppliers or customers—to conform to one's will.

For example, the degree to which information is accepted by a customer might depend on the perceived expertise of the seller. Additionally, if the information is useful or positively valued by the customer, it would constitute a reward. If the salesperson is the sole representative in a given territory for making a much-needed product available (say, perhaps, a critical component in a production process), the customer may recognize a salesperson's coercive power.

The additional traits on this list include a global customer orientation characteristic as well as a number of traits that are commonly associated with salesperson effectiveness such as enthusiasm, persuasiveness, and sincerity.

From Table 6.5, it can be seen that 65+ users of direct selling are *more* likely than any of the nonuser groups to attribute to direct sellers customer orientation, reward power, and being considerate and are *less* likely to see direct sellers as having a job orientation. These 65+ users, compared with all other groups, also attribute to direct sellers more sincerity.

Both the 65+ users and the 65+ nonusers attribute more legitimate power, more organization, more persuasiveness and less persistence to direct sellers than do younger groups. Finally, 65+ users see direct salespeople as more friendly than do the 65+ nonusers.

The analysis (Table 6.6) indicates that while 65+ users see direct salespeople as high in expert power, referent power, legitimate power, and experience, these users also rank the salespeople low in enthusiasm, persistence, reward power, and job orientation. The 65+ nonusers rank direct salespeople as high in persuasiveness and organization.

SALESPERSON TRAITS AND SHOPPING ORIENTATIONS

Table 6.7 presents a correlation matrix of direct salesperson traits by customer shopping orientations. While implications of causality should not be drawn, several interesting items stand out. For example, attitudes toward direct sellers' customer orientation were negatively correlated with statements that expressed a suspicious nature and those that expressed distrust of in-home selling. There was also a large positive correlation between these two shopping orientations and the attitude toward direct sellers' job orientation.

A global measure of power was associated with low mobility, personalizing shopper, social shopping, and surprisingly, loyalty to local merchants. Of particular interest were relatively high correlations between reward power and low mobility, personalizing shopper, social shopping, loyalty to local merchants, and getting what you order. High correlations are evidenced between coercive power and negative toward merchants and loyalty to local merchants; between legitimate power and low mobility; between referent power and low mobility, personalizing shopper, and loyalty to local merchants. The recurring high correlations between various components of power and certain of the shopping orientations indicates strong associations between direct sellers' power and customers who have low mobility; who like to have a close, personal relationship with salespeople; who view shopping as a social activity; and who are, surprisingly, loyal to local merchants.

Among other traits that are positively associated with good selling skills several strong correlations are evident. Persuasiveness attributed to direct sellers is associated with price-conscious shoppers, suspicious nature, and a distrust of in-home shopping. Friendliness is inversely correlated with negative toward merchants and positively correlated with get what you order. Sincerity is associated with low mobility, social shopping, loyalty to local merchants, and get what you order. Not surprisingly, sincerity is negatively correlated with suspicious nature and distrust of in-home shopping.

For direct salespeople attributions of being considerate are negatively correlated with respondents who express a suspicious nature and are positively correlated with those who believe that they get what they order when shopping in-home. Persistence shows a strong correlation with suspicious nature and distrust of in-home shopping. A similar situation exists between experience correlated with suspicious nature and distrust of in-home shopping. Experience is also negatively correlated with getting what you order through in-home shopping. Apparently respondents who view direct sellers as experienced and persuasive are also those who view these selling skills in a negative light. Perhaps these respondents assume that direct sellers are out to make a sale regardless of whether the customer actually receives the desired benefits.

The other traits that are examined in this section have to do with customer orientation. These traits include an all-inclusive term "customer orientation" that represents a set of scale items including positive responses toward the salesperson having the customer's best interests in mind, offering products that meet needs, not using pressure tactics, following up on the sale, being interested in the customer and easy to talk with, and wanting to do a good job. As early as 1925, Strong (1925) emphasized that personal selling strategies should be directed toward securing customer satisfaction as well as purchase orders. The purpose of soliciting responses to these traits with respect to direct-selling salespeople is to determine the extent to which these positive selling traits are associated with direct selling. Customer-oriented selling refers to the degree to which people practice the marketing concept by trying to help customers achieve need-satisfaction through appropriate purchases. In fact, some writers have proposed interpersonal behavior models with a two-dimensional (concern for self/concern for others) focus (Blake and Mouton 1970; Buzzotta, Lefton, and Sherberg 1972; Thomas 1976).

The SOCO (Selling Orientation-Customer Orientation) scale was developed and introduced in 1982 (Saxe and Weitz). In terms of reliability, the coefficient alpha (Cronbach 1951) for the SOCO scale's first sample of salespeople was .86. This demonstrates a high level of internal consistency, an important indication of reliability (Peter 1979). Test-retest reliability was measured after a six-week interval. Forty-six salespeople in the second sample were retested, and a correlation of .67 (p < .001, one-tailed) indicated moderate stability over time.

In terms of factor structure, a principal axes factor analysis resulted in two factors. One, accounting for 53 percent of the variance, was a general factor representing customer orientation. All items had a moderate positive correlation with this factor, while 271 of 276 between-item correlations were in the expected direction and most were significant. The second factor accounted for 20 percent of the variance. This factor separated the positively stated items from the negatively stated items, a frequent characteristic of the analyses of scales consisting of both positive and negative items (e.g., Christie and Geis 1970, Robinson and Shaver 1973, Welsh 1956).

Content validity cannot be assessed statistically, but results from a broad representative range of items. Expert judges, a common method of "validation," averaged 79 percent agreement on item inclusion.

Convergent and discriminant validity were examined using data collected in the second sample of salespeople. The SOCO scale correlated ($r = .56$, $p < .001$) with a measure of long-term versus short-term orientation developed by Saxe (1979).

Table 6.8 shows the results of a recursive regression analysis using customer orientation (modified from SOCO) as the dependent variable. As seen in the table the relative contributions of five variables (or variable sets) were assessed with respect to the incremental explained variance accounted for by each variable in different selected combinations. These variables (and variable sets) include age, power (overall), power (five types), shopping orientation, and sales variables.

It can be seen at a glance that sales variables produce the highest R^2 (.63) and that age produces the lowest R^2 (.04) when these are assessed individually rather than in combination with other variables. In additional equations where various variable combinations are used, the sales variables continue to reflect the highest marginal R^2s. Conversely, it appears that the age of the respondent exerts negligible impact on respondents' perceptions of salespeople's customer orientations.

The dependent variable in Table 6.9 is job orientation. Job orientation conveys attitudes that are opposite to that of a customer orientation. For example, where the customer-oriented salesperson is concentrating on meeting the customer's needs and providing satisfaction, the job-oriented salesperson's focus is in completing the sale and in trying to sell as much as possible. Where the customer-oriented salesperson is interested in listening to the customer, the job-oriented salesperson is more interested in what he or she has to say.

Not surprisingly, of the five variable sets, sales variables overwhelmingly account for the largest amount of the variance ($R^2 = .72$). Age, again, has a negligible effect, but shopping orientation also contributes a fairly large marginal R^2 as shown in equation 24.

Table 6.10 depicts the R^2s accounted for by age, shopping orientation, and sales variables regressed against power (overall). Sales variables continue to account for the largest explained variance, both in an absolute sense and in terms of marginal contribution to the R^2.

Tables 6.11 through 6.16 depict the regression coefficients for the various equations. In Table 6.11 it can be seen that strong associations exist between customer orientation and power, particularly reward power and expert power. Respondents here are indicating a willingness to follow salespeople's advice when the salespeople are perceived as having the customer's best interest in mind and are experts in their field. As might be expected, strong negative relationships exist between job orientation and reward power. Salespeople with job orientations are not viewed as offering the most satisfying solutions to the customer's problems. Interestingly, there is also a significant negative relationship perceived between job orientation and expert power. Respondents apparently feel that salespeople who are more job-oriented than customer-oriented are not good sources of product knowledge.

Table 6.12 depicts the relationships between the dependent variables customer orientation, job orientation, and power and the various shopping orientation characteristics. Respondents tend to associate customer orientation with preferring purchasing a service over purchasing a product via in-home shopping. Also associated with customer orientation are getting what you order, low mobility, and loyalty to local merchants. A strong negative relationship occurs between customer orientation and suspicious nature. Apparently suspicious respondents are reluctant to attribute positive characteristics to salespeople.

For job orientation significant positive findings were linked with suspicious nature and distrust of in-home shopping. Finally power is associated with low mobility, negative toward merchants, and, conversely, loyalty toward local merchants.

Table 6.13 shows salespersons' characteristics regressed against the same three dependent variables. Sincerity and considerateness are strongly linked to customer orientation, while experience and persistence are associated with job orientation. Interestingly, a negative relationship exists between persistence and power. Sincerity, persuasiveness, and creativity are both strongly linked to power.

Table 6.14 depicts the marginal contribution to R^2 that is realized by sequentially adding variables while controlling for age. The selected variables that are added include power, salesperson characteristics, and respondent shopping orientations.

While equation 6 suggests that power makes a significant contribution to the R^2, equations 7, 11, 13, and 15 show that reward power and expert power specifically make the largest contribution.

With respect to a salesperson's personal characteristics, it can be seen that creativity, considerateness, and sincerity are the most important attributes linked to customer orientation. These variables also make the largest marginal contribution to R^2. Negatively associated with customer orientation are persistence and experience. Customers apparently associated persistence with a hard-sell approach that ignores the best interests of the customer. Unfortunately, rather than being seen as a valuable asset to helping them solve problems, respondents seemed to view experience as a negative characteristic associated with job orientation rather than as a tool to better serve the customer.

This pattern is reversed in Table 6.15 where job orientation is the dependent variable. Here considerateness and sincerity are negatively associated with job orientation while experience and persistence are positively associated. In this case, ambitiousness also shows a significant relationship to job orientation.

Power, in general, shows a negative relationship to job orientation. Equations 22, 25, 27, and 29 indicate that reward power shows the strongest negative association with job orientation. However, the set of variables that make the largest marginal contribution to R^2 are the salesperson's characteristics, particularly experience and persistence.

Table 6.16 shows that, again, salesperson characteristics make the largest marginal contribution to R^2. In this case, power is the dependent variable. The most important personal attributes appear to be creativity and sincerity, although age also has an impact. Persistence is negatively associated with power.

The most important shopping orientations are negative toward merchants, loyalty to local merchants, and low mobility. It is interesting that both negative attitudes toward merchants and loyalty to local merchants occur among respondents who perceived power to be associated with salespeople. However, the loyalty to local merchants attitude indicates a willingness to shop with local merchants even though the respondent is not necessarily entirely pleased with the shopping experience.

Table 6.1

Willingness to Purchase: Direct-Selling Users and Nonusers by Age Group Compared[1]

	Users			Nonusers			Level of Significance[2]
	65+	50-64	$\leq$49	65+	50-64	$\leq$49	
Door-to-Door							
$8-$10	4.10	4.13	4.39	4.49	4.50	4.41	.001
$25-$50	3.98	3.90	4.34	4.55	4.55	4.45	.001
$200-$350	4.51	4.43	4.62	4.69	4.73	4.64	.001
Party Plan							
$8-$10	2.82	2.57	2.34	3.70	3.60	3.25	.001
$25-$50	3.03	2.82	2.44	3.87	3.84	3.43	.001
$200-$300	3.81	3.71	3.53	4.23	4.22	3.96	.001
In-Home Demonstration							
$8-$10	3.16	3.35	3.41	3.77	3.83	3.82	.001
$25-$50	3.19	3.39	3.32	3.92	3.97	3.85	.001
$200-$300	3.73	3.85	3.93	4.15	4.18	4.09	.001

[1]On a 5 point scale where: 1 = very willing, 2 = somewhat willing, 3 = neither willing nor unwilling, 4 = somewhat unwilling, 5 = unwilling so that high scores indicate less willingness.

[2]Analysis of variance.

Table 6.2
Perception of Extent to Which Consumers Perceive Direct-Selling Modes to Have Purchase Characteristics[1]

Purchase Characteristic	Mode[3]	Users			Nonusers			Level of Significance[2]
		65+	50-64	$\leq$49	65+	50-64	$\leq$49	
Credible product claims	1	2.17	2.21	2.31	1.90	1.98	2.02	.001
	2	2.91	3.10	2.99	2.52	2.58	2.59	.001
	3	2.93	2.99	2.95	2.54	2.59	2.55	.001
	4	3.40	3.46	3.49	3.46	3.52	3.30	N.S.
Provides wide selection	1	1.67	1.86	1.77	1.61	1.52	1.61	N.S.
	2	2.53	2.65	2.64	2.16	2.19	2.19	.001
	3	2.20	2.33	2.20	1.97	1.98	1.83	.001
	4	3.45	3.69	3.66	3.51	3.61	3.53	.01
Good quality products	1	2.15	2.21	2.33	1.98	2.06	2.13	.001
	2	2.93	3.02	2.99	2.55	2.56	2.55	.001
	3	2.87	2.93	2.96	2.57	2.56	2.51	.001
	4	3.44	3.51	3.56	3.48	3.53	3.45	N.S.
Price matches quality	1	2.12	2.32	2.20	2.01	2.05	2.08	N.S.
	2	2.82	2.96	2.76	2.43	2.44	2.42	.001
	3	2.71	2.86	2.68	2.46	2.43	2.31	.001
	4	3.37	3.40	3.44	3.37	3.40	3.24	N.S.
Provides sufficient information about product	1	2.36	2.33	2.61	2.17	2.33	2.42	.001
	2	3.06	3.04	3.09	2.64	2.74	2.72	.001
	3	3.11	3.08	3.14	2.75	2.81	2.74	.001
	4	3.20	3.24	3.24	3.29	3.36	3.06	.001
Accurate portrayal of products	1	2.25	2.26	2.31	2.13	2.20	2.22	N.S.
	2	3.04	3.06	2.98	2.64	2.72	2.62	.001
	3	3.05	3.05	2.92	2.70	2.74	2.66	.001
	4	3.34	3.33	3.31	3.36	3.45	3.31	N.S.
Fills order requests accurately	1	2.62	2.55	2.80	2.40	2.61	2.59	.001
	2	3.29	3.27	3.39	2.88	3.01	2.93	.001
	3	3.22	3.28	3.32	2.90	3.01	2.91	.001
	4	3.50	3.51	3.59	3.50	3.56	3.44	N.S.
Quality consistent from one order to next	1	2.36	2.47	2.43	2.25	2.34	2.32	N.S.
	2	3.16	3.29	3.17	2.73	2.82	2.72	.001
	3	3.04	3.14	3.04	2.74	2.81	2.64	.001
	4	3.30	3.46	3.45	3.36	3.43	3.20	.01
Order filled in timely manner	1	2.46	2.58	2.54	2.29	2.33	2.43	.01
	2	3.12	3.20	3.07	2.70	2.79	2.68	.001
	3	2.99	3.20	2.97	2.70	2.79	2.65	.001
	4	3.39	3.37	3.58	3.44	3.50	3.33	N.S.
Order delivered when promised	1	2.45	2.55	2.58	2.28	2.38	2.40	.01
	2	3.15	3.22	3.09	2.74	2.83	2.76	.001
	3	3.07	3.18	3.05	2.72	2.82	2.71	.001
	4	3.36	3.33	3.51	3.36	3.41	3.28	N.S.
Competitive prices	1	2.20	2.32	2.21	2.09	2.16	2.02	N.S.
	2	2.62	2.72	2.61	2.32	2.36	2.17	.001
	3	2.56	2.65	2.47	2.34	2.33	2.12	.001
	4	3.35	3.45	3.46	3.36	3.38	3.29	N.S.

Table 6.2 (continued)

Money-back guarantee	1	2.19	2.37	2.45	2.06	2.13	2.11	.001
	2	2.86	3.32	3.07	2.50	2.59	2.51	.001
	3	2.79	3.11	3.11	2.50	2.60	2.47	.001
	4	3.32	3.49	3.49	3.37	3.46	3.30	N.S.
Well-known brand name	1	2.18	2.37	2.29	2.04	2.15	2.12	.01
	2	2.87	3.03	2.96	2.55	2.62	2.54	.001
	3	2.78	2.89	2.93	2.52	2.59	2.44	.001
	4	3.33	3.48	3.51	3.43	3.51	3.47	N.S.
Company pays for call/	1	1.72	1.78	2.12	1.68	1.78	1.88	.001
postage when ordering	2	2.10	2.10	2.28	1.89	1.99	2.01	.001
	3	2.06	2.14	2.21	1.89	1.99	1.97	.01
	4	2.18	2.22	2.51	2.23	2.79	2.32	N.S.
Delivery direct to home	1	2.98	3.25	3.12	2.90	3.13	3.16	.001
	2	3.24	3.29	3.14	3.02	3.09	2.87	.01
	3	3.37	3.46	3.27	3.08	3.22	3.16	.001
	4	2.65	2.85	2.64	2.86	2.92	2.64	.01
Company pays postage for	1	1.70	1.93	2.03	1.66	1.72	1.74	.01
returned goods	2	2.09	2.41	2.34	1.89	1.90	1.92	.001
	3	2.08	2.35	2.34	1.87	1.87	1.92	.001
	4	1.96	2.31	2.31	2.17	2.10	1.97	N.S.
Ability to get products	1	1.99	2.30	2.24	1.95	2.05	2.03	.01
not readily available	2	2.55	2.72	2.74	2.29	2.32	2.29	.001
	3	2.52	2.67	2.51	2.25	2.30	2.17	.001
	4	2.70	2.79	2.84	2.79	2.83	2.61	N.S.
Number to call with	1	1.91	2.16	2.14	1.86	1.88	1.89	N.S.
complaints/questions	2	2.61	2.85	2.64	2.30	2.29	2.23	.001
	3	2.66	2.83	2.55	2.30	2.31	2.18	.001
	4	3.00	3.16	2.99	3.08	3.20	3.00	N.S.
Ability to charge purchases	1	1.53	1.94	2.39	1.75	1.92	2.31	.001
	2	1.67	1.88	2.26	1.76	1.86	2.07	.001
	3	1.85	1.92	2.38	1.89	1.99	2.19	.001
	4	2.86	3.19	3.39	3.12	3.29	3.49	.001
Availability of	1	1.56	1.63	1.88	1.55	1.67	1.69	.01
alteration/repair	2	1.98	2.18	2.28	1.73	1.86	1.84	.001
	3	2.08	2.11	2.26	1.78	1.86	1.90	.001
	4	2.73	2.88	3.01	2.84	3.07	2.94	N.S.
Ability to make exchange	1	1.78	1.88	2.02	1.79	1.89	1.76	N.S.
	2	2.33	2.66	2.51	2.08	2.24	2.18	.001
	3	2.02	2.73	2.34	2.07	2.20	2.04	.001
	4	3.28	3.50	3.53	3.40	3.54	3.44	.01
Capability of buying	1	2.23	2.44	2.11	2.11	2.14	2.24	N.S.
several things at a time	2	3.16	3.08	3.11	2.74	2.85	2.85	.001
	3	2.75	2.84	2.59	2.43	2.53	2.44	.001
	4	3.68	3.77	3.74	3.65	3.74	3.64	N.S.

---

[1] On a four point scale where 1 = not at all, 2 = slightly, 3 = somewhat, 4 = very much so.

[2] Analysis of variance.

[3] 1 = Door-to-door, 2 = Party plan, 3 = In-home demonstration, 4 = Retail.

101

Table 6.3
Shopping Orientations of Direct-Selling Users and Nonusers by Age Group[1]

Trait	Users			Nonusers			Level of Significance[2]
	65+	50-64	$\leq$49	65+	50-64	$\leq$49	
Low mobility	2.12	1.90	1.65	2.09	1.70	1.61	.001
Price-conscious shopper	3.81	3.95	3.94	3.78	3.81	3.91	N.S.
Personalizing shopper	3.73	3.60	3.30	3.65	3.50	3.26	.001
Negative toward merchants	1.96	2.09	2.13	1.99	2.03	2.13	.001
Suspicious nature	3.30	3.28	3.36	3.44	3.36	3.42	.001
Shopping self-confidence	3.29	3.38	3.39	3.28	3.36	3.60	.001
Shopping propensity	3.10	3.13	3.15	3.13	3.10	3.12	N.S.
Social shopping	3.17	3.06	3.12	3.03	2.97	2.93	N.S.
Time pressure shopping	2.84	3.22	3.33	2.71	3.00	3.32	.001
Shopping innovator	3.48	3.57	3.67	3.37	3.48	3.62	.001
Negative toward local shopping	2.67	2.78	2.76	2.69	2.70	2.76	N.S.
Loyalty to local merchants	2.70	2.48	2.33	2.66	2.59	2.32	.001
Distrust of in-home	3.42	3.45	3.23	3.58	3.50	3.38	.001
Positive toward convenience	3.32	3.34	3.46	3.11	3.10	3.37	.001
Positive toward price/quality/selection	3.00	2.93	2.91	2.88	2.79	3.02	.001
Get what you order	3.31	3.29	3.26	3.24	3.15	3.26	N.S.
Service over product in-home	3.20	3.11	2.82	3.31	3.18	2.88	.001

[1]On a 5 point scale where 1 = strongly disagree, 2 = disagree, 3 = neither agree nor disagree, 4 = agree, 5 = strongly agree.

[2]Analysis of variance.

Table 6.4
Perceptions of the Importance of Source Traits by Users and Nonusers[1]

Source Trait	Users 65+	Users 50-64	Users ≤49	Non-Users 65+	Non-Users 50-64	Non-Users ≤49	Level of Significance[2]
Money-back guarantee	4.37	4.43	4.30	4.35	4.40	4.31	N.S.
Well-known brand name	3.83	3.61	3.50	3.87	3.81	3.78	.001 (3-1, 4, 5, 6)[3]
Well-known company name	3.97	3.73	3.63	4.03	3.96	3.87	.001 (3-1, 4, 5, 6) (2, 4)
Previous experience with brand	3.92	3.91	3.61	3.86	3.85	3.72	.01 (3-1, 4, 5)
Previous experience with product	3.90	3.93	3.63	3.90	3.87	3.75	.01 (3-1, 4, 5) (4-6)
Company recommended by friends/family	3.30	3.38	3.14	3.30	3.15	3.22	N.S.
Company pays for call/postage when you order	3.44	3.66	3.56	3.40	3.51	3.43	N.S.
Access to salesperson	3.64	3.60	3.26	3.59	3.58	3.31	.001 (3-1, 4, 5) (6-1, 4, 5)
Delivery direct to home/workplace	3.86	3.84	3.64	3.89	3.79	3.89	N.S.
Company pays postage for returns	3.96	4.03	3.92	3.89	3.95	3.76	N.S.
Ability to get products not readily available in stores	3.81	3.75	3.78	3.76	3.77	3.71	N.S.
Ability to decide on purchase in my home	3.29	3.27	3.25	3.16	3.14	3.23	N.S.
Number to call with complaints/ questions	4.07	4.11	3.90	4.00	3.98	3.88	N.S.
Availability of C.O.D.	2.55	2.66	2.47	2.53	2.41	2.34	N.S.
Ability to charge purchase	2.79	2.90	3.12	2.82	2.98	3.18	.001 (1-6) (3, 4-6)
Convenience of access	3.93	3.82	3.70	3.94	3.94	3.77	N.S.
Repeated solicitation at home	1.67	1.63	1.62	1.64	1.50	1.71	N.S.
No obligation trial period	2.85	3.07	3.08	2.84	2.74	2.82	N.S.
Having product right away	3.64	3.65	3.78	3.62	3.66	3.70	N.S.
Wide selection	4.02	4.05	4.17	4.04	4.11	4.16	N.S.
Availability of information about product	4.29	4.16	4.14	4.25	4.25	4.18	N.S.
Previous experience with company	4.01	3.93	3.61	3.97	3.86	3.75	.001 (3-1, 2, 4, 5) (6-1, 4)
Ability to examine product before purchasing	4.08	4.10	3.95	4.05	4.06	3.91	N.S.
Getting what I ordered without substitutions	4.53	4.40	4.52	4.49	4.55	4.50	N.S.
Availability of first/second choice	3.71	3.77	3.42	3.51	3.60	3.56	N.S.
Samples for evaluation	3.70	3.72	3.64	3.63	3.63	3.64	N.S.
Personalized demonstration of product	3.08	3.19	2.94	2.83	2.86	2.76	.001 (1, 2-6) (1, 2-4) (1-5)
Having salesperson come to my house	2.17	2.03	1.92	1.87	1.82	1.78	.001 (1-3, 4, 5, 6)
Post-purchase follow-up by salesperson	2.23	2.09	2.00	1.98	1.90	1.90	.01 (1-4, 5, 6)
Post-purchase follow-up by phone	2.11	2.14	1.96	1.92	1.82	1.94	.01 (1-4, 5)
Post-purchase follow-up by mail	2.28	2.31	2.47	2.10	2.08	2.35	N.S.

[1]On a 5 point scale where 1 = not at all important, 2 = not too important, 3 = somewhat important, 4= very important, 5 = extremely important.

[2]Analysis of variance, Scheffe Test.

[3]Read: For well known brand names, group 3 (≤49 users) differs from groups 1 (65+ nonusers), 4 (65+ nonusers), 5 (50-64 nonusers) and 6 (≤49 nonusers).

103

Table 6.5
Perceptions of Salespeople by Direct-Selling Users and Nonusers[1]

Sales Traits	Users			Nonusers			Level of Significance[2]
	65+	50-64	$\leq$49	65+	50-64	$\leq$49	
Customer orientation	3.04	2.91	2.69	2.90	2.75	2.64	.001 (1-3, 4, 5, 6)[3] (2-3, 5, 6) (4-3, 5, 6)
Job orientation	3.55	3.64	3.71	3.65	3.70	3.82	.001 (1-4, 5, 6) (4-6)
Reward power	2.83	2.63	2.45	2.58	2.41	2.28	.001 (4-5, 6) (2-6) (1-3, 4, 5, 6)
Coercive power	2.19	1.91	2.15	2.12	1.90	2.03	.001 (1, 4-5)
Legitimate power	2.23	2.09	2.04	2.19	2.02	1.92	.001 (1-5, 6) (4-5, 6)
Referent power	2.62	2.51	2.33	2.51	2.49	2.27	.01 (1, 4, 5-6)
Expert power	2.56	2.24	2.19	2.36	2.17	1.96	.001 (1-2, 3, 4, 5,6) (4-5, 6) (5-6)
Enthusiasm	3.80	3.87	3.77	3.77	3.68	3.77	N.S.
Well-organized	3.36	3.42	3.15	3.29	3.18	3.12	.001 (1-5, 6) (4-5)
Ambitious	3.61	3.74	3.80	3.62	3.57	3.67	N.S.
Persuasive	3.67	3.66	3.58	3.78	3.65	3.44	.001 (4, 5-6)
Friendly	3.82	3.81	3.67	3.70	3.69	3.49	.001 (1, 2, 4, 5-6) (1-4)
Sincere	3.06	2.79	2.64	2.90	2.73	2.41	.001 (1-2, 3, 4, 5, 6) (4-3, 5, 6) (6-2, 3, 5)
Considerate	3.30	3.15	3.08	3.09	3.02	2.94	.001 (1-4, 5 6)
Creative	3.08	3.15	2.91	2.94	2.95	2.97	N.S.
Persistent	3.74	3.79	4.04	3.86	3.93	4.02	.001 (1-3, 5, 6) (4-6)
Experienced	3.47	3.46	3.57	3.59	3.63	3.70	N.S.
Good verbal skills	3.45	3.35	3.44	3.43	3.28	3.35	N.S.

---

[1]On a 5 point scale where 1 = strongly disagree, 2 = disagree, 3 = neither agree nor disagree, 4 = agree, 5 = strongly agree.

[2]Analysis of variance, Scheffe Test.

[3]Read: For customer orientation, group 1 (65+ users) differs from group 3 ($\leq$49 users), 4 (65+ nonusers), 5 (50-64 nonusers), and 6 ($\leq$49 nonusers); also, group 2 differs from groups 3, 5 and 6; also, group 4 differs from groups 3, 5, and 6.

Table 6.6
Six Group Discriminant Analysis: Perceptions of Salesperson Traits across Buyer Categories[1]

	Discriminant Function Weights				
Salesperson Characteristics[4]	Func 1	Func 2	Func 3	Func 4	Func 5
Persuasive[2]	0.62	-0.31	0.08	-0.04	-0.09
Well-organized	0.40	0.01	-0.39	-010	-0.26
Creative	-0.12	0.74	0.01	-0.09	-0.03
Customer orientation2	0.40	-0.59	0.26	-0.27	-0.39
Friendly[3]	0.01	0.42	0.41	0.16	-0.20
Considerate	0.06	0.16	-0.83	0.07	0.13
Sincere[2]	0.21	0.24	0.74	0.13	0.11
Ambitious	0.01	0.24	0.28	0.17	-0.04
Expert power[2]	-0.03	-0.09	0.06	0.68	-0.03
Enthusiasm	0.03	-0.08	0.08	-0.42	0.37
Persistent	-0.21	-0.29	0.10	-0.35	-0.16
Referent power[3]	-0.23	-0.17	0.05	0.33	-0.25
Reward Power[2]	0.13	-0.28	-0.24	-0.30	0.19
Legitimate power[3]	-0.17	-0.07	0.08	0.24	0.04
Experience	0.08	0.16	0.16	0.17	0.08
Job orientation	-0.11	-0.06	0.04	-0.16	-0.04
Coercive power	-0.02	0.01	-0.03	-0.10	0.69
Good verbal skills	-0.07	-0.03	0.07	0.14	0.64
Chi Square	192.0[2]	61.7	31.0	16.4	4.3
Percent Variance	68.7	15.6	7.3	6.1	2.2
Percent correctly classified: 29.7%					

[1]Group 1 = direct-selling nonusers (65+), Group 2 = direct-selling nonusers (50-64); Group 3 = direct-selling nonusers ($\leq$49); Group 4 = users (65+), Group 5 = users (50-64), Group 6 = users ($\leq$49).

[2]Wilkes lambda level of significance = .001.

[3]Wilkes lambda level of significance = .01.

[4]On a 5 point scale where: 1 = very willing, 2 = somewhat willing, 3 = neither willing nor unwilling, 4 = somewhat unwilling, 5 = unwilling so that high scores indicate less willingness.

Table 6.7
Pearson Correlations: Salesperson Traits with Shopping Orientations

	Low Mobility	Price-conscious Shopper	Personalizing Shopper	Negative Toward Merchants	Suspicious Nature	Shopping Self-Confidence	Shopping Propensity	Social Shopping	Time Pressure Shopping	Shopping Innovator	Negative Toward Local Shopping	Loyalty to Local Merchants	Distrust of In-Home	Positive Toward Convenience	Positive Toward Price	Get What You Order	Service Over Product In-Home
Customer orientation	$.16^1$	$.01^1$	$.14^1$	$-.12^1$	$-.21^1$	$.03^2$	$.09^1$	$.16^1$	$-.02$	$.03$	$-.04^1$	$.17^1$	$-.16^1$	$.13^1$	$.14^1$	$.26^1$	$.06^2$
Job orientation	$-.10^1$	$.12^1$	$.02$	$.04$	$.36^1$	$.06^2$	$.12^1$	$-.04$	$.01$	$-.01$	$.09^1$	$-.01$	$.30^1$	$-.07$	$-.08$	$-.16^1$	$.06$
Power (overall)	$.20^1$	$.01$	$.18^1$	$.10^1$	$-.03$	$-.03$	$.10^1$	$.16^1$	$.03$	$.01$	$.06^2$	$.23^1$	$.03$	$.08^1$	$.11^1$	$.08^1$	$.13^1$
Reward power	$.17^1$	$.01$	$.14^1$	$.04$	$-.09$	$.01$	$.09^1$	$.16^1$	$.01$	$.03$	$.03^2$	$.16^1$	$-.08$	$.11^1$	$.11^1$	$.13^1$	$.08$
Coercive power	$.10^1$	$.02$	$.06^2$	$.14^1$	$-.04$	$-.03$	$.09^2$	$.06$	$.04$	$-.04$	$.05^1$	$.14^1$	$.09^1$	$.06^2$	$.06^2$	$-.01^2$	$.08$
Legitimate power	$.14^1$	$-.02$	$.10^1$	$.09^2$	$-.01$	$-.04$	$.06^2$	$.11^1$	$.04$	$-.01$	$.08^1$	$.12^1$	$.01^2$	$.07$	$.09$	$.06^2$	$.07$
Referent power	$.12^1$	$-.01$	$.19^1$	$.06$	$-.01$	$-.01$	$.06^1$	$.12^1$	$.04$	$-.01$	$.04$	$.21^1$	$.06$	$.04$	$.09$	$.01$	$.09^1$
Expert power	$.13^1$	$-.01$	$.11^1$	$.04$	$-.02$	$-.01$	$.07$	$.11^1$	$-.01$	$-.03$	$.02$	$.15^1$	$-.01$	$.08$	$.09$	$.11^1$	$.11$
Enthusiasm	$-.04$	$.08^1$	$.04$	$-.10^1$	$.05$	$.01$	$.06^2$	$-.04$	$.03$	$-.03$	$-.03$	$.04$	$.06$	$.08^1$	$.01$	$.09^1$	$.09^1$
Organized	$.01$	$.10^1$	$.03$	$-.07$	$-.01$	$-.04$	$-.04$	$.02$	$-.01$	$-.01$	$.01$	$.06$	$-.03^2$	$.07$	$.07$	$.17^1$	$.09$
Ambitious	$-.05^2$	$.09^1$	$.03$	$-.04$	$.09^1$	$-.03$	$.09^1$	$-.01^2$	$-.01$	$-.04$	$-.01$	$.02$	$.05^1$	$.06$	$.02$	$.05^1$	$.04$
Persuasive	$.01$	$.13^1$	$.10^2$	$-.01$	$.15^1$	$-.01$	$.12$	$.05^2$	$-.01$	$.01$	$-.01^2$	$.07^1$	$.15^1$	$-.02$	$-.03$	$.01$	$.10^1$
Friendly	$.01$	$.02$	$.06^1$	$-.12^1$	$-.02$	$-.04$	$.03^2$	$.05^1$	$-.03$	$.02$	$-.05^1$	$.14^1$	$-.01$	$-.08$	$-.04$	$.13^1$	$.08$
Sincere	$.13^1$	$-.01$	$.10^2$	$-.05^1$	$-.15$	$-.01$	$.06^1$	$.13^1$	$.04$	$.01$	$-.01$	$.08$	$-.14^1$	$.11^1$	$.09$	$.21^1$	$.03$
Considerate	$.07$	$.01$	$.06^2$	$-.12^1$	$-.15$	$-.01$	$.04$	$.08^1$	$-.01^2$	$.01$	$-.03$	$.08$	$-.09^2$	$.06$	$.01$	$.17^1$	$.03$
Creative	$.03$	$.01$	$.07^1$	$-.02$	$-.06$	$.03$	$.07^1$	$-.06^2$	$.05^2$	$-.01$	$-.01$	$.01$	$-.06^2$	$.08$	$.10^1$	$-.12^1$	$.04$
Persistent	$-.08^2$	$.10^1$	$.01$	$.02$	$.26^1$	$.03^2$	$.09^1$	$.06^2$	$-.04$	$.02$	$-.03$	$-.03$	$.21^1$	$-.02$	$-.05^2$	$-.12^1$	$.01^2$
Experienced	$-.05$	$.07^1$	$.05^2$	$.04^1$	$.27$	$.08^1$	$.08^2$	$-.03$	$.01$	$.01$	$.06$	$.03$	$.22^1$	$.05^2$	$.04$	$-.13^1$	$.05^2$
Good verbal skills	$-.01$	$.04$	$.06^1$	$-.08^1$	$.04$	$.01$	$.06$	$-.04$	$-.01$	$-.01$	$-.02$	$.07$	$.01$	$.05^1$	$.06$	$.07$	$.04$

^{1}Level of significance $= .001$

^{2}Level of significance $= .01$

106

Table 6.8
Regressions of Age, Power, Shopping Orientation, and Sales Variables against Customer Orientation

Dependent Variable	Equation	Variables in Equation	R^2	Marginal R^2
Customer	1	Age	.04	
Orientation	2	Power (overall)	.25	
	3	Power (5 types)	.39	
	4	Shopping orientation	.19	
	5	Sales variables	.63	
	6	Age, then power (overall)	.27	.23
	7	Age, then power (5 types)	.40	.36
	8	Age, then sales variables	.63	.59
	9	Age, then shopping orientation	.20	.16
	10	Age, then power (overall), then sales variables	.66	.39
	11	Age, then power (5 types) then sales variables	.68	.41
	12	Age, then shopping orientation, then power (overall)	.36	.16
	13	Age, then shopping orientation, then power (5 types)	.40	.20
	14	Age, then shopping orientation, then power (overall), then sales variables	.67	.31
	15	Age, then shopping orientation, then power (5 types) then sales variables	.69	.33

Note: There are 15 different equations represented here. In equation 1, age explained 4 percent ($R^2 = .04$) of the variance in customer orientation. Equations 2 through 5 are interpreted similarly.

In equation 6, age was entered first followed by power. The two variables explain 27 percent ($R^2 = .27$) of the variance in customer orientation.

The addition of power to the equation adds 23 percent (marginal $R^2 = .23$) to explained variation in customer orientation.

107

Table 6.9
Regressions of Age, Power, Shopping Orientation, and Sales Variables against Job Orientation

Dependent Variable	Equation	Variables in Equation	R^2	Marginal R^2
Job	16	Age	.01	
Orientation	17	Power (overall)	.05	
	18	Power (5 types)	.14	
	19	Shopping orientation	.19	
	20	Sales variables	.72	
	21	Age, then power (overall)	.06	.05
	22	Age, then power (5 types)	.14	.13
	23	Age, then sales variables	.71	.70
	24	Age, then shopping orientation	.19	.18
	25	Age, then power (overall) then sales variables	.63	.57
	26	Age, then power (5 types) then sales variables	.72	.59
	27	Age, then shopping orientation, then power (overall)	.24	.11
	28	Age, then shopping orientation, then power (5 types)	.29	.16
	29	Age, then shopping orientation, then power (overall) then sales variables	.73	.60
	30	Age, then shopping orientation, then power (5 types) then sales variables	.73	.44

Note: There are 15 different equations represented here. In equation 16, age explained 1 percent (R^2 =.01) of the variance in job orientation. Equations 17 through 20 are interpreted similarly.

In equation 21, age was entered first followed by power. The two variables explain 6 percent (R^2 = .06) of the variance in job orientation.

The addition of power to the equation adds 5 percent (marginal R^2 = .05) to explained variation in job orientation.

Table 6.10
Regressions of Age, Shopping Orientation, and Sales Variables against Power

Dependent Variable	Equation	Variables in Equation	R^2	Marginal R^2
Power	31	Age	.03	
(Overall)	32	Shopping Orientation	.15	
	33	Sales variables	.21	
	34	Age, sales variables	.21	.18
	35	Age, shopping orientation	.15	.12
	36	Age, then shopping orientation, then sales variables	.28	.13

Note: In equation 31, age by itself explains 3 percent (R^2 = .03) of the variance in power. Equations 32 and 33 are interpreted similarly.

In equation 34, age and sales variables explain 21 percent (R^2 = .21) in power, with sales variables accounting for 18 percent (marginal R^2 = .18) of the variance explained.

108

Table 6.11
Regressions of Age and Power against Customer Orientation, Job Orientation, and Power

Dependent Variable	Age 1	Age 2	Age 3	Power	Reward	Coercive	Legitimate	Referent	Expert	R^2	F
EQ. 1 Customer orientation	$-.08^1$		.14							.04	32.4^1
EQ. 16 Job orientation	+.05		-.04							.01	5.7^1
EQ. 31 Power	-.03		$.16^1$							.03	25.1^1
EQ. 2 Customer orientation				$.50^1$						.25	52.02
EQ. 17 Job orientation				$-.23^1$						.05	86.4^1
EQ. 3 Customer Orientation					$.44^1$	$-.06^1$	.03	$.07^1$	$.25^1$	.39	196.1^1
EQ. 18 Job Orientation					$-.30^1$	$.14^1$	.06	.01	$-.11^1$	.14	50.3^1

Types of Power

----

^{1}Level of significance = .001.

^{2}Level of significance = .01.

Table 6.12

Regressions of Shopping Orientation against Customer Orientation, Job Orientation, and Power

	Dependent Variables		
Idependent Variables	EQ. 4 Customer Orientation	EQ.19 Job Orientation	EQ. 32 Power
Service over product in-home	$.12^1$	$-.06_1$	$.11^1$
Negative toward local shopping	.02	$.07^1$	.05
Shopping self-confidence	$.02_1$	.01	$-.02_1$
Social shopping	$.09_1$	-.03	$.09_1$
Get what you order	$.17^1$	-.04	$.07^1$
Time pressure shopping	$-.03_1$	$.01_1$	$-.02_1$
Low mobility	$.12^1$	$-.08^1$	$.13^1$
Personalizing shopper	$.07_1^2$	$.01_1$	$.09_1$
Suspicious nature	$-.17^1$	$.30^1$	$-.09_1^1$
Positive toward price/ quality/selection	.03	.03	$.09^1$
Shopping propensity	$.08^1$	.02	.04
Shopping innovator	-.01	-.01	-.03
Price-conscious shopper	.01	.02	$.01_1$
Negative toward merchants	$-.05_1$	-.04	$.12_1^1$
Loyalty to local merchants	$.12^1$	-.04	$.16^1$
Positive toward convenience	.03	$-.01_1$	.05
Distrust of in-home	-.07	$.21^1$	.04
R^2	$.19_1$	$.19_1$	$.15_1$
F	20.4^1	21.1^1	15.7^1
Constant	1.71	2.04	.28

^{1}Level of significance = .001.

^{2}Level of significance = .01.

Table 6.13

Regressions of Salespersons' Characteristics against Customer Orientation, Job Orientation, and Power

	Dependent Variables		
Independent Variables	EQ.5 Customer Orientation	EQ.20 Job Orientation	EQ.33 Power
Verbal skills	$.05_1^1$	$.03_1$	.05
Experience	$-.12^1$	$.49_1^1$	-.04
Ambitious	$.01_1$	$.09_1^1$	$-.02_1$
Sincerity	$.33^1$	$-.09^1$	.22
Enthusiasm	$.04_1$	.04	$-.05_1$
Creative	$.16^1$	-.01	$.15_1$
Persuasive	$.03_1$	.04	$.14^1$
Friendly	$.08^1$	-.01	$-.04_1$
Organized	$.07_1^1$	$-.02_1$	$.10_1^1$
Persistent	$-.16^1$	$.40_1^1$	$-.12_1^1$
Considerate	$.27^1$	$-.05^1$	$.07^1$
R^2	$.63_1$	.72	.21
F	231.1^1	350.2	35.9
Constant	1.36	1.22	7.21

^{1}Level of significance = .001.

110

Table 6.14
Regressions of Selected Power, Salesperson Characteristics, and Shopping Orientation against Customer Orientation Controlling for Age

	Customer Orientation									
	EQ. 6	EQ. 7	EQ. 8	EQ. 9	EQ. 10	EQ. 11	EQ. 12	EQ. 13	EQ. 14	EQ. 15
Age 3	$.06_2$	$.05$	$.06^1$	$.10^1$	$.04$	$.03$	$.06_2$	$.05$	$.03$	$.02$
Age 1	$-.07^2_1$	$-.05$	$-.04$	$-.06$	$-.03_1$	$-.03$	$-.06^2_1$	$-.05$	$-.03_1$	$-.03$
Power	$.48^1$				$.21^1$		$.42^1$		$.19^1$	
$R^2 =$	$.27$									
$F_* =$	185.9^1									
$C =$	1.81									
Coercive power		$-.05^1_1$				$.01_1$		$-.04$		$-.01_1$
Reward power		$.44^1_1$				$.17^1$		$.39$		$.17^1$
Referent power		$.07^1_1$				$.01_1$		$.07$		$.01_1$
Expert power		$.25^1$				$.15^1$		$.21$		$.13^1$
	$R^2 =$	$.40$								
	$F_* =$	168.2^1								
	$C =$	1.73								
Creative			$-.17^1_1$		$.14^1_1$	$.13^2_1$			$.14^1_1$	$.14^1_1$
Persistent			$-.14^1_1$		$-.13^1_1$	$-.11^1_1$			$-.12^1_1$	$-.09^1_1$
Friendly			$.09^1_2$		$.10^1_1$	$.09^1_1$			$.09^1_2$	$.08^1_1$
Good verbal skills			$.05^2_1$		$.04^1_1$	$.05^1_1$			$.05^2_1$	$.06^1_1$
Experienced			$-.11^1_1$		$-.11^1_1$	$-.09^1_1$			$-.10^1$	$-.08^1$
Well-organized			$.08^1_1$		$.06^1_1$	$.05^1_1$			$.06^1_1$	$.07^1_1$
Considerate			$.27^1_1$		$.25^1_1$	$.24^1_1$			$.25^1$	$.25^1$
Sincerity			$.31^1$		$.27^1$	$.24^1$			$.25$	$.24$
		$R^2 =$	$.63$		$.66$	$.68$				
		$F_* =$	259.56		273.2^1	233.8				
		$C =$	1.39		1.14	1.10				
Social shopping				$.10^1_1$			$.06^2_1$	$.04_1$	$.03_2$	$.02_2$
Get what you order				$.19^1_1$			$.15^1_1$	$.13^2_1$	$.05^2$	$.05^2$
Shopping propensity				$.10^1_1$			$.08^1_1$	$.06^2_1$	$.04$	$.03$
Service over product in-home				$.11^1$			$.07^1$	$.06^2$	$.02$	$.02$
Low mobility				$.08^1_1$			$.02_2$	$.01_1$	$.03_2$	$.03_2$
Suspicious nature				$-.18^1_1$			$-.16^1_1$	$-.13^1_1$	$-.04^2$	$-.04^2$
Loyalty to local merchants				$.10^1$			$.04$	$.04$	$.02$	$.02$
Personalizing shopper				$.06^1_1$			$.03_1$	$.02$	$.03$	$.03$
Distrust of in-home				$-.09^1$			$-.09^1$	$-.05$	$-.01$	$.01$
			$R^2 =$	$.20$			$.36$	$.45$	$.67$	$.67$
			$F_* =$	34.5^1			70.1^1	83.9^1	156.1	1.50
			$C =$	1.93			1.65	1.52	$.83$	$.91$

---

[1] Level of significance = .001.

[2] Level of significance = .01.

* C = Constant

111

Table 6.15
Regressions of Selected Power, Salesperson Characteristics, and Shopping Orientation against Job Orientation Controlling for Age

Job Orientation

	EQ. 21	EQ.22	EQ. 23	EQ. 24	EQ. 25	EQ. 26	EQ. 27	EQ. 28	EQ. 29	EQ. 30
Age 3	-.01	.01	.01	-.05	.02	.01	-.02	-.02	.01	.01
Age 1	.05[1]	.02	.03	.06	.04	.03	.06[1]	.04	.03[1]	.03
Power	-.22[1]				-.19		-.21[1]		-.05[1]	
R^2 = .06										
F_* = 30.2										
C = 4.16										
Coercive power	.14[1]					.03[1]		.09[1]		.02[1]
Reward power	-.30[1]					-.06[1]		-.25[1]		-.06[2]
Legitimate power	-.06[1]					-.04		-.06		-.04[2]
Expert power	-.11					-.01		-.09[1]		-.01
R^2 = .14										
F_* = 42.0[1]										
C = 4.25										
Experienced				.51[1]	.51[1]	.50[1]			.48[1]	.47[1]
Ambitious				.10[1]	.10[1]	.10[1]			.11	.10[1]
Considerate				-.04[2]	-.03	-.03			-.04	-.03[1]
Persistent				.41[1]	.40[1]	.39[1]			.38[1]	.37[2]
Sincerity				-.09[1]	-.07[1]	-.06[1]			-.06[1]	-.05[2]
R^2 = .71					.63	.72				
F_* = 544.9[1]					384.21	353.7				
C = 1.24						1.35				
Suspicious nature				.30[1]			.29[1]	.26[1]	.08[1]	.07[1]
Low mobility				-.07[2]			-.03	-.03[1]	-.02	-.02[2]
Negative toward local shopping				.06[2]			.07[1]	.08[1]	.04[1]	.04[2]
Distrust of in-home				.22[1]			.22[1]	.19[1]	.06[1]	.06[1]
R^2 = .19							.24	.29	.73	.73
F_* = 60.9[1]							66.8[1]	60.7	339.1	274.9
C = 1.83							2.20	2.42	.85	.88

---

[1]Level of significance = .001.

[2]Level of significance = .01.

*C = Constant

112

Table 6.16
Regressions of Age, Salesperson Characteristics, and Shopping Orientation against Power

Independent Variables	EQ. 34	EQ. 35	EQ. 36
Age 3	$.11^1$	$.11^1$	$.08^2$
Age 1	$.01_1$	$.01$	$.03_1$
Creative	$.16_1^1$		$.14_1$
Persistent	$-.13_1^1$		$-.12_1^1$
Well-organized	$.08_1^1$		$.09_1^1$
Persuasive	$.10^1$		$.08_1^1$
Considerate	$.07_1$		$.08_1^1$
Sincerity	$.20^1$		$.17^1$

$$R^2 = .21$$
$$F_* = 50.7^1$$
$$C = 6.16$$

		EQ. 35	EQ. 36
Social shopping		$.09_1^1$	$.06^2$
Get what you order		$.07_1^2$	$-.02_1$
Negative toward merchants		$.15_1^1$	$.14_2$
Service over product in-home		$.11_1^1$	$.07_1^2$
Loyalty to local merchants		$.14_2^1$	$.11^1$
Suspicious nature		$-.07_1^2$	$-.01_1$
Low mobility		$.11_1^1$	$.11_2^1$
Positive toward price/ quality/selection		$.09^1$	$.07^2$
Personalizing shopper		$.09^1$	$.07^2$

$$R^2 = .15 \qquad R^2 = .28$$
$$F_* = 25.0 \qquad F_* = 35.4$$
$$C = 1.88 \qquad C = -.58$$

---

^{1}Level of significance = .001.

^{2}Level of significance = .01.

*C = Constant

CHAPTER 7

Perceptions and Preferences of Mature Consumers

The objective of this chapter is to discuss the perceptions of and preferences for each direct-marketing and direct-selling mode as they compare to each other and to retail stores in general. Because perceptions/preferences may differ depending upon the degree of contact with the various modes, "user" groups were utilized in the analysis as were the four age groups.

Multidimensional scaling (MDS) was the analysis procedure used. The interested reader may refer to Appendix C for a non-mathematical discussion of the analysis plan and the various statistical procedures used. The perceptions of the respondents were best represented in two dimensions regardless of age or user category. The general conclusion can therefore be drawn that perceptions of direct-selling and direct-marketing modes are universal with respect to the user and age criteria (see Figures 7.1 and 7.2).

However, just because respondents perceive the various modes relative to one another in a similar way does not necessarily mean that each mode will be preferred to the same degree by all groups. Therefore, each groups' (user and age) preferences were combined separately with the MDS solution to form an ideal point (most preferred point for a mode) for each product category. Product categories ranged from low price/low involvement to high price/high involvement as it seemed likely that the preferred mode may differ depending upon the type of product or the cost of the specified product.

Three product categories were used: a hardware item or kitchen utensil valued at \$8-\$10, a cosmetic item valued at \$25-\$50, and a set of luggage valued at \$250-\$350. The ideal points were established for (1) all three products for given user/age groups and (2) all user/age groups for a given product.

Subsequent analysis indicated that there were not significant differences in ideal point (using the coordinates) for *any* of the analyses. Therefore, it must be concluded that the "ideal" mode is also universal and does not change either across user/age groups or across product categories. Consequently, the preferences for the entire sample were used in the final presentation (Figures 7.1 and 7.2).

Figures 7.1 and 7.2 are perceptual maps that show the relationship of each mode to the others, including retail stores and ideal points for all three product categories. In Figure 7.1, it can be seen that door-to-door is distinctively different from party plans and in-home demonstrations, both of which are similar to each other. Store catalogues and specialty catalogues are also relatively similar, while telephone solicitation is the most dissimilar of all (Figure 7.2). It should be noted that the ideal points in both figures are very close to the position of the retail store, although store catalogues are very close to the ideal point.

Nevertheless, retail stores occupy a relatively unique position on at least one dimension. It can be concluded that retailers are considered quite different from most of the direct-selling/direct-marketing modes and are so dominantly preferred that the analysis is simply overwhelmed.

Table 7.1 shows the similarities between the various direct-selling/ direct-marketing modes across the four user groups. Telephone solicitation is the most dissimilar when compared to the other shopping modes. This tendency held for all user groups.

Since scores of 3.0 or higher indicate a relatively high degree of similarity, it would be well to note those modes with these higher scores. For all groups, store catalogues were similar to specialty catalogues, specialty catalogues to direct mail, direct mail to advertisements, door-to-door to in-home demonstrations, and party plans to in-home demonstrations. However, all direct-selling/direct-marketing modes scored fairly low—1.7 to 2.3 range—when compared to retail stores. Therefore, little similarity was perceived between the direct modes and retailing.

In Table 7.2 direct modes are rank-ordered according to similarities for each of the four user groups. Specialty catalogues are closest to retail stores for all groups, and telephone solicitation is most dissimilar. For direct-selling users, in-home demos are second closest to retailers; for direct-marketing users and users of both specialty catalogues are second closest; and for nonusers advertisements are second closest. Door-to-door and direct mail are not perceived as similar to retail outlets for any of the four groups.

To investigate the perceptual relationship between the direct-marketing modes and direct-selling modes without the retail alternative, the MDS analysis was conducted separately for the four age groups and the four user groups, and separately for the direct-marketing modes and the direct-selling modes. For the direct-marketing modes the three-dimensional solution was most appropriate. For the direct-selling modes the two-dimensional solution was appropriate. Figures 7.3 through 7.6 show the three-dimensional solution for direct marketing (without retail) for the four age groups. Figures 7.7 through 7.10 show the two-dimensional solutions for the direct-selling modes (without retail) for the four age groups. Note that for the direct-selling modes, the perceptual map does not differ with respect to the age groups. However, for the direct-marketing modes, there are some differences in the perceptual map according to age group. Age groups 1 and 2 are almost identical, but there are some differences in age groups 3 and 4. There are also differences in the labeling of the dimensions themselves, especially with age group 4.

For Figures 7.3 and 7.5 the three dimensions obtained with respect to direct-marketing modes include personal contact (I), variety (II), and specialized products (III). In Figure 7.6, personal contact (I) and specialized products (III) were also obtained, but in this case a third dimension, price, appeared. In Figure 7.3, it can again be seen that department store catalogues are closest to the "ideal" for all three product categories for age group 1 (≤ 34). Store catalogues are also closest to ideal for all three products for age group 2 (35-49). However, advertisements, specialty catalogues, and store catalogues are closest for age group 3 (50-64), and, surprisingly, telephone solicitation is closest for age group 4 (65+).

The latter finding, as can be seen from Figure 7.6, is related to the high priority placed on personal contact by the mature consumer. Telephone solicitation loads heavily on this particular dimension, a circumstance that sharply differentiates this mode from other direct-marketing modes.

It is interesting to note how the ideal points change across age groups. For example, for age groups 1 and 2, the ideal points for all three product categories are negatively related to personal contact, a characteristic that closely related the ideal points to department store catalogues. However, for age group 3, the ideal points move rather dramatically toward the other end of dimension I, that is, toward personal contact. For both age groups 3 and 4 (people over 50 years of age) the ideal points approach the telephone solicitation mode. This finding is both interesting and important as it appears that older consumers will be amenable to phone solicitation and personal contact as opposed to ordering from the catalogues that younger consumers prefer.

Figures 7.7 through 7.10 illustrate the differences in age groups with respect to direct-selling modes. Although the perceptual maps do not change across age groups, nor do the labelings of the dimensions change, the ideal points *do* change with age groups. The two dimensions of interest in these figures are group/social/invitation (I) and pressure (II).

For age group 1, the ideal point is very close to door-to-door sales. For age groups 2 and 3, the ideal points are not only completely different from door-to-door, but are also extremely different from the other two direct-selling modes. However, for age group 4 the ideal points are again closely linked to door-to-door. Therefore, the youngest and the oldest respondent age groups are more amenable to buying from the door-to-door mode than are either of the other two age groups.

The middle-age groups 2 and 3, those between 35 and 64, lean much more toward the in-home demonstration or the party plan, both of which are "invitation only" type modes.

Figures 7.11 through 7.14 address direct-marketing modes across user groups. Some differences across these groups are noteworthy. First, telephone solicitation, department store catalogues, and specialty catalogues remain in approximately the same position across the four user groups. However, advertising and direct mail positioning differ somewhat across groups. For direct-selling users, advertising is negatively related to variety while direct mail is positively related. For direct-marketing users, on the other hand, both are positively related to variety, and for users of both *and* users of neither advertising and direct mail are negatively related.

With respect to ideal points for the user groups, groups 3 and 4 have unique ideal points, both sets being "off the map" with respect to all three dimensions. For the first two user groups the ideal points also are reversed with respect to dimensions 1 and 3, while they do not differ dramatically with respect to dimension 2. For direct-selling users, the ideal points reflect a lack of personal contact and more specialized products. In contrast, user group 2, direct-marketing users, do enjoy personal contact but are less interested in specialized products.

It is interesting to note that the direct-marketing users' ideal points are somewhat opposed to the catalogue sources on dimension 1. For those who use direct-selling only, their ideal points approach catalogues on the perceptual map.

For direct–selling modes, Figures 7.15 through 7.18, there are almost no differences across user groups. Perceptual maps are almost identical with ideal points closely grouped but relatively distant from the direct-selling modes themselves. The ideal points indicate that respondents prefer less pressure and more of an "invitation only" format to the selling mode.

Figure 7.1
Perceptual Map of Direct-Selling Modes (vs. Retail Store) and Ideal Points (Most Preferred Mode) for Three Product Categories: Total Sample

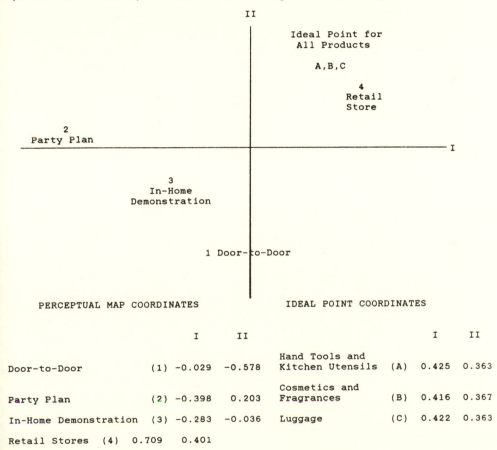

PERCEPTUAL MAP COORDINATES

		I	II
Door-to-Door	(1)	-0.029	-0.578
Party Plan	(2)	-0.398	0.203
In-Home Demonstration	(3)	-0.283	-0.036
Retail Stores	(4)	0.709	0.401

IDEAL POINT COORDINATES

		I	II
Hand Tools and Kitchen Utensils	(A)	0.425	0.363
Cosmetics and Fragrances	(B)	0.416	0.367
Luggage	(C)	0.422	0.363

Figure 7.2
Perceptual Map of Direct-Marketing Modes (vs. Retail Store) and Ideal Points (Most Preferred Mode) for Three Product Categories: Total Sample

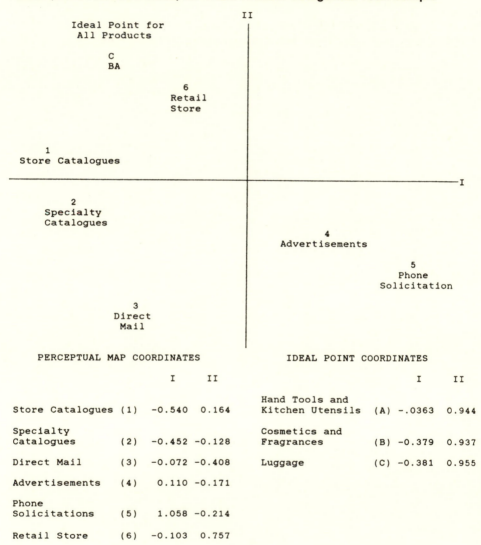

PERCEPTUAL MAP COORDINATES

		I	II
Store Catalogues	(1)	-0.540	0.164
Specialty Catalogues	(2)	-0.452	-0.128
Direct Mail	(3)	-0.072	-0.408
Advertisements	(4)	0.110	-0.171
Phone Solicitations	(5)	1.058	-0.214
Retail Store	(6)	-0.103	0.757

IDEAL POINT COORDINATES

		I	II
Hand Tools and Kitchen Utensils	(A)	-.0363	0.944
Cosmetics and Fragrances	(B)	-0.379	0.937
Luggage	(C)	-0.381	0.955

Table 7.1
Mean Similarities between Modes: Four User Groups[1]

Sources Compared	Direct-Selling Users	Direct-Marketing Users	Users of Both	Users of Neither
1. Store Catalogues vs. Specialty Catalogues	3.38	3.31	3.28	3.26
2. Store Catalogues vs. Direct Mail	2.81	2.68	2.75	2.84
3. Store Catalogues vs. Advertisement	2.69	2.66	2.58	2.80
4. Store Catalogues vs. Phone Solicitation	1.74	1.63	1.64	1.89
5. Store Catalogues vs. Retail Outlet	2.32	2.76	2.87	2.63
6. Specialty Catalogues vs. Direct Mail	3.02	3.01	3.03	3.01
7. Specialty Catalogues vs. Advertisement	2.76	2.82	2.84	2.96
8. Specialty Catalogues vs. Phone Solicitation	1.62	1.74	1.78	1.99
9. Specialty Catalogues vs. Retail Outlet	2.21	2.39	2.40	2.40
10. Direct Mail vs. Advertisement	3.27	3.23	3.34	3.21
11. Direct Mail vs. Phone Solicitation	2.29	2.20	2.27	2.32
12. Direct Mail vs. Retail Outlet	2.04	2.20	2.21	2.28
13. Advertisement vs. Phone Solicitation	2.40	2.26	2.31	2.28
14. Advertisement vs. Retail Outlet	2.14	2.22	2.37	2.43
15. Phone Solicitation vs. Retail Outlet	1.72	1.71	1.78	1.89
16. Door-to-Door vs. Party Plan	2.89	2.85	2.85	2.94
17. Door-to-Door vs. In-Home Demonstrations	3.29	3.26	3.21	3.17
18. Door-to-Door vs. Retail Outlet	2.11	1.96	2.07	2.15
19. Party Plan vs. In-Home Demonstrations	3.70	3.54	3.57	3.55
20. Party Plan vs. Retail Outlet	2.23	2.07	2.28	2.24
21. In-Home Demonstrations vs. Retail Outlet	2.25	2.08	2.32	2.22

[1] On a 5 point scale where 1 = very dissimilar, 5 = very similar. High numbers indicate high perceived similarity.

121

Table 7.2
Rank Order of Similarity Scores: Direct Sources and Retailers Compared

Sources Compared	Direct-Selling Users	Direct-Marketing Users	Users of Both	Users of Neither
1. Store Catalogues vs. Retail Outlet	1	1	1	1
2. Specialty Catalogues vs. Retail Outlet	4	2	2	3
3. Direct Mail vs. Retail Outlet	7	4	6	4
4. Advertisement vs. Retail Outlet	5	3	3	2
5. Phone Solicitation vs. Retail Outlet	8	8	8	8
6. Door-to-Door vs. Retail Outlet	6	7	7	7
7. Party Plan vs. Retail Outlet	3	6	5	5
8. In-Home Demonstrations vs. Retail Outlet	2	5	4	6

Figure 7.3
Direct Marketing without Retail: Age-1 ($\leq$34)

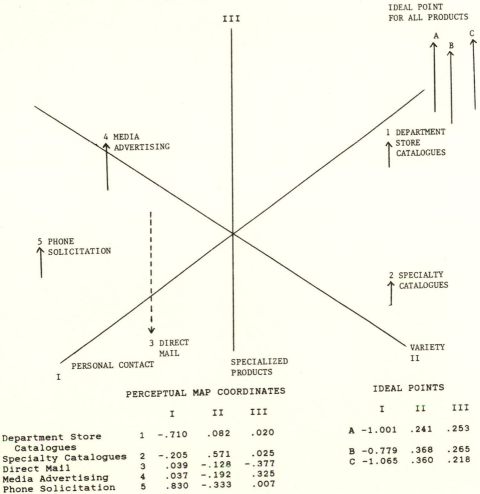

		I	II	III

PERCEPTUAL MAP COORDINATES

		I	II	III
Department Store Catalogues	1	-.710	.082	.020
Specialty Catalogues	2	-.205	.571	.025
Direct Mail	3	.039	-.128	-.377
Media Advertising	4	.037	-.192	.325
Phone Solicitation	5	.830	-.333	.007

IDEAL POINTS

	I	II	III
A	-1.001	.241	.253
B	-0.779	.368	.265
C	-1.065	.360	.218

123

Figure 7.4
Direct Marketing without Retail: Age-2 (35-49)

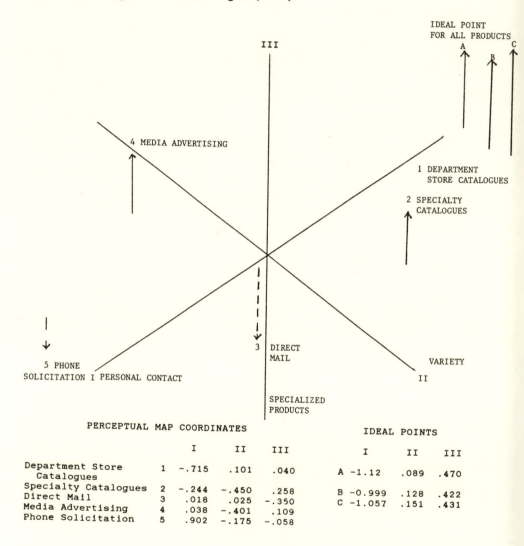

PERCEPTUAL MAP COORDINATES

		I	II	III
Department Store Catalogues	1	-.715	.101	.040
Specialty Catalogues	2	-.244	-.450	.258
Direct Mail	3	.018	.025	-.350
Media Advertising	4	.038	-.401	.109
Phone Solicitation	5	.902	-.175	-.058

IDEAL POINTS

	I	II	III
A	-1.12	.089	.470
B	-0.999	.128	.422
C	-1.057	.151	.431

124

Figure 7.5
Direct Marketing without Retail: Age-3 (50-64)

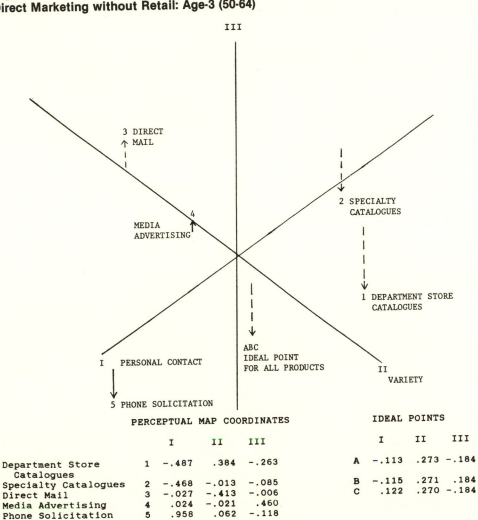

PERCEPTUAL MAP COORDINATES

		I	II	III
Department Store Catalogues	1	−.487	.384	−.263
Specialty Catalogues	2	−.468	−.013	−.085
Direct Mail	3	−.027	−.413	−.006
Media Advertising	4	.024	−.021	.460
Phone Solicitation	5	.958	.062	−.118

IDEAL POINTS

	I	II	III
A	−.113	.273	−.184
B	−.115	.271	.184
C	.122	.270	−.184

125

Figure 7.6
Direct Marketing without Retail: Age-4 (65+)

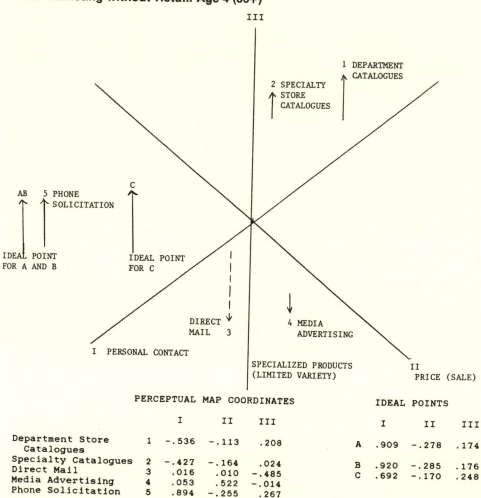

		I	II	III		I	II	III
Department Store Catalogues	1	-.536	-.113	.208	A	.909	-.278	.174
Specialty Catalogues	2	-.427	-.164	.024	B	.920	-.285	.176
Direct Mail	3	.016	.010	-.485	C	.692	-.170	.248
Media Advertising	4	.053	.522	-.014				
Phone Solicitation	5	.894	-.255	.267				

PERCEPTUAL MAP COORDINATES   IDEAL POINTS

126

Figure 7.7
Direct Selling without Retail: Age-1 (≤ 34)

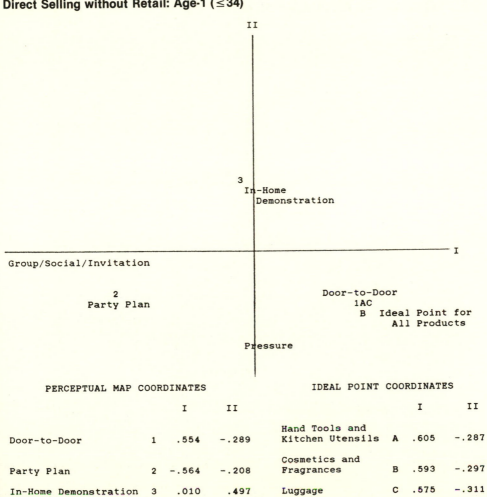

PERCEPTUAL MAP COORDINATES				
		I	II	
Door-to-Door	1	.554	-.289	
Party Plan	2	-.564	-.208	
In-Home Demonstration	3	.010	.497	

IDEAL POINT COORDINATES			
		I	II
Hand Tools and Kitchen Utensils	A	.605	-.287
Cosmetics and Fragrances	B	.593	-.297
Luggage	C	.575	-.311

Figure 7.8
Direct Selling without Retail: Age-2 (35-49)

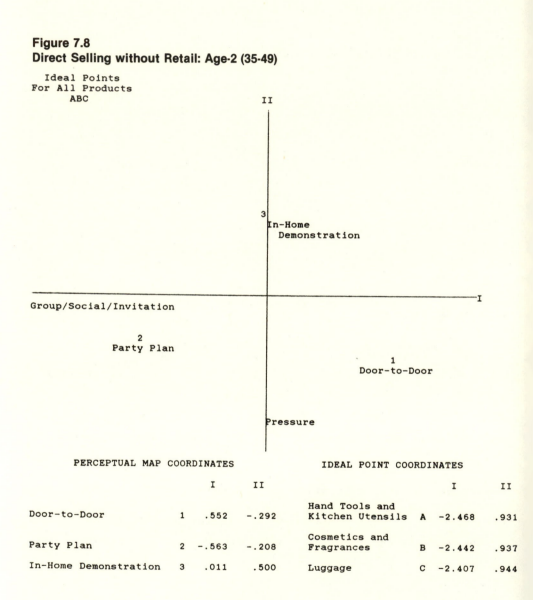

Ideal Points
For All Products
   ABC

II

3
In-Home
  Demonstration

Group/Social/Invitation ——————————————————————I

2
Party Plan

1
Door-to-Door

Pressure

PERCEPTUAL MAP COORDINATES					IDEAL POINT COORDINATES			
		I	II				I	II
Door-to-Door	1	.552	-.292	Hand Tools and Kitchen Utensils	A	-2.468	.931
Party Plan	2	-.563	-.208	Cosmetics and Fragrances	B	-2.442	.937
In-Home Demonstration	3	.011	.500	Luggage	C	-2.407	.944

128

Figure 7.9
Direct Selling without Retail: Age-3 (50-64)

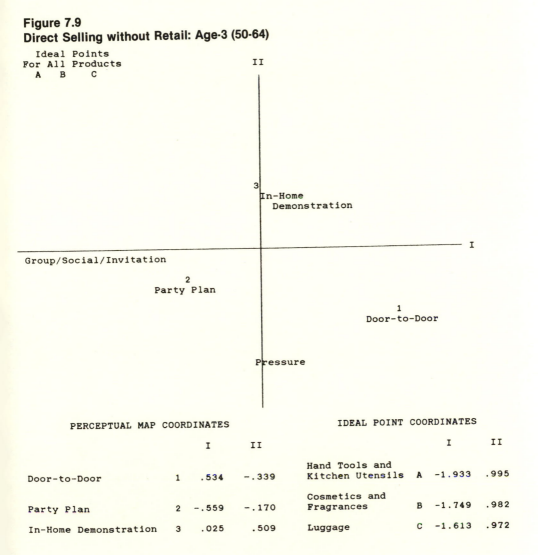

Ideal Points
For All Products
A   B   C

II

3
In-Home
Demonstration

I

Group/Social/Invitation

2
Party Plan

1
Door-to-Door

Pressure

PERCEPTUAL MAP COORDINATES

		I	II
Door-to-Door	1	.534	−.339
Party Plan	2	−.559	−.170
In-Home Demonstration	3	.025	.509

IDEAL POINT COORDINATES

		I	II
Hand Tools and Kitchen Utensils	A	−1.933	.995
Cosmetics and Fragrances	B	−1.749	.982
Luggage	C	−1.613	.972

129

Figure 7.10
Direct Selling without Retail: Age-4 (65+)

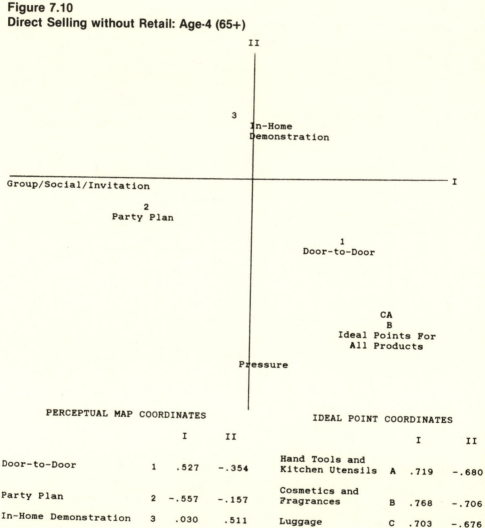

PERCEPTUAL MAP COORDINATES

		I	II
Door-to-Door	1	.527	-.354
Party Plan	2	-.557	-.157
In-Home Demonstration	3	.030	.511

IDEAL POINT COORDINATES

		I	II
Hand Tools and Kitchen Utensils	A	.719	-.680
Cosmetics and Fragrances	B	.768	-.706
Luggage	C	.703	-.676

130

Figure 7.11
Direct Marketing without Retail: Users-1 (Direct Selling Users)

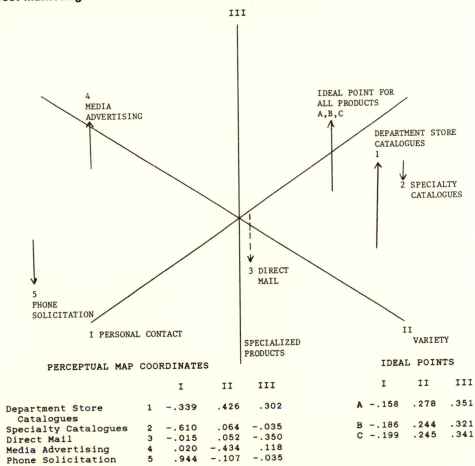

PERCEPTUAL MAP COORDINATES

		I	II	III
Department Store Catalogues	1	-.339	.426	.302
Specialty Catalogues	2	-.610	.064	-.035
Direct Mail	3	-.015	.052	-.350
Media Advertising	4	.020	-.434	.118
Phone Solicitation	5	.944	-.107	-.035

IDEAL POINTS

	I	II	III
A	-.158	.278	.351
B	-.186	.244	.321
C	-.199	.245	.341

131

Figure 7.12
Direct Marketing without Retail: Users-2 (Direct Marketing Users)

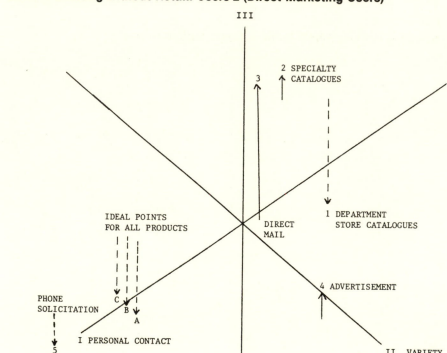

PERCEPTUAL MAP COORDINATES

		I	II	III
Department Stores Catalogues	1	−.563	−.109	−.315
Specialty Catalogues	2	−.417	−.261	.054
Direct Mail	3	−.011	.007	.385
Media Advertising	4	.033	.472	.025
Phone Solicitation	5	.958	−.108	−.149

IDEAL POINTS

	I	II	III
A	.453	−.230	−.342
B	.530	−.246	−.345
C	.571	−.256	−.339

132

Figure 7.13
Direct Marketing without Retail: Users-3 ("Both")

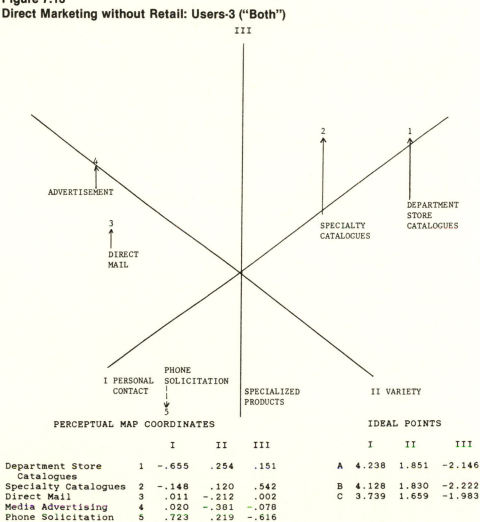

PERCEPTUAL MAP COORDINATES

		I	II	III
Department Store Catalogues	1	−.655	.254	.151
Specialty Catalogues	2	−.148	.120	.542
Direct Mail	3	.011	−.212	.002
Media Advertising	4	.020	−.381	−.078
Phone Solicitation	5	.723	.219	−.616

IDEAL POINTS

	I	II	III
A	4.238	1.851	−2.146
B	4.128	1.830	−2.222
C	3.739	1.659	−1.983

Figure 7.14
Direct Marketing without Retail: Users-4 ("Neither")

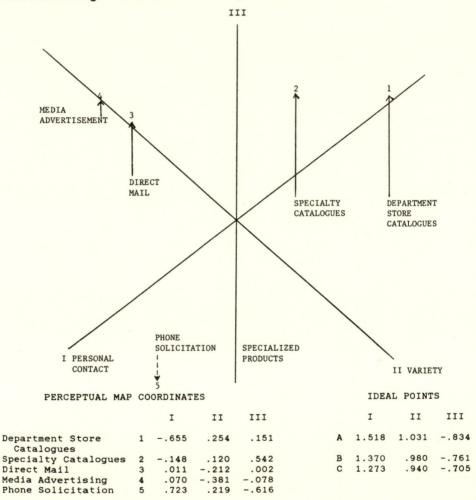

PERCEPTUAL MAP COORDINATES					IDEAL POINTS			
		I	II	III		I	II	III
Department Store Catalogues	1	-.655	.254	.151	A	1.518	1.031	-.834
Specialty Catalogues	2	-.148	.120	.542	B	1.370	.980	-.761
Direct Mail	3	.011	-.212	.002	C	1.273	.940	-.705
Media Advertising	4	.070	-.381	-.078				
Phone Solicitation	5	.723	.219	-.616				

134

Figure 7.15
Direct Selling without Retail: Users-1 (Direct Selling Users)

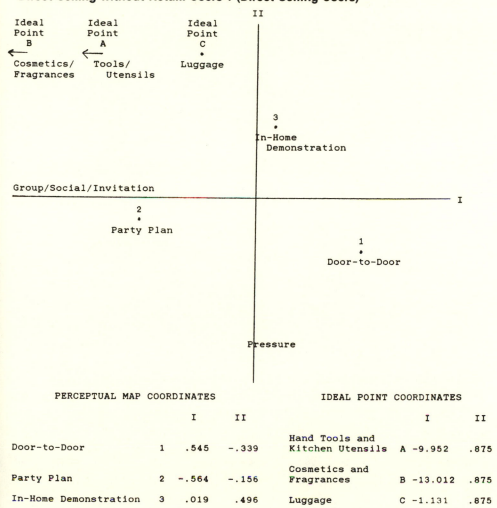

PERCEPTUAL MAP COORDINATES		I	II		IDEAL POINT COORDINATES		I	II
Door-to-Door	1	.545	-.339	Hand Tools and Kitchen Utensils	A	-9.952	.875
Party Plan	2	-.564	-.156	Cosmetics and Fragrances	B	-13.012	.875
In-Home Demonstration	3	.019	.496	Luggage	C	-1.131	.875

135

Figure 7.16
Direct Selling without Retail: Users-2 (Direct Marketing Users)

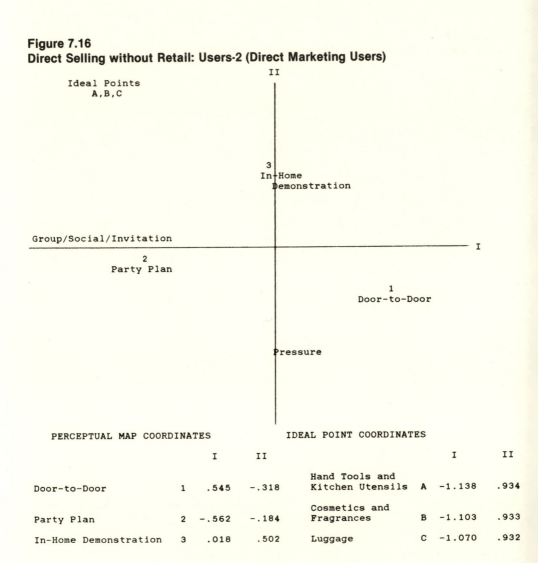

Ideal Points
A,B,C

II

3
In-Home
Demonstration

Group/Social/Invitation

I

2
Party Plan

1
Door-to-Door

Pressure

PERCEPTUAL MAP COORDINATES				IDEAL POINT COORDINATES			
		I	II			I	II
Door-to-Door	1	.545	−.318	Hand Tools and Kitchen Utensils	A	−1.138	.934
Party Plan	2	−.562	−.184	Cosmetics and Fragrances	B	−1.103	.933
In-Home Demonstration	3	.018	.502	Luggage	C	−1.070	.932

136

Figure 7.17
Direct Selling without Retail: Users-3 ("Both")

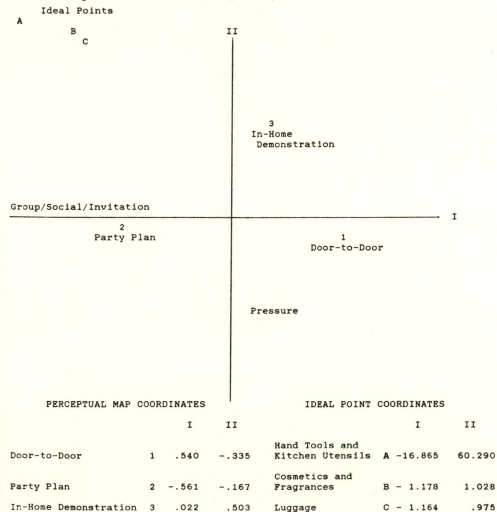

PERCEPTUAL MAP COORDINATES

		I	II
Door-to-Door	1	.540	−.335
Party Plan	2	−.561	−.167
In-Home Demonstration	3	.022	.503

IDEAL POINT COORDINATES

		I	II
Hand Tools and Kitchen Utensils	A	−16.865	60.290
Cosmetics and Fragrances	B	− 1.178	1.028
Luggage	C	− 1.164	.975

137

Figure 7.18
Direct Selling without Retail: Users-4 ("Neither")

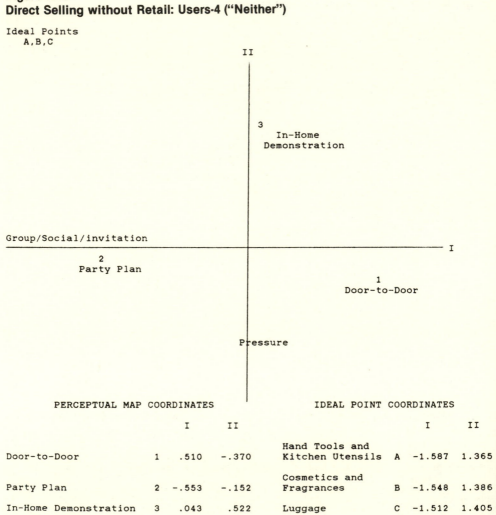

Ideal Points
   A,B,C

II

3
   In-Home
Demonstration

Group/Social/invitation
—— I

2
Party Plan

1
Door-to-Door

Pressure

PERCEPTUAL MAP COORDINATES | IDEAL POINT COORDINATES

		I	II				I	II
Door-to-Door	1	.510	-.370	Hand Tools and Kitchen Utensils	A	-1.587	1.365
Party Plan	2	-.553	-.152	Cosmetics and Fragrances	B	-1.548	1.386
In-Home Demonstration	3	.043	.522	Luggage	C	-1.512	1.405

CHAPTER 8

Profiling Users and Nonusers

The analysis in this chapter reveals demographic and psychographic profiles of those who purchase via direct-selling and direct-marketing modes. The psychographics include shopping orientation scales related to both in-store and in-home purchasing:

mobility	suspicious nature
price consciousness	attitude toward retail merchants
personal contact desirability	self-confidence
shopping propensity	social shopping
shopping time pressure	shopping innovation
loyalty to local merchants	attitude toward local merchants

Other scales deal specifically with in-home shopping: convenience, service vs. product, price/selection/quality, general attitude toward in-home shopping, and, obtaining what was ordered. The mature consumers (50-64 and 65+) will be contrasted with younger consumers. Within the mature segment the contrast will be between users and nonusers.

DEMOGRAPHIC PROFILES ACROSS AGE GROUPS

Tables 8.1 through 8.7 present a demographic profile of respondents on several dimensions across the age groups. The older two age groups are more likely than the ≤ 49 group to own a home, but the entire group of respondents are predominantly home-owners.

In Table 8.2 the education distribution is shown to have included a large number of respondents in each group that have only high school or less. However, nearly half the sample has at least some college.

The distribution by household size in Table 8.3 shows that (as expected) as age increases, the size of the household tends to become smaller. Table 8.4 also provides few surprises; younger respondents tend to be employed while the 65+ age group is predominantly retired (79.3%).

Table 8.5 shows that the 65+ group has a larger percentage than the other two groups of respondents in the lower income brackets, although more than one-third of these respondents have annual incomes greater than $20,000.

Of the three age groups, the 50-64 group is most likely to be married (Table 8.6), while approximately half of the 65+ group are married. According to Table 8.7, the respondent group was primarily female regardless of age group.

DEMOGRAPHIC PROFILES OF USERS ≤49

Tables 8.8 through 8.14 portray the demographic composition of the ≤49 user segment of the sample. These users tend to own their own homes, particularly the direct-selling users and the users of both (Table 8.8). The largest percentages of direct-selling users and users of both have no more than a high school education. However, this finding also holds for users of neither mode. Conversely, the largest category of direct-marketing users (37.9%) were college graduates (Table 8.9).

The largest category of direct-selling users was found in a household size of four persons; this was also true for users of both and users of neither (Table 8.10). However, the largest group of direct-marketing users was in the single-person household (29.5%). As expected, Table 8.11 shows that most of the ≤49 groups—regardless of user category—are employed. They also tend to have annual incomes in excess of $20,000 as portrayed in Table 8.12.

While most ≤49 respondents are married, a fairly large percentage of direct-marketing users (45.2%) are not married, even in this younger age group. Further, more than half the singles (53.2%) are direct-marketing users. This finding may encourage some direct marketers to develop campaigns targeted especially to the growing singles market (Table 8.13). Finally, in the ≤49 age group the majority of respondents in each user group are female (Table 8.14). Interestingly, however, 61.2 percent of the males are direct-marketing users, but practically none (2%) are direct-selling users. A large percentage of the females (75.7%) are either direct-marketing users or users of both. Only 17.2 percent are users of neither.

PROFILE OF USERS 50-64

The 50-64 age group typically are married, empty nest, and still in the work force. These are often their peak income years, those immediately preceding retirement. Tables 8.15 through 8.21 present a demographic profile of the 50-64 year old respondents in this sample.

It can be seen from Table 8.15 that, as is typical for this age group, most respondents are home owners, regardless of their purchasing mode behavior. Table 8.16 shows that the highest percentage of those with at least some college are direct-marketing users. Direct-selling users, by contrast, show no college graduates and represent the highest percentage of those having only high school education. Household size (Table 8.17) tends to be small among all groups, no doubt reflecting the empty nest characteristic of this age group.

A surprisingly large percentage (25+ %) of the 50-64's are retired, but the majority are still employed (Table 8.18). Here again, buying modes appear to be unrelated to this variable. The higher income levels of this group are reflected in Table 8.19. As was true for the ≤ 49 group, the 50-64 group also shows a substantial level of direct-marketing usage among singles (Table 8.20). Fully 55.1 percent of the users of direct marketing are single even though 75.9 percent of this segment of the sample are married.

Respondents in this age group are predominantly female (Table 8.21). Males show no usage of direct selling, but 53.1 percent of them have used direct marketing.

PROFILE OF USERS 65+

Consumers in the 65+ age bracket tend to be retired, empty nest, and on lower incomes. Many of them own their own homes. Tables 8.22 through 8.28 show a breakdown of the demographic characteristics of this segment of respondents.

From Table 8.22, it can be seen that 86.7 percent of respondents aged 65+ own their own homes. The residence type of these respondents has no bearing on the purchasing modes that they prefer to use. Nor do mature consumers differ from the ≤ 49 group. However, both of these are slightly higher than the 50-64 group (75.1%) in home ownership.

With respect to education (Table 8.23), the 65+ is similar to the ≤ 49 group again. Slightly more than half (54.8%) have only a high school education. The 50-64 group shows fewer respondents having only high school (40.2%).

As might be expected, 65+ respondents live overwhelmingly (93.7%) in household sizes of only one or two (Table 8.24). The majority (79.3%) are also retired, a dramatic increase over the 50-64 group (Table 8.25). The loss in income—only 35.7 percent in the $20k+ category (Table 8.26)—clearly shows the drop in buying power compared to the younger age groups. Although there is an increased usage of direct marketing in the 65+ higher income group over the ≤ 49 higher income group, there is also a decrease in direct-selling usage and usage of both. Overall, usage of neither rises from 18.2 percent in the ≤ 49 group to 38.5 percent in the 65+ age group.

Table 8.27 shows usage of direct marketing almost equally split between the married and the unmarried with the unmarried having a slight edge. Usage patterns among all shopping modes are more evenly divided for the 65+ group than for any other age group based on the variable marital status.

According to Table 8.28, males are again more willing to use direct marketing than direct selling. However, this bias may stem from the fact that direct-selling plans have been traditionally geared toward females. The 65+ men in this study tended to use either direct marketing (54.7%) or neither (38.5%). Females followed a similar pattern.

DEMOGRAPHIC PROFILE BY AGE AND USAGE CATEGORIES

The first part of this section deals with demographics of mature consumers with respect to catalogue shopping. Three groups of mature consumers are defined as a basis for comparison: nonusers, light users, and heavy users. The second part of this section examines characteristics of light and heavy catalogue shoppers as a group and also across four age categories: ≤ 34, 35-49, 50-64, and 65+.

Table 8.29 presents a comparison of light and heavy catalogue users on a variety of dimensions as well as incorporating a comparison of nonuser characteristics. Few differences were observed across the three groups with respect to basic demographic data. However, two exceptions are noteworthy.

First, nonusers are less educated than either of the two user groups. Sepcifically, catalogue users are more likely than nonusers to have had at least some college. There are several possible explanations for this finding. Those with more education typically are more internally-oriented in their locus of control; consequently they may feel able to handle the uncertainties associated with catalogue shopping.

A second possible explanation is related to various forms of risk-taking. As can be seen from Table 8.29, nonusers also have lower incomes. While lower income usually correlates with lower education, both of these findings may be specifically related to willingness to take financial risk. Catalogue shopping may be seen as more risky financially because of an inability to examine a product directly before one invests in it. This drawback may reasonably be expected to act as more of a deterrent to catalogue shopping among lower educated/lower income consumers than among other groups.

Other aspects of risk aversion among nonusers may include functional risk, psychological risk, and social risk. Any or all of these are likely to be associated with catalogue shopping, and may be a more salient deterrent among lower socioeconomic groups.

DEMOGRAPHICS OF CATALOGUE USERS ACROSS AGE CATEGORIES

From Table 8.30, one can see that younger catalogue users tend to rent multiple-unit dwellings. They are better educated than other age categories, and they tend to work for another person, be temporarily unemployed, or work as a homemaker. Similar statements characterize the spouses of these young respondents. Middle-age groups tend to be self-employed or work part-time; their spouses are temporarily unemployed or self-employed. On the other hand, while many mature consumers also live in multiple-unit dwellings, unlike younger catalogue users, they are retired as are their spouses. Younger and middle-aged users also have higher incomes than mature consumers. Not surprisingly, income peaks during middle age. As might be expected, the younger users are married or never married, middle-aged group members are more likely to be divorced or separated, and the mature consumers are more likely to be widowed. In general, users tend to be either ≤ 49 or $65+$ and male.

DIRECT MAIL

This first section deals with significant demographic characteristics attached to direct mail shoppers. Two groups of the mature consumers are defined as a basis for comparison: nonusers and users. Each of these two groups can also be compared against the total group of mature consumers. The likes and dislikes with respect to in-home shopping of all elderly, nonusers, and users are also examined.

The second section examines characteristics of direct mail users comparing mature consumers with younger consumers. The likes and dislikes with respect to in-home shopping are also compared across all users, younger users, and older users.

Older users of direct mail shopping differ from older nonusers in several respects. First, nonusers are more likely to own their own homes, although they also have lower income than users. Owning their own homes may be related to the fact that they are more likely than users to be married, while users are more likely to have never been married. Nonusers are also more likely to be male; users are more likely to be female (Table 8.31).

The younger users of direct mail are more likely to work than mature users. If mature consumers do work, they are likely to be self-employed or full-time homemakers. Younger consumers, on the other hand, are likely to work for someone else either full or part-time. As might be expected, younger consumers enjoy higher incomes. Mature consumers are also more likely to be widowed (expected) or never married (unexpected). They are also more likely than younger consumers to be white (Table 8.32).

MEDIA ADS

The first section deals with the demographic characteristics of those who respond to direct response media ads. All 65+ are compared with 65+ users of media ads and 65+ nonusers. These groups are also compared on the basis of their likes and dislikes with respect to in-home shopping.

The second section also begins with a comparison of demographic characteristics. This time the groups of interest include all users, mature (65+) users, and younger (≤ 65) users. Similar contrasts will be cited with respect to the likes and dislikes of these groups regarding in-home shopping.

Table 8.33 indicates that there are few differences in demographic characteristics between mature users of direct response media advertising and mature nonusers of media ads. The only significant difference was related to income: nonusers tend to have lower incomes and users tend to have higher incomes. This might be easily explained in terms of nonusers being less willing to assume the risk of ordering a product which they have not had the opportunity to examine first hand.

Now we take a closer look at the characteristics of all users of direct response media advertising. For purposes of comparison, this group is divided into two subgroups: the 65+ and the ≤ 65.

As may be seen from Table 8.34, the 65+ group and the ≤ 65 differ on several key demographic dimensions. Among the younger respondents, both spouses tend to work; among mature consumers, married couples tend not to work, and singles may or may not work. Younger consumers work for someone else full time, but mature consumers tend to be self-employed or retired. Spouses of younger consumers usually work for someone else or are self-employed, but the mature spouse tends to be a homemaker. Here again, the younger group tends to have higher incomes, and the mature tend to be widowed, divorced, or separated.

TELEPHONE SOLICITATION

The first section covers a comparison of all mature consumers against two subgroups, one containing users of telephone solicitation direct response buying and the other made up of nonusers. These groups are also compared with respect to their likes and dislikes regarding in-home shopping.

The second section has to do only with those who do purchase from marketers that use telephone solicitation. The group of all users has been further subdivided into a group of mature consumers and a group of younger consumers. As in all previous sections, comparisons will be made on the basis of demographic characteristics and with respect to the likes and dislikes of each group.

This section deals exclusively with mature consumers, subdividing them into users and nonusers of purchasing through telephone solicitation. As shown in Table 8.35, there were no significant differences between elderly users and nonusers of telephone solicitation with respect to any of the demographic characteristics. Such a lack of demographic differences makes effective segmentation much more difficult for in-home marketers. Basically, one must conclude that purchasers via telephone solicitation may equally be expected to come from any demographic subgroup of the mature consumer group.

As can be seen from Table 8.36, mature telephone solicitation buyers tend to be retired while younger consumers work for others on a full-time basis. The same findings held for both heads of households and for their spouses.

DIRECT SELLING

The first part of this section covers a comparison of mature users and nonusers of direct selling as a means of product purchase. Comparisons will be made on the basis of demographic differences between these groups as well as on differences between the groups with respect to what they like and what they dislike about in-home shopping.

The second part of this section is restricted to users of direct selling only. This group is subdivided into mature and younger groups. Again, comparisons are made with respect to demographic characteristics as well as likes and dislikes of attributes of in-home shopping.

Mature users of direct selling as a purchasing mode are more likely to be self-employed or full-time homemakers. If they do work, users are likely to be clerical or sales workers. Nonusers, on the other hand, tend to be professionals or managers. Users also tend to be female and nonusers male (Table 8.37).

From Table 8.38, we can glean a few demographic differences between the 65+ group and the <65 group users of direct-selling purchasing. The <65 group tends to have higher incomes, and the 65+ group tends to be widowed or separated. With respect to employment status, the <65 group tends to work for someone else full time, and the 65+ group tends to be retired. These findings also held for the respondents' spouses.

PARTY PLAN

In the first part of this section, we examine characteristics of mature consumers—both users and nonusers of party plans—to see how they differ demographically and in their likes and dislikes of in-home shopping. The second part of this section covers comparisons of older and younger users of party plans. Differences in demographic characteristics as well as likes and dislikes of in-home shopping will be examined.

As can be seen from Table 8.39, there are several demographic differences between the two mature groups of users and nonusers of party plans. In general, heads of nonuser households are single and work, while users tend to be married with both working. With respect to the employment status of nonuser spouses, they work for others on either a full- or part-time basis or they are self-employed.

Nonusers tend to be older, and users tend to be younger. Nonusers also have higher incomes than users. Nonusers are more likely to have never married, while users are more likely to be widowed. Finally, users tend to be female.

These findings are consistent with what is known about party plans. Marrieds who both work are more likely to have discretionary income to spend at parties. Users would have to be mobile in order to attend, and, thus, one would expect them to be younger and more able to get out. Finally, the users' widowed status may give them an impetus to attend parties for the social contact. Also, females are far more likely to participate in party plans than are males.

The second part of this section looks at party plan users.

Table 8.40 shows a comparison of demographic characteristics of older and younger consumers. With respect to the employment status of the head of the household, the younger consumers tend to work, and the older ones tend not to work. Younger consumers generally work for someone else full time or are full-time homemakers. Older respondents tend to be retired. The younger group has higher income than the older group, as one might expect. The younger group is also more likely to be married or divorced.

IN-HOME DEMONSTRATIONS

The first part of this section covers demographic and attitudinal information concerning mature consumers' perceptions of in-home shopping. Specifically, two mature groups—users and nonusers of in-home demonstrations as a purchasing mode—will be compared with respect to demographic characteristics and with respect to what each group likes and does not like about in-home shopping.

The second part of this section covers only users of in-home demonstrations. Here, users are divided into two subgroups—the older and younger—in order to compare demographic characteristics and likes and dislikes concerning in-home shopping.

As shown in Table 8.41, differences in mature elderly users of in-home demonstrations versus mature nonusers are confined to only one demographic characteristic: race. Nonusers tend to be white. This finding in isolation from other demographic traits is not very enlightening. One would expect race effects to be highly correlated with other demographic effects.

In the second part of this section characteristics of mature users versus younger users are examined.

For users of in-home demonstrations, Table 8.42 shows some demographic distinctions between mature and younger consumers. Younger consumers are likely to have some college; mature consumers tend to polarize at either a grade school education or, at the opposite extreme, having had graduate work. Among the younger consumers, the head of the household is married or single, and at least one member works. Older consumers tend to be married also but neither work, while younger consumers either work for someone else or are full-time homemakers. A similar situation holds for spouses. The household incomes of younger consumers are higher than those of older consumers.

SHOPPING ORIENTATIONS

The mean shopping orientation scores for the total sample are shown in Table 8.43 along with significant differences among the three age groups. Table 8.44 shows a discriminant analysis for shopping orientation across the three age groups.

Respondents in the 65+ age group are more likely to cite low mobility as a problem than are the other two age groups. Respondents in this group are also more personalizing shoppers than are the others. However, the 65+ group feels less time pressure when shopping, are more favorable toward merchants, and are less price conscious. They do tend to have less shopping self-confidence, and they are less convenience-oriented.

With respect to the four user groups, direct-selling users were less likely to distrust in-home shopping, or be concerned with low mobility or with loyalty to local merchants, not a surprising finding given the nature of direct selling. These users are also more positive toward convenience, one of the big advantages of in-home shopping. Direct-selling users are more positive than the other groups toward statements that support good price/quality benefits from in-home shopping. Finally, direct-selling users are more likely to be shopping innovators. That is, they enjoy finding unique products and locating new places to shop.

In contrast to direct-selling users, direct-marketing users are more likely to feel the time pressure of shopping and to exhibit negative attitudes toward merchants. Those who shop via direct marketing agreed more with statements indicating that merchants do not like having them in the store and take advantage of them when they are in the store.

Direct-marketing users are less likely to have been dissatisfied with the

match of the product ordered and customer expectations. Not surprisingly, these users are also less prone to evince a suspicious nature toward
unusual persons and situations.

SHOPPING ORIENTATION SCORES: 65+ AGE GROUP

Table 8.45 displays the mean shopping orientations scores for the 65+
age group across the four user categories.

Direct-selling users were significantly more positive than other users
and nonusers with respect to the convenience of in-home shopping. These
users were also more likely to be shopping innovators, but were less
fearful of the risk associated with in-home shopping such as products not
being worth what was paid or turning out to be a disappointment upon
receipt.

Direct-marketing users were more likely to be personalizing shoppers.
They like to shop where they are known and where they are acquainted
with sales personnel. These users are also more price conscious than other
shoppers and more negative toward local merchants.

Direct-marketing users are less positive than other users toward statements that reflect a positive price/quality/selection relationship for
products sold via in-home distribution. Direct-marketing users in the 65+
group also reflect a lack of shopping self-confidence which is perhaps a
reason for choosing direct marketing as an alternative purchasing route.

SHOPPING ORIENTATION SCORES: 50-64 AGE GROUP

In Table 8.46 mean shopping orientation scores across four user groups
have been completed for the 50-64 age group. The only significant differences are those observed for Group 4, those who use neither direct selling
nor direct marketing. The "neither" group differs from the direct
marketing and "both" groups in that it is more likely to be concerned
about the "workings" of in-home buying. That is, this group is more likely
to agree that ordering in-home is risky on several accounts: more risky to
order expensive products, to order from an unfamiliar company, and to
order without seeing and touching the product. They are also more likely
to be concerned that prices are too high and the goods are not worth the
asking price.

Users of neither are also less likely than the direct marketing and "both"
groups to be positive toward convenience, toward the price/quality/
selection relationship, and toward getting what is ordered.

SHOPPING ORIENTATION SCORES: ≤49 AGE GROUP

Table 8.47 shows that only five variables yielded significant differences
for the ≤49 groups across the four user groups. Users of both were more

likely than direct-marketing users to express a lack of shopping self-confidence. Users of neither were more likely to express opinions of distrust and risk concerning in-home shopping, and, surprisingly, were more likely to be positive toward the convenience of in-home shopping than were direct-marketing users and users of both. However, as opposed to these two groups, nonusers expressed more willingness to purchase a service via in-home shopping than a product. Finally direct-selling users were less positive than direct-marketing users toward the price/quality/selection aspects of in-home shopping.

Although few differentiating characteristics were observed for the younger two age groups, analysis of the 65+ age group versus other age groups yielded some interesting results. The problems of low mobility and less shopping self-confidence have been associated with the mature consumer in previous studies. These findings are again confirmed. The 65+ group's propensity to regard shopping as recreation and an opportunity for socializing with store personnel has also been documented. Since they experience less time pressure, it is not surprising that they are less convenience-oriented than the younger age groups.

In the 65+ group direct-selling users are differentiated by a desire for the convenience of in-home shopping and by a lack of distrust for in-home shopping that was evidenced by other user groups. Although direct marketing users were likely to be personalizing shoppers—a characteristic at variance with in-home shopping modes—they were also more negative toward local merchants, a characteristic which may help explain their use of direct marketing. Additionally, they lack shopping self-confidence which indicates that they are unsure of making satisfying purchases in a traditional shopping environment. Use of direct marketing may be seen as a vehicle to help them find better deals.

Table 8.1
Cross-tabulation of Respondent Age by Residence

Row Pct[1] Col Pct	Own	Rent	No Rent Paid	Row Total
$\leq$49	75.1[2] 12.7[3]	21.8 26.0	3.1 18.6	14.4
50-64	89.1 20.5	9.0 14.7	1.8 15.3	19.7
65+	86.7 66.8	10.9 59.3	2.4 66.1	65.9
Column Total	85.5	12.1	2.4	100.0

[1]Read: "Row Percent" and "Column Percent." See footnotes 2 and 3 for interpretation. Use throughout chapter.

[2]Read: "75.1 percent of respondents aged $\leq$49 own their homes."

[3]Read: "12.7 percent of respondents who own their homes are in the $\leq$49 age group."

Table 8.2
Cross-tabulation of Respondent Age by Education

Row Pct Col Pct	<HS	Some College	College Grad	Row Total
$\leq$49	40.2 10.7	31.2 18.4	28.7 19.1	14.4
50-64	60.9 22.2	20.6 16.6	18.5 16.8	19.7
65+	54.8 67.0	24.1 65.1	21.1 64.1	65.9
Column Total	53.9	24.5	21.7	100.0

Table 8.3
Cross-tabulation of Respondent Age by Household Size

Row Pct Col Pct	Household Size					Row Total
	1	2	3	4	5+	
$\leq$49	19.9	19.6	17.1	26.9	16.5	14.4
	8.7	5.7	29.3	64.9	69.4	
50-64	16.8	58.3	14.5	7.8	2.7	19.7
	10.0	23.2	34.1	25.7	15.3	
65+	40.6	53.1	4.6	.9	.8	66.0
	81.3	71.1	36.5	9.5	15.3	
Column Total	32.9	49.3	8.4	6.0	3.4	100.0

Table 8.4
Cross-tabulation of Respondent Age by Employment Status

Row Pc Col Pct	Retired	Employed	Unemployed	Row Total
$\leq$49	.6	92.2	7.2	14.6
	.1	34.3	30.1	
50-64	26.5	66.3	7.2	19.9
	9.2	33.7	41.0	
65+	79.3	19.1	1.5	65.5
	90.6	32.0	28.9	
Column Total	57.3	39.2	3.5	100.0

Table 8.5
Cross-tabulation of Respondent Age by Income Category

Row Pct Col Pct	<$10K	$10K-$20K	$20K+	Row Total
<49	12.0	22.1	65.8	14.4
	7.6	9.9	20.9	
50-64	12.7	25.2	62.2	19.7
	11.0	15.4	27.0	
65+	28.0	36.3	35.7	66.0
	81.4	74.7	52.1	
Column Total	22.7	32.1	45.2	100.0

Table 8.6
Cross-tabulation of Respondent Age by Marital Status

Row Pct Col Pct	Married	Not Married	Row Total
≤ 49	65.3 16.0	34.7 12.0	14.4
50-64	75.9 25.5	24.1 11.4	19.7
65+	51.8 58.5	48.2 76.6	66.0
Column Total	58.5	41.5	100.0

Table 8.7
Cross-tabulation of Respondent Age by Sex

Row Pct Col Pct	Male	Female	Row Total
≤ 49	13.7 17.9	86.3 13.9	14.4
50-64	6.5 11.7	93.5 20.6	19.7
65+	11.7 70.3	88.3 65.4	66.0
Column Total	11.0	89.0	100.0

Table 8.8
Cross-tabulation of ≤ 49 Users by Residence

Row Pct Col Pct	Own	Rent	No Rent Paid	Row Total
Direct-Selling Users	82.6 7.1	13.0 3.8	4.3 9.1	6.4
Direct-Marketing Users	69.9 38.1	26.0 48.7	4.1 54.5	40.9
Both	83.7 38.4	13.0 20.5	3.3 36.4	34.5
Neither	67.7 16.4	32.3 26.9		18.2
Column Total	75.1	21.8	3.1	100.0

Table 8.9
Cross-tabulation of ≤ 49 Users by Education

Row Pct Col Pct	<H.S.	Some College	College Grad	Row Total
Direct-Selling Users	47.8 7.7	39.1 8.1	13.0 2.9	6.5
Direct-Marketing Users	33.8 34.3	28.3 36.9	37.9 53.9	40.7
Both	43.9 37.8	35.0 38.7	21.1 25.5	34.6
Neither	44.6 20.3	27.7 16.2	27.7 17.6	18.3
Column Total	40.2	31.2	28.7	100.0

Table 8.10
Cross-tabulation of ≤ 49 Users by Household Size

Row Pct Col Pct	1	Household Size 2	3	4	5	Row Total
Direct-Selling Users		13.0 4.3	26.1 9.8	39.1 9.4	21.7 8.5	6.4
Direct-Marketing Users	29.5 60.6	18.5 38.6	14.4 34.4	24.7 37.5	13.0 32.2	40.9
Both	11.4 19.7	21.1 37.1	19.5 39.3	29.3 37.5	18.7 39.0	34.5
Neither	21.5 19.7	21.5 20.0	15.4 16.4	23.1 15.6	18.5 20.3	18.2
Column Total	19.9	19.6	17.1	26.9	16.5	100.0

Table 8.11
Cross-tabulation of ≤49 Users by Employment Status

Row Pct Col Pct	Retired	Employed	Unemployed	Row Total
Direct-Selling Users		91.3 6.6	8.7 8.0	6.7
Direct-Marketing Users		95.0 41.5	5.0 28.0	40.3
Both	.8 50.0	93.3 35.2	5.8 28.0	34.8
Neither	1.6 50.0	84.1 16.7	14.3 36.0	18.3
Column Total	.6	92.2	7.2	100.0

Table 8.12
Cross-tabulation of ≤49 Users by Income

Row Pct Col Pct	<$10K	$10K-$20K	$20 K+	Row Total
Direct-Selling Users	13.0 7.0	26.1 7.6	60.9 6.0	6.4
Direct-Marketing Users	13.7 46.5	18.5 34.2	67.8 42.1	40.9
Both	6.5 18.6	26.8 41.8	66.7 34.9	34.5
Neither	18.5 27.9	20.0 16.5	61.5 17.0	18.2
Column Total	12.0	22.1	65.8	100.0

Table 8.13
Cross-tabulation of ≤49 Users by Marital Status

Row Pct Col Pct	Married	Not Married	Row Total
Direct-Selling Users	78.3 7.7	21.7 4.0	6.4
Direct-Marketing Users	54.8 34.3	45.2 53.2	40.9
Both	75.6 39.9	24.4 24.2	34.5
Neither	64.6 18.0	35.4 18.5	18.2
Column Total	65.3	34.7	100.0

Table 8.14
Cross-tabulation of ≤49 Users by Sex

Row Pct Col Pct	Male	Female	Row Total
Direct-Selling Users	4.3 2.0	95.7 7.1	6.4
Direct-Marketing Users	20.5 61.2	79.5 37.7	40.9
Both	4.9 12.2	95.1 38.0	34.5
Neither	18.5 24.5	81.5 17.2	18.2
Column Total	13.7	86.3	100.00

Table 8.15
Cross-tabulation of 50-64 Users by Residence

Row Pct Col Pct	Own	Rent	No Rent Paid	Row Total
Direct-Selling Users	81.8 4.1	18.2 9.1		4.5
Direct-Marketing Users	90.8 47.7	8.3 43.2	.9 22.2	46.8
Both	87.0 15.4	9.1 15.9	3.9 33.3	15.8
Neither	88.8 32.7	8.8 31.8	2.5 44.4	32.9
Column Total	89.1	9.0	1.8	100.0

Table 8.16
Cross-tabulation of 50-64 Users by Education

Row Pct Col Pct	$\leq$H.S.	Some College	College Grad	Row Total
Direct-Selling Users	72.7 5.4	27.3 6.0		4.5
Direct-Marketing Users	54.6 41.9	22.0 50.0	23.3 58.9	46.7
Both	62.3 16.2	27.3 21.0	10.4 8.9	15.8
Neither	67.5 36.5	14.4 23.0	18.1 32.2	32.9
Column Total	60.9	20.6	18.5	100.0

Table 8.17
Cross-tabulation of 50-64 Users by Household Size

Row Pct Col Pct	Household Size					Row Total
	1	2	3	4	5	
Direct-Selling	9.1	68.2	18.2		4.5	4.5
Users	2.4	5.3	5.6		7.7	
Direct-Marketing	18.9	57.9	15.4	6.1	1.8	46.6
Users	52.4	46.3	49.3	36.8	30.8	
Both	12.8	52.6	20.5	10.3	3.8	16.0
	12.2	14.4	22.5	21.1	23.1	
Neither	16.8	60.2	9.9	9.9	3.1	32.9
	32.9	34.0	22.5	42.1	38.5	
Column Total	16.8	58.3	14.5	7.8	2.7	100.0

Table 8.18
Cross-tabulation of 50-64 Users by Employment Status

Row Pct Col Pct	Retired	Employed	Unemployed	Row Total
Direct-Selling	27.3	63.6	9.1	4.7
Users	4.8	4.5	5.9	
Direct-Marketing	25.5	66.8	7.7	46.6
Users	44.8	47.0	50.0	
Both	25.0	71.1	3.9	16.1
	15.2	17.3	8.8	
Neither	28.6	63.6	7.8	32.6
	35.2	31.3	35.3	
Column Total	26.5	66.3	7.2	100.0

Table 8.19
Cross-tabulation of 50-64 Users by Income

Row Pct Col Pct	<$10K	$10K-$20K	$20 K+	Total
Direct-Selling	9.1	36.4	54.5	4.5
Users	3.2	6.5	3.9	
Direct-Marketing	11.0	25.0	64.0	40.9
Users	40.3	46.3	48.0	
Both	7.7	24.4	67.9	34.5
	9.7	15.4	17.4	
Neither	18.0	24.2	57.8	18.2
	46.8	31.7	30.6	
Column Total	12.7	25.2	62.2	100.0

Table 8.20
Cross-tabulation of 50-64 Users by Marital Status

Row Pct Col Pct	Married	Not Married	Row Total
Direct-Selling	77.3	22.7	4.5
Users	4.6	4.2	
Direct-Marketing	71.5	28.5	46.6
Users	43.9	55.1	
Both	78.2	21.8	16.0
	16.4	14.4	
Neither	80.7	19.3	32.9
	35.0	26.3	
Column Total	75.9	24.1	100.0

Table 8.21
Cross-tabulation of 50-64 Users by Sex

Row Pct Col Pct	Male	Female	Row Total
Direct-Selling Users		100.0 4.8	4.5
Direct-Marketing Users	7.5 53.1	92.5 46.2	46.6
Both	2.6 6.3	97.4 16.6	16.0
Neither	8.1 40.6	91.9 32.4	32.9
Column Total	6.5	93.5	100.00

Table 8.22
Cross-tabulation of 65+ Users by Residence

Row Pct Col Pct	Own	Rent	No Rent Paid	Row Total
Direct-Selling Users	92.0 5.7	6.9 3.4	1.1 2.6	5.3
Direct-Marketing Users	84.4 43.4	12.9 52.8	2.6 48.7	44.6
Both	91.1 12.4	8.3 9.0	.5 2.6	11.8
Neither	87.2 38.5	10.0 34.8	2.9 46.2	38.3
Column Total	86.7	10.9	2.4	100.0

Table 8.23
Cross-tabulation of 65+ Users by Education

Row Pct Col Pct	$\leq$H.S.	Some College	College Grad	Row Total
Direct-Selling Users	63.6 6.3	20.5 4.6	15.9 4.1	5.4
Direct-Marketing Users	49.4 40.1	25.4 46.8	25.1 53.1	44.5
Both	47.7 10.3	28.5 14.0	23.8 13.4	11.9
Neither	62.0 43.3	21.8 34.6	16.2 29.4	38.3
Column Total	54.8	24.1	21.1	100.0

Table 8.24
Cross-tabulation of 65+ Users by Household Size

Row Pct Col Pct	Household Size					Row Total
	1	2	3	4	5	
Direct-Selling Users	38.6 5.1	52.3 5.3	5.7 6.6	1.1 7.1	2.3 15.4	5.4
Direct-Marketing Users	42.2 46.2	52.0 43.5	4.5 43.4	.4 21.4	.8 46.2	44.4
Both	40.9 11.9	50.8 11.2	4.7 11.8	3.1 42.9	.5 7.7	11.8
Neither	38.8 36.8	55.3 40.0	4.6 38.2	.6 28.6	.6 30.8	38.5
Column Total	40.6	53.1	4.6	.9	.8	100.0

Table 8.25
Cross-tabulation of 65+ Users by Employment Status

Row Pct Col Pct	Retired	Employed	Unemployed	Row Total
Direct-Selling	75.3	22.4	2.4	5.5
Users	5.2	6.4	8.3	
Direct-Marketing	78.6	20.5	.9	44.8
Users	44.4	48.1	25.0	
Both	80.5	17.8	1.6	11.9
	12.1	11.1	12.5	
Neither	80.4	17.4	2.2	37.8
	38.3	34.3	54.2	
Column Total	79.3	19.1	1.5	100.0

Table 8.26
Cross-tabulation of 65+ Users by Income

Row Pct Col Pct	<$10K	$10K-$20K	$20 K+	Row Total
Direct-Selling	33.0	42.0	25.0	5.4
Users	6.3	6.2	3.8	
Direct-Marketing	23.6	36.1	40.3	44.4
Users	37.5	44.1	50.2	
Both	24.9	38.3	36.8	11.8
	10.5	12.4	12.1	
Neither	33.3	35.2	31.5	38.5
	45.8	37.2	34.0	
Column Total	28.0	36.3	35.7	100.0

Table 8.27
Cross-tabulation of 65+ Users by Marital Status

Row Pct Col Pct	Married	Not Married	Row Total
Direct-Selling Users	52.3 5.4	47.7 5.3	5.4
Direct-Marketing Users	48.1 41.3	51.9 47.8	44.4
Both	53.9 12.2	46.1 11.3	11.8
Neither	55.3 41.1	44.7 35.7	38.5
Column Total	51.8	48.2	100.0

Table 8.28
Cross-tabulation of 65+ Users by Sex

Row Pct Col Pct	Male	Female	Row Total
Direct-Selling Users	1.1 .5	98.9 6.0	5.4
Direct-Marketing Users	14.4 54.7	85.6 43.1	44.4
Both	6.2 6.3	93.8 12.5	11.8
Neither	11.7 38.5	88.3 38.4	38.5
Column Total	11.7	88.3	100.00

Table 8.29
Demographic Comparison across Non/Light/Heavy Catalogue Users:
65+ Only

VARIABLE	CHI SQUARE	LEVEL OF SIGNIFICANCE	INTERPRETATION
Population Density	16.40	.173	
Type of Dwelling Unit	15.01	.132	
Ownership of Residence	1.55	.818	
Education of Respondent	49.82	.000	Nonusers are less educated
Employment of Household	6.18	.627	
Employment of Respondent	13.22	.353	
Employment of Spouse	11.74	.467	
Occupation of Respondent	13.17	.215	
Occupation of Spouse	9.50	.486	
Age of Respondent	8.14	.228	
Age of Spouse	9.03	.172	
Household Income	20.39	.060	Nonusers have lower incomes
Marital Status	4.62	.796	
Race	4.00	.677	
Sex of Respondent	3.91	.142	

Table 8.30
Demographics of Catalogue Users Only across Age Categories

VARIABLE	CHI SQUARE	LEVEL OF SIGNIFICANCE	INTERPRETATION
Population Density	17.50	.489	Young: multiple-unit dwellings
Type of Dwelling Unit	33.56	.004	Older: multiple-unit dwellings
Ownership of Residence	40.20	.000	Young: rent
Education of Respondent	39.40	.003	Young: more educated
Employment of Household	602.37	.000	Young: 1 or both work Young: single/work
Employment of Respondent	602.22	.000	Young: work for other Young: temporarily unemployed Young: homemaker
Employment of Spouse	336.36	.000	Young: work for other Young: self-employed Older: retired
Occupation of Respondent	15.01	.451	
Occupation of Spouse	26.29	.035	Young: sales, craft, other Middle: manager, sales, craft Older: professional, clerical
Household Income	139.03	.000	Younger: higher income than elderly Middle: higher than younger
Marital Status	157.64	.000	Older: widowed Younger: married/never married Middle: divorced/separated
Race	11.72	.230	
Sex of Respondent	11.96	.008	Younger/Older: male

164

Table 8.31
Demographics of Direct Mail Users vs. Nonusers: 65+ Only

VARIABLE	CHI SQUARE	LEVEL OF SIGNIFICANCE	INTERPRETATION
Population Density	3.119	.794	
Residence Type	4.596	.467	
Residence Ownership	6.824	.033	Nonusers: own home
Education of Respondent	26.194	.000	
Employment Status of Household	4.852	.303	
Employment Status of Respondent	4.426	.619	
Employment Status of Spouse	4.297	.637	
Occupation of Respondent	2.803	.730	
Occupation of Spouse	2.384	.794	
Age of Respondent	4.681	.197	
Age of Spouse	2.848	.416	
Household Income	16.810	.010	Nonusers: lower income Users: higher income
Marital Status	13.207	.010	Nonusers: married Users: never married
Race	.809	.847	
Sex of Respondent	7.711	.005	Nonusers: male Users: female

Table 8.32
Demographics of Direct Mail Users: 65+ vs. <65

VARIABLE	CHI SQUARE	LEVEL OF SIGNIFICANCE	INTERPRETATION
Population Density	7.266	.297	
Residence Type	2.178	.824	
Ownership of Residence	.639	.727	
Education of Respondent	7.183	.207	
Employment Status of Household	158.583	.000	<65: married (1 or 2 work); single (work) 65+: married/single (0 work)
Employment Status of Respondent	157.666	.000	<65: work for other (full/part) 65+: self-employed; retired; full-time homemakers
Employment Status of Spouse	87.015	.000	<65: work for other (full); self-employed 65+: retired
Occupation of Respondent	7.486	.187	
Occupation of Spouse	1.847	.870	
Household Income	13.155	.041	<65: higher 65+: lower
Marital Status	43.347	.000	65+: widowed; never married
Race	7.088	.029	65+: white
Sex of Respondent	1.667	.197	

165

Table 8.33
Demographics of Media Ad Users vs. Nonusers: 65+ Only

VARIABLE	CHI SQUARE	LEVEL OF SIGNIFICANCE	INTERPRETATION
Population Density	9.695	.138	
Residence Type	4.952	.422	
Ownership of Residence	3.513	.173	
Education of Respondent	9.972	.126	
Employment Status of Household	.594	.964	
Employment Status of Respondent	10.485	.106	
Employment Status of Spouse	6.935	.327	
Occupation of Respondent	5.819	.324	
Occupation of Spouse	2.701	.746	
Age of Respondent	1.484	.686	
Age of Spouse	4.017	.260	
Household Income	13.090	.042	Nonusers: lower income Users: higher income
Marital Status	2.902	.574	
Race	1.374	.712	
Sex of Respondent	.334	.563	

Table 8.34
Demographics of Media Ad Users: 65+ vs. <65

VARIABLE	CHI SQUARE	LEVEL OF SIGNIFICANCE	INTERPRETATION
Population Density	16.682	.011	Non-MSA, outside central city (2m+) all 65+ All other 65+
Residence Type	4.707	.453	
Ownership of Residence	2.213	.331	
Education of Respondent	7.872	.248	
Employment Status of Household	92.519	.000	Both work: <65 65+: married (neither work; single (0 or 1 works)
Employment Status of Respondent	104.573	.000	<65: work for someone else (full, part) 65+: self-employed; retired
Employment Status of Spouse	70.170	.000	<65: works for someone else; self-employed 65+: homemaker
Occupation of Respondent	5.645	.342	
Occupation of Spouse	8.672	.123	
Household Income	13.978	.030	<65: higher income
Marital Status	22.976	.000	65+: widowed; divorced; separated
Race	.149	.700	
Sex of Respondent	.716	.398	

166

Table 8.35
Demographics of Users vs. Nonusers of Phone Solicitation: 65+ Only

VARIABLE	CHI SQUARE	LEVEL OF SIGNIFICANCE
Population Density	4.569	.600
Residence Type	6.885	.229
Ownership of Residence	1.686	.430
Education of Respondent	10.353	.111
Employment Status of Household	2.703	.609
Employment Status of Respondent	6.173	.404
Employment Status of Spouse	1.171	.978
Occupation of Respondent	3.006	.699
Occupation of Spouse	2.058	.841
Age of Respondent	.695	.874
Age of Spouse	.104	.991
Household Income	1.814	.936
Marital Status	.191	.996
Race	.682	.877
Sex of Respondent	.013	.910

Table 8.36
Demographics of Users of Phone Solicitation: 65+ vs. <65

VARIABLE	CHI SQUARE	LEVEL OF SIGNIFICANCE	INTERPRETATION
Population Density	4.180	.524	
Residence Type	5.722	.221	
Ownership of Residence	1.403	.496	
Education of Respondent	7.455	.114	
Employment Status of Household	38.648	.000	<65: married (1 or 2 work); single (work) 65+: married/single (0 work)
Employment Status of Respondent	46.251	.000	<65: work full time 65+: retired
Employment Status of Spouse	21.484	.000	<65: work full time 65+: retired
Occupation of Respondent	1.904	.753	
Occupation of Spouse	4.221	.377	
Household Income	5.259	.511	
Marital Status	5.747	.125	
Race	.002	.965	
Sex of Respondent	.077	.782	

Table 8.37
Demographics of Users vs. Nonusers of Direct Selling: 65+ Only

VARIABLE	CHI SQUARE	LEVEL OF SIGNIFICANCE	INTERPRETATION
Population Density	7.431	.283	
Residence Type	3.583	.611	
Ownership of Residence	2.821	.244	
Education of Respondent	5.564	.474	
Employment Status of Household	1.703	.790	
Employment Status of Respondent	13.201	.040	Users: Self-employed; Full-time homemaker
Employment Status of Spouse	15.796	.015	Nonuser: works for others (full); full-time homemaker
Occupation of Respondent	10.410	.064	Nonuser: professional; managers Users: clerical; sales workers
Occupation of Spouse	6.479	.262	
Age of Respondent	1.805	.614	
Age of Spouse	2.779	.427	
Household Income	4.334	.632	
Marital Status	3.950	.413	
Race	3.402	.334	
Sex of Respondent	10.509	.001	Nonusers: male Users: female

Table 8.38
Demographics of Direct-Selling Users: 65+ vs. <65

VARIABLE	CHI SQUARE	LEVEL OF SIGNIFICANCE	INTERPRETATION
Population Density	6.568	.363	
Residence Type	1.849	.870	
Ownership of Residence	5.995	.050	
Education of Respondent	8.239	.144	
Employment Status of Household	72.542	.000	<65: married (1 or 2 work); single (work) 65+: married/single (0 work)
Employment Status of Respondent	59.192	.000	<65: work for other (full/part) 65+: retired
Employment Status of Spouse	59.091	.000	<65: work for someone else (full)
Occupation of Respondent	6.359	.273	
Occupation of Spouse	4.618	.329	
Household Income	16.344	.012	<65: higher 65+: lower
Marital Status	18.610	.000	65+: widowed/separated
Race	.798	.671	
Sex of Respondent	.325	.569	

Table 8.39
Demographics of Party Plan Users vs. Nonusers: 65+ Only

VARIABLE	CHI SQUARE	LEVEL OF SIGNIFICANCE	INTERPRETATION
Population Density	12.178	.058	
Residence Type	5.920	.314	
Ownership of Residence	2.441	.295	
Education of Respondent	3.251	.777	
Employment Status of Household	7.751	.101	Nonusers: single (work) Users: married (both work)
Employment Status of Respondent	5.932	.431	
Employment Status of Spouse	2.164	.821	
Occupation of Respondent	2.445	.785	
Occupation of Spouse	4.533	.475	
Age of Respondent	11.716	.008	Nonusers: older User: younger
Age of Spouse	4.174	.243	
Household Income	11.666	.070	Nonusers: highest income Users: middle income
Marital Status	16.973	.002	Nonusers: never married Users: widowed
Race	3.244	.356	
Sex of Respondent	32.255	.000	Users: female

Table 8.40
Demographics of Party Plan Users: 65+ vs. <65

VARIABLE	CHI SQUARE	LEVEL OF SIGNIFICANCE	INTERPRETATION
Population Density	6.352	.385	
Residence Type	4.053	.542	
Ownership of Residence	2.387	.274	
Education of Respondent	7.731	.259	
Employment Status of Household	164.176	.000	<65: married (1 or 2 work); single (work) 65+: married/single (0 work)
Employment Status of Respondent	164.651	.000	<65: work for someone else (full/part); full-time homemaker 65+: retired
Employment Status of Spouse	85.356	.000	<65: work for someone else (full); full-time homemaker 65+: retired; part-time work for other
Occupation of Respondent	3.418	.636	
Occupation of Spouse	4.647	.460	
Household Income	49.256	.000	<65: higher income 65+: lower income
Marital Status	51.248	.000	<65: married/divorced 65+: widowed
Race	1.825	.402	
Sex of Respondent	.029	.864	

169

Table 8.41
Demographics of In-Home Demonstration Users vs. Nonusers: 65+ Only

VARIABLE	CHI SQUARE	LEVEL OF SIGNIFICANCE	INTERPRETATION
Population Density	9.772	.135	
Residence Type	1.756	.882	
Ownership of Residence	2.019	.364	
Education of Respondent	6.363	.356	
Employment Statement of Household	3.943	.414	
Employment Status of Respondent	5.008	.543	
Employment Status of Spouse	2.843	.828	
Occupation of Respondent	5.423	.367	
Occupation of Spouse	3.047	.693	
Age of Respondent	2.351	.503	
Age of Spouse	.458	.928	
Household Income	2.344	.885	
Marital Status	2.201	.699	
Race	25.992	.000	Nonusers: white
Sex of Respondent	.891	.346	

Table 8.42
Demographics of In-Home Demonstration Users: 65+ vs. <65

VARIABLE	CHI SQUARE	LEVEL OF SIGNIFICANCE	INTERPRETATION
Population Density	8.332	.215	
Residence Type	5.059	.281	
Ownership of Residence	4.027	.134	
Education of Respondent	9.509	.090	<65: some college 65+: grade school; graduate work
Employment Status of Household	68.149	.000	<65: married (1 or 2 work); single (works) 65+: married (neither work)
Employment Status of Respondent	77.895	.000	<65: works for someone else (full, part); full-time homemakers 65+: retired
Employment Status of Spouse	42.722	.000	<65: works for someone else 65+: retired
Occupation of Respondent	7.043	.217	
Occupation of Spouse	6.101	.297	
Household Income	20,593	.002	<65: higher income 65+: lower income
Marital Status	25.113	.000	<65: married/divorced 65+: widowed/separated
Race	2.326	.507	
Sex of Respondent	1.082	.298	

Table 8.43
Mean Shopping Orientation Scores: Total Sample

Shopping Orientations[1]	Age Group 1 ≤ 49	2 50-64	3 65 +	
Time pressure-shopping	3.33	3.04	2.73	All three groups differ
Low mobility	1.58	1.69	2.02	Group 3 differs from groups 1, 2
Shopping self-confidence	3.50	3.35	3.27	Group 3 and 2 differ from group 1
Personalizing shopper	3.27	3.52	3.65	All three groups differ
Negative toward merchants	2.13	2.02	1.99	Group 3 differs from group 1
Shopping innovator	3.64	3.50	3.39	All three groups differ
Positive toward convenience	3.39	3.18	3.17	Groups 3, 2 differs from group 1
Price-conscious shopper	3.90	3.81	3.77	Group 3 differs from group 1
Negative toward local shopping	2.74	2.72	2.68	Group 3 differs from group 1
Loyalty to local merchants	2.31	2.56	2.66	All three groups differ
Positive toward price/quality/selection	2.98	2.82	2.88	Group 2 differs from group 1
Suspicious nature	3.40	3.35	3.42	No two groups differ
Social shopping	3.01	2.95	3.01	No groups differ
Get what you order	3.30	3.21	3.25	No two groups differ
Distrust of in-home	3.32	3.47	3.55	Groups 3, 2 differ from group 1
Shopping propensity	3.13	3.09	3.12	No two groups differ
Service over product in-home	2.83	3.14	3.24	Groups 3, 2 differ from group 1

[1]On a 5-point scale where 1 = strongly disagree, 2 = disagree, 3 = neither, 4 = agree, and 5 = strongly agree. High numbers represent more of the trait.

171

Table 8.44
Discriminant Analysis: Shopping Orientations across Three Age Groups

Shopping Orientations[1]	Discriminant Function Coefficients		Discriminant Function Loadings	
	1	2	1	2
Time pressure-shopping[2]	-.61	-.15	-.50	.18
Low mobility[2]	.50	.46	.57	.21
Shopping self-confidence[2]	-.33	.07	-.17	.18
Personalizing shopper[2]	.27	-.18	.24	-.39
Negative toward merchants[2]	-.21	-.03	-.13	.14
Shopping innovator[2]	-.10	-.02	-.15	.17
Positive toward convenience[2]	-.08	.08	-.01	.35
Price-conscious shopper[3]	-.05	-.01	-.08	.11
Negative toward local shopping[3]	.08	-.46	-.17	-.08
Loyalty to local merchants[2]	.34	-.46	.20	-.54
Positive toward price/quality/selection[3]	.02	.45	.18	.45
Suspicious nature	.06	.34	.15	.19
Social shopping	-.14	.25	.11	.16
Get what you order	.07	.24	.12	.27
Distrust of in-home[2]	.21	.22	.13	-.21
Shopping propensity	.03	.20	.09	.15
Service over product in-home[2]	.12	-.15	.11	-.30

Chi Square 503.4[2]
Percent Variance Explained 28.8
Percent of Respondents Correctly Classified: 66.3%

[1]On a 5-point scale where 1 = strongly disagree, 2 = disagree, 3 = neither, 4 = agree, and 5 = strongly agree. High numbers represent more of the trait.

[2]Wilkes' lambda level of significance = .001

[3]Wilkes' lambda level of significance = .01

172

Table 8.45
Mean Shopping Orientation Scores across Four User Groups: 65+ Only

Shopping Orientations[1]	Direct Selling	Direct Marketing	Both	Neither	
Time pressure-shopping	3.12	3.42	3.35	3.20	No two groups differ
Low mobility	1.73	1.54	1.63	1.55	No two groups differ
Shopping self-confidence	3.53	3.61	3.36	3.52	Group 3 differs from group 2
Personalizing shopper	3.06	3.28	3.29	3.26	No two groups differ
Negative toward merchants	2.16	2.12	2.13	2.16	No two groups differ
Shopping innovator	3.38	3.68	3.75	3.44	No two groups differ
Positive toward convenience	3.40	3.53	3.48	3.94	Group 4 differs from groups 3, 2
Price-conscious shopper	3.92	3.90	3.95	3.81	No two groups differ
Negative toward local shopping	2.73	2.74	2.75	2.75	No two groups differ
Loyalty to local merchants	2.35	2.32	2.30	2.33	No two groups differ
Positive toward price/quality/selection	2.67	3.09	2.96	2.88	Group 1 differs from group 2
Suspicious nature	3.51	3.43	3.34	3.38	No two groups differ
Social shopping	3.53	2.90	3.07	3.00	No two groups differ
Get what you order	3.12	3.37	3.37	3.07	No two groups differ
Distrust of in-home	3.52	3.27	3.17	3.69	Group 4 differs from groups 3, 2; Group 1 differs from group 3
Shopping propensity	3.00	3.15	3.16	3.06	No two groups differ
Service over product in-home	3.12	2.67	2.74	3.26	Group 4 differs from groups 3, 2

[1] On a 5-point scale where 1 = strongly disagree, 2 = disagree, 3 = neither, 4 = agree, and 5 = strongly agree. High numbers represent more of the trait.

173

Table 8.46
Mean Shopping Orientation Scores across Four User Groups: 50-64

Shopping Orientations[1]	Direct Selling	Direct Marketing	Both	Neither	
Time pressure-shopping	2.92	3.00	2.35	2.95	No two groups differ
Low mobility	2.21	1.66	1.75	1.64	No two groups differ
Shopping self-confidence	3.42	3.35	3.33	3.42	No two groups differ
Personalizing shopper	3.83	3.44	3.58	3.56	No two groups differ
Negative toward merchants	2.00	2.03	2.08	1.98	No two groups differ
Shopping innovator	3.62	3.49	3.50	3.50	No two groups differ
Positive toward convenience	3.27	3.30	3.47	2.80	Group 4 differs from groups 2, 3
Price-conscious shopper	3.83	3.81	3.98	3.73	No two groups differ
Negative toward local shopping	2.71	2.70	2.82	2.72	No two groups differ
Loyalty to local merchants	2.59	2.54	2.45	2.66	No two groups differ
Positive toward price/quality/selection	2.77	2.88	2.92	2.67	Group 4 differs from groups 2, 3
Suspicious nature	3.44	3.31	2.21	3.47	No two groups differ
Social shopping	2.91	2.90	2.96	3.04	No two groups differ
Get what you order	2.94	3.32	3.42	2.94	Group 4 differs from groups 2, 3
Distrust of in-home	3.73	3.27	3.30	3.82	Group 4 differs from groups 2, 3
Shopping propensity	3.14	3.05	3.11	3.14	No two groups differ
Service over product in-home	3.25	3.04	3.05	3.34	No two groups differ

[1] On a 5-point scale where 1 = strongly disagree, 2 = disagree, 3 = neither, 4 = agree, and 5 = strongly agree. High numbers represent more of the trait.

174

Table 8.47
Mean Shopping Orientation Scores across Four User Groups: ≤49

Shopping Orientations[1]	Direct Selling	Direct Marketing	Both	Neither	
Time pressure-shopping	2.90	2.71	2.81	2.70	No two groups differ
Low mobility	1.89	2.00	2.08	2.06	No two groups differ
Shopping self-confidence	3.23	3.26	3.29	3.26	No two groups differ
Personalizing shopper	3.70	3.58	3.77	3.69	Groups 4 and 3 differ from group 2
Negative toward merchants	1.92	1.98	1.96	2.03	No two groups differ
Shopping innovator	3.42	3.41	3.54	3.31	No two groups differs
Positive toward convenience	2.97	3.31	3.46	2.87	Group 3 differs from groups 1, 4; Group 4 differs from group 2
Price-conscious shopper	3.65	3.68	3.85	3.88	Group 4 differs from group 2
Negative toward local shopping	2.57	2.68	2.70	2.71	No two groups differ
Loyalty to local merchants	2.79	2.61	2.65	2.70	No two groups differ
Positive toward price/quality/selection	2.89	2.97	3.06	2.71	Group 4 differs from groups 2, 3
Suspicious nature	3.30	3.41	3.32	3.49	Group 4 differs from groups 1, 2, 3
Social shopping	3.20	2.94	3.09	3.05	No two groups differ
Get what you order	3.14	3.42	3.40	3.00	Group 4 differs from groups 2, 3; Groups 3, 2 differ from 1
Distrust of in-home	3.56	3.44	3.29	3.79	Group 3 differs from groups 1, 4; Group 4 differs from group 2
Shopping propensity	3.08	3.06	3.13	3.19	Group 4 differs from group 2
Service over product in-home	3.09	3.20	3.07	3.40	Group 4 differs from group 1

[1]On a 5-point scale where 1 = strongly disagree, 2 = disagree, 3 = neither, 4 = agree, and 5 = strongly agree. High numbers represent more of the trait.

175

CHAPTER 9

Reaching the Mature Consumer

The mature consumer continues to dislike high-pressure sales tactics and the uncertainty of shopping by pictures. However many mature consumers do like the convenience of in-home shopping, although most direct-marketing modes are not perceived favorably when compared to retailing.

Mature users felt that catalogues were as good as or better than retailers on several dimensions including credibility of product claims, price and quality of goods, ability to make exchanges, and the accurate portrayal of products. However, the same cannot be said for other direct-marketing modes which fared less favorably when compared to retailers.

This research also identified shopping orientations and examined their relationships to various demographic descriptors of patronage behavior. Of particular interest were the shopping orientations of mature consumers who use direct marketing and direct selling. Also investigated were the relationships of these orientations to other aspects of shopping behavior.

In contrast to the findings of other research (e.g., Martin 1975), this study indicates that mature consumers tend to enjoy shopping. More importantly our research shows that they like to shop where well-known brands and products are carried. They are reluctant to try new outlets and are not very self-confident when shopping. The mature consumer does seem to be a recreational type of shopper, shopping for social reasons as well as purchasing reasons.

This research indicates that attitudinal postures tend to differentiate mature users and nonusers with respect to various shopping modes. For example: "Distrust of in-home shopping" defines a series of statements such as "I am taking a chance if I order something instead of buying it from a store" and "I would never consider ordering expensive items." Agreement with these statements indicates a distrust of in-home shopping and that the respondent believes that in-home shopping is risky, probably riskier than patronizing traditional retail stores. Not surprisingly, mature nonusers of certain in-home shopping modes scored higher agreement than users. These modes include catalogue, direct mail, media ads, direct selling, and party plan.

Mature users of catalogues, direct mail, media ads, phone solicitation, and party plans were in agreement with statements that dealt with the convenience and relaxation of shopping at home. Those who use catalogues, direct mail, and media ads agree that portrayal of products is generally accurate and that they have been satisfied with the products that they receive. Mature users of catalogues, direct mail, media ads, phone solicitation, and direct selling are also positive toward price, quality, and selection of items obtained through these shopping modes. Nonusers of catalogues and media ads tended to agree with statements that indicate a loyalty to local merchants. Interestingly, the statements can also be used to identify the users of telephone solicitation. This may not be surprising since much telephone solicitation involves patronage of local businesses.

Mature nonusers of catalogues agreed with statements suggesting that they would prefer to buy a service rather than a product through in-home shopping, that they price shop, and that they tend to shop around before making a decision. Apparently these buyers find catalogue shopping too limiting in these respects. Nonusers of catalogues are also personalizing shoppers. That is, interaction with store personnel is an important facet of the shopping experience for them and may explain their reluctance to engage in catalogue shopping. These mature nonusers of catalogues are also suspicious in nature, again suggesting that they would rather do business with people and stores that they are familiar with.

As a group, mature consumers are more inclined to associate risk with direct mail and in-home demonstrations than were the younger groups. They were also distinguished by their loyalty to local merchants and by their need for personal contact when shopping. This latter trait distinguished mature consumers from all other age groups except in the direct-selling shopping modes.

On the other hand, for several in-home shopping modes, younger consumers were distinguished from the older consumers by being more price-conscious shoppers, by being more negative toward merchants, and by being negative toward local shopping. For all modes but telephone solicitation, the younger consumer tended to feel time pressure when shopping. This may reflect the largely retired nature of the mature consumer group which allows them greater leisure time and more scheduling flexibility.

Mature users of direct selling also desired availability of information and a wide selection of items. It is these specific qualities that induce the elderly consumer to shop direct. Also, having the product right away was a determinant characteristic for users of media ads. This suggests that expedited delivery should be stressed in these advertisements.

When considering users by age category, we found that younger catalogue shoppers desire wide selection and the ability to charge purchases. In fact, the ability to charge was a determinant for younger consumers across all shopping modes except media ads and direct selling.

Mature users of direct selling, party plans, and in-home demonstrations are all concerned about well-known name brands, and the party plan users are also concerned about availability of information and the company paying postage or shipping costs.

It was also reported that the importance of shopping attributes will discriminate between various user categories. For example, and not surprisingly, mature catalogue users felt that the ability to decide in-home was important, but mature nonusers cited as important all of the following attributes: availability of C.O.D., repeated solicitation, availability of samples, see product before trying, phone follow-up after purchase, access to salesperson, personal demonstration, trial period, another choice available, and mail follow-up after purchase. Many of these characteristics are lacking, at least to some extent, in catalogue shopping.

Users of phone solicitation were interested in phone or personal follow-up and access to the sales representative. Party plan users also wanted follow-up along with a personal demonstration, a trial period, and having a sales representative in their home.

The attributes that appear to be of interest to the mature across several shopping modes and that distinguish them from their younger counterparts include access to the sales representative, a well-known company, and previous experience with the brand and company.

Before we proceed to some thoughts on how to market to the mature consumer, it is necessary to discuss a couple of characteristics often associated with mature consumers. These concern: 1) information recipient's characteristics, 2) age differences and influenceability, and 3) mobility.

Information Recipient's Characteristics

Although older adults often have greater difficulty in learning than do younger adults, and certain modes of stimulus presentation and contextual cues may magnify the deficit, mature consumers may compensate for this loss by relying on their lifelong experience in processing diverse types of information. It has been demonstrated that, in comparison with the performance of new skills, adults in their fifties and sixties show only minor deficits in performing tasks which they continued to practice throughout their life. Some investigators have hypothesized that the experience acquired with age enables older adults to process information with increased efficiency. According to Birren (1974) when individuals group their past experience into new categories, the categories become larger, so that as the individual grows older, he/she may process fewer units of information per unit of time, but the categories become larger. The result of this is that effectiveness may stay the same and even improve.

Thus mature consumers may compensate for their diminished speed in processing information by using their experience as a basis for abstracting the stimulus input. Accordingly, the efficiency with which the mature process a given information load is enhanced and learning is facilitated. In situations with which they have had prior experience, mature adults' learning abilities are likely to be comparable to those of younger individuals.

Despite the lack of direct evidence for the assertion that older individuals are able to process information more efficiently than younger adults, Birren (1969) has marshalled data that are congenial to this hypothesis. He interviewed people between the ages of 30 and 60 about decisions they had made in important spheres of their lives such as career, family, and organizational participation. These data were used to develop protocols that indicated that older individuals had great facility in distinguishing information that was relevant to their goals from information that was less salient. Older subjects processed less information than younger adults, but the information that was processed was of central importance to the decision at hand.

The data collected from these protocols appear to contradict laboratory findings of an age decrement in the ability to ignore irrelevant information. However, in those laboratory studies in which a positive age-distractibility relationship was found, the experimental task uniquely involved a decision situation unfamiliar to all age groups. In such situations, where the elderly's experience is not useful in developing efficient processing strategies, the impairment of their ability to suppress irrelevant stimuli is magnified by the comparison with other age groups because of their diminished processing faculties.

In summary, it appears that a decline in the speed of processing information reduces the older person's ability to learn. This learning difficulty is magnified by rapid stimulus pacing and the presence of irrelevant information, particularly if the older person has had little experience with the issue. However, if experience is considerable, it enhances the elderly's information processing efficiency, which compensates for the slowness of processing. In these instances, the elderly may not show a learning deficit in relation to younger adults, even if irrelevant stimuli are present.

Age Differences and Influenceability

Three approaches have been used to investigate the age-influenceability relationship: suggestibility, persuasion, and conformity. Suggestibility involves the repeated presentation of an advocacy until a person adopts an attitude or behavior that is consistent with this advocacy. Typically the suggestion is made without providing the message recipient reasons for carrying it out. Using this approach, suggestibility has been found to increase until the age of eight or nine, then to decline sharply until adolescence, after which it levels off.

Investigations involving a persuasion approach have yielded a somewhat different finding. Persuasion entails presenting detailed arguments to convince a message recipient to adopt the position advocated. Although persuasion studies have sampled only individuals ranging in age from 14 to 32, they are univocal in reporting a consistent decline in persuasibility as a function of increasing age.

The findings of suggestibility and persuasion studies appear to provide inconsistent evidence with regard to the age-influenceability relationship. Whereas suggestibility studies indicate that from adolescence on there are no age-related differences in influenceability, persuasion research suggests that resistance to influence increases with age, at least until after the age of 30. This disparity is most likely attributable to differences in the cognitive skills required to resist suggestion relative to that required to resist persuasion. Because suggestibility involves no arguments in support of the advocacy, relatively little cognitive skill is needed to resist influence. As a result, adolescents are as resistant to suggestion as adults. In contrast, in persuasion situations, the message recipients must have the skill to defend themselves against the arguments presented if they are to resist influence. Because this skill is likely to develop with age, people may become less susceptible to persuasion as they grow older.

Still at issue is the mature consumer's susceptibility to persuasion compared to that of younger adults. Though the persuasion findings indicate that for adults there is a decline in influenceability with age, this conclusion is based on research which samples individuals of middle age or younger. Possibly the decline in susceptibility to persuasion continues beyond middle age, levels off at some point, or is reversed in old age.

The conclusions that, for adults, age has no systematic effect on persuasion requires qualification. Conformity studies indicate that the age-influenceability relationship depends on the circumstances in which influence occurs. These investigations involved: (1) presenting the subjects with an ambiguous stimulus, (2) asking subjects to make a judgment about the stimulus, (3) communicating to the subjects that there was a disparity between their initial judgment and that made by a peer group, and (4) measuring the extent to which subjects changed their judgment toward that attributed to the group. Using this approach, Klein and Birren (1972a) found that older subjects (60 to 86 years old) conformed to the group's opinion significantly more often than did younger subjects (16 to 21 years old), whether the task involved visual perceptual judgment, auditory perceptual judgment, auditory signal detection, problem solving, or social attitudes. In a follow-up study, Klein and Birren (1972b) attempted to determine whether perception of self-competence mediated the effects of age on conformity. They found that when subjects were labeled as competent in performing judgments (achieved by telling them that their performance was much better than that of persons previously tested) older subjects showed decreased conformity to a greater extent than did younger subjects such that age had no systematic effect on conformity.

Thus it appears that when older individuals perceive themselves to be competent they are no more susceptible to social influence than younger adults. However, when the mature perceive themselves to lack the competence to make a decision they manifest greater influenceability than younger people. The research reported here indicates that the mature consumer feels less confident about shopping than younger consumers. Furthermore, the lack of resistance to influence attempts is likely to be most acute for those older persons who are isolated from contact with others; in such situations there may be a lack of exposure to the social reinforcement necessary to enhance individuals' perception of their own self-confidence.

On the basis of the evidence reviewed a scenario of how older consumers process information can be constructed. First, with retirement generally between the ages of 60 and 65, a contraction begins in the mature individual's life space—a contraction that becomes particularly pronounced after the age of 75. Although the result is a reduction in the variety of interpersonal sources of information to which the older consumers are exposed, it is compensated for by increased reliance on mass media, the extended family, and friends who live in physical proximity. Second, starting at about age 45 individuals show a reduced ability to learn when the information presentation is rapid and externally paced, is given in a context that includes irrelevant information, and addresses an issue with which message recipients have had little experiences. In contrast, older individuals do not show learning deficits in tasks for which they have developed related skills in earlier life. Third, older individuals appear to be no more influenceable than other adults, unless they perceive themselves to lack the competence necessary to make a judgment. In the latter situation, or when older individuals are socially isolated they show a greater susceptibility to social influences than younger adults. The foregoing scenario has implications for communication strategies, product strategies, and other mix variables.

Mobility

Because mature consumers may be handicapped, in poor health, or suffer from poor eyesight, they often suffer from mobility problems.

Nearly 40 percent of older households do not own an automobile. Public transportation usage is relatively infrequent among seniors because they have difficulty boarding and leaving buses and walking back and forth to bus stops. Many fear crime on public transportation or walking home. When seniors reach a public building, they encounter architectural barriers that restrict their mobility (Harris 1978).

Direct marketers and direct sellers can respond to these mobility problems by bringing seniors to their goods or by bringing their goods to seniors. Both approaches appear to have profit potential. Goods can be brought to older persons by mail. The marketer can also bring goods to senior citizens by delivery or mobile stores. Lambert (1979) found that seniors want retailers to provide delivery services, a shopper service whereby they could telephone in their orders and have a store employee make product and brand selections, and a home-call service whereby sales personnel call on the elderly with samples and product information.

Several studies have shown that senior citizens shop nearby their residences since many lack personal transportation. In addition, substantial store loyalty has been exhibited by this group for items with small unit values (e.g., food and magazines) or for products about which the store owner may give advice (e.g., drugs and medicines). Store loyalty disappears as unit value of the item increases and frequency of purchase decreases (e.g., appliances). Greater store loyalty is also exhibited by those at higher incomes and older ages (Samli 1967; Samli and Palubinskas 1972).

Some of this country's important retail institutions, such as shopping centers and supermarkets, have features that make them quite attractive to senior shoppers. The generally favorable prices and the safe, comfortable atmosphere of these stores contribute to their appeal. At the same time, however, Reinecke (1975) notes that certain other features of these institutions inhibit older consumers from taking advantage of them. First, these stores are generally located away from older neighborhoods where many aged and most poor live. Transportation, either public (which is typically poor or nonexistent) or private (which is typically unavailable to older shoppers on a regular basis), is necessary to reach these outlets. Moreover, there are problems of the right merchandise assortment to satisfy the needs of older consumers. For these and other reasons such retail institutions have not adequately met the needs of senior citizens.

There are a number of ways in which shopping center associations and the management of department stores, clothing stores, and supermarkets can take the following actions to expand their business among senior attract more senior citizens to shop at their facilities. Reinecke (1975) suggests occupants of shopping centers, in some cases acting as a group, can takes the following actions to expand their business among senior citizens: (1) sponsor low-cost or free bus transportation from "senior" centers to shopping centers; (2) expand telephone shopping and promote it; (3) provide free or low-cost bus tokens for patrons; (4) provide lounges or rest areas; (5) provide larger print on labels and price-tags; and (6) experiment with senior clothing departments.

Mason and Bearden (1978a; 1978b) found most elderly prefer to shop in the mornings, given the opportunity, which is consistent with previous research. However, infrequent catalogue use was reported. This is contrary to the stereotype often presented of the homebound senior citizen with little social interaction and limited shopping alternatives. Instead, as has been found for other market segments, catalogue shopping appears to be a voluntary activity and is simply viewed as part of the total array of shopping alternatives available.

The physical environment of many retail stores and shopping centers does not meet the needs of senior citizens. Lambert (1979) found that a substantial proportion of seniors need personal assistance in locating products. They also mentioned a need for improved store directories and for frequently needed products to be grouped together. Provision of rest facilities, like chairs and benches, were also desired since they could shop longer if there were places to rest. Some retailers (e.g., K-mart and Price Chopper Discount Foods) currently provide rest facilities within their stores. In a survey of Houston's older citizens, Gelb (1978) found that 29 percent of seniors cut "shopping trips short at least half the time because of getting tired." Some of Lambert's (1979) respondents suggested that retailers have special checkout lines for older patrons. These lines should be staffed by personnel trained to be patient and courteous in counting and changing money and in answering customer questions.

Retailers could improve access to their stores for older patrons by adopting the following actions: provide special events or special shopping days/times for only senior citizens, and set up information booths to assist seniors with their shopping (Lumpkin and Greenberg 1982); reserve parking spaces for seniors near the store or mall entrance; avoid heavy doors, turnstiles, or steps, but provide handrails and ramps; provide package carry-out service; furnish walkers and wheelchairs; keep aisles clear of boxes, special displays, and unattended shopping carts; and offer special assistance to older persons (e.g., in locating products, removing products from shelves, and carrying products) (Lambert 1979).

Gelb (1978) revealed some interesting findings with respect to store location and staffing. Her conclusions suggested that for retailers interested in older buyers or for manufacturers appraising a current or proposed channel structure, store location and staffing may be relevant factors. Proximity to public transportation and senior housing appears to be most critical. A location near a recreation center or a church with active retirement-age groups also may be desirable.

No clear-cut direction emerges from the study for retail staffing decisions. Only one-third of the respondents said they preferred to deal with sales clerks younger than themselves. One-third said they would be attracted to a newly opened store in their neighborhood if someone their age worked there. This is a significant but hardly overwhelming percentage.

More relevant than rushing out to hire seniors as salespersons, however, may be the treatment that a firm gives to its own retirees who will interact with potential 65+ consumers. Fifty-six percent of respondents failed to agree that store owners—representative of the marketing community—were glad to see them as customers. This perception suggests that more than staffing policies may be communicating indifference from marketers. Areas to be considered here include credit, support for public transportation, the age mix of models used in advertising, and in short, anything that represents the marketer to the retirement-age consumer.

INFORMATION SOURCES

One area of concern regarding the mature consumer that has received limited study, yet is of particular interest to advertisers, involves the sources of information that mature consumers use.

Lumpkin and Festervand (1987) provide a typology of information sources used by the mature consumers, shown in Table 9.1. Eight informational dimensions were identified: advertisements, product/store recognition, family, guarantees, salespeople, friends and experiences, evaluation at home and store, and independent sources.

A comparison of mature and younger consumer sources of information resulted in similar dimensions. Five of the eight informational sources identified for mature were similarly identified for younger consumers.

Using the information typology of mature consumers as a guide, a review of research provides insight into this important area.

Schiffman (1971) was among the first to examine the various sources of product information used by the elderly. The study examined the impact of information and informational sources on the new product trial decisions of the elderly. A primary focus of the research was the suitability of personal experiences as a source of internal information.

The following conclusions were reached: (1) there is a strong positive association between interest (need) and trial of the new product, (2) there is a strong positive association between initiation of product-related conversation and trial, and (3) there is a strong positive association between past experience and new product trial.

Schiffman (1972) investigated the relationship between product-related social interaction and three related marketing variables: (1) extent of social involvement, (2) exposure to mass media, and (3) product innovativeness.

The findings suggested that older individuals who were most involved in product-related social interaction are also: (1) more involved in other forms of social interaction, (2) more exposed to those mass media providing them with news and current events information, and (3) more innovative when it comes to trying new food products. They are also seen to value innovative behavior more and are perceived by their peers to be more innovative. Additionally, our findings indicate that many mature consumers like the personal aspects associated with shopping.

Klippel and Sweeney (1974) investigated the use of information sources by the mature consumer. The primary purpose of their research was to increase the knowledge of the information sources used by the mature consumer in learning about products. The information sources were classified as formal sources (newspaper, television, and radio advertisements) or informal sources (friends, neighbors, family, and retail sales representatives).

The findings suggested that for the mature consumers surveyed the importance of various information sources is stable across product classes. The analysis suggested that a significant difference does exist between the importance of informal and formal information sources in learning about products. Informal information sources (friends and neighbors and immediate family) were the most important sources.

The present research results indicated that mature consumers do perceive risk in direct shopping situations. This finding conflicts with earlier research (Schiffman 1971) which reported: (1) there were no differences in interest in types and number of risk-reducing information between elderly women who exhibit high perceived risk and those who exhibit low perceived risk, and (2) there were no significant differences between the high and low perceived risk groups in the types of information used.

We found that there are strong indications of risk in mature consumers and that they do rely on different sources of information than younger consumers.

All consumers place the most emphasis on guarantees, product and store reputation, and personal evaluation at home and in the store. The mature group, however, places more value on product and source reputations—as these relate to the guarantees. They also place more value on the ability to examine a product before purchasing it. Research on the mature shopper's complaining behavior (Warland, Herrman, and Willits 1975; Bearden and Mason 1979; Bearden, Teel, and Crockett 1980; Bernhardt 1981; Manzer, Gentry, and Wilson 1982) indicates they are less likely to complain when dissatisfied. It may be that the mature consumer uses guarantees and product/store reputation to help minimize the need to complain. Our research indicates that the availability of complaint mechanisms is equally important for all age groups.

PRODUCT STRATEGIES

Older adults are often among the last to adopt a new product, service, or idea. Our findings suggest the utility of certain strategies for gaining more rapid and greater acceptance of new products among older adults. Though the strategies suggested are applicable in gaining adoption among all age segments, the ways in which these strategies are implemented differ when mature consumers are of focal concern. One such strategy entails minimizing the complexity that mature consumers perceive a new product to have. Because the mature learn new tasks or skills most readily when they can rely on their past experiences, they should be less hesitant in adopting a new product and they should have greater dexterity in its use when the innovation does not depart greatly from past product experiences. Radically new product innovations, therefore, should be avoided when mature consumers constitute an important segment of the market.

A second product strategy is to direct marketing efforts at increasing the divisibility of a new product for older consumers. In comparison with other age groups, mature consumers have fewer economic resources and are more cautious in making decisions. As a result, the degree to which they can try a new product on a limited basis (i.e., its divisibility) is likely to be a crucial factor in determining their new product adoption. To facilitate trial by the elderly, product sampling procedures might be instituted, particularly in locales where residential concentration of the aged is greatest. Product sampling also may serve to reduce the mature consumer's perception of product complexity, because sampling allows learning about the product to be self-paced. And this approach may help to overcome the mature consumer's perceptions of risk associated with direct shopping modes.

COMMUNICATION STRATEGY

The major practical implications of this review pertain to communication strategy. In particular, the findings indicate that mature consumers do not constitute a homogeneous age segment. Rather, what constitutes a mature consumer segment depends on the strategist's objective. If reaching the mature consumer is of focal concern, then the over-60 or 65+ classification can be used. Because the contraction in life space generally begins between these ages, the sources of information are often similar for people defined as mature in this way. If the objective is to ensure learning, then individuals over the age of 45 should be distinguished from younger adults. At this age, deficits in information processing become prominent. Finally, if the aim is to gain acceptance of a persuasive appeal and if message recipients perceive themselves to be competent in coping with an issue, no age-based segmentation seems appropriate. In this situation, older adults are no more susceptible to social influence than younger adults. In contrast, if the audience has a perception of little competence, mature consumers show greater influenceability than younger adults, though the age at which this occurs is problematic.

Since multiple communication objectives typically exist, classification of mature consumers as those who have reached a particular chronological age has little utility. This is not to say that knowledge about age differences is devoid of practical implications. Indeed, a substantial number of strategies are likely to enhance the information base on which mature consumers make decisions without adversely affecting the processing of younger segments of the population.

Specifically, the following communication strategies are suggested:

1. If the communication criterion is information exposure, emphasis should be placed on reaching the mature consumer's extended family. Not only do mature consumers have substantial contact with their extended family, but they also rely on their extended family for information. Use of this approach eliminates the need for lengthy arguments in support of an advocacy that are unlikely to be learned by the mature consumer because of their diminished processing speed.

   Attention should be given to mature consumers per se, particularly if the market is characterized by residential concentration of the aged. In such situations, the mature consumers' exposure to and reliance on their age peers as sources of information are likely to be substantial. However, this strategy should not be pursued to the exclusion of reaching the mature consumer's extended family. Even if the mature consumer's peers are an important reference group, they also rely on their extended family for information.

   Finally, the mature consumer can be reached efficiently by television and newspapers, because older individuals are heavy consumers of these mass media.

2. Newspapers are the most appropriate medium if the objective is to have mature consumers learn new information. Older people are not only heavy consumers of this medium, but they also consider it the most important mass media source of information. Further, newspapers allow information processing to be self-paced, reducing the chance of learning deficits that often result from externally paced presentations.

   In the dissemination of information to the mature, distracting materials should be avoided. Though it has been demonstrated that low levels of distraction may enhance persuasion of the population in general, given the older individual's inability to ignore irrelevant stimuli, even mild distraction is likely to inhibit their comprehension of information. Thus humor, quick cuts (i.e., rapid movement from one scene to another in audiovisual presentations), and other such distracting devices may be inappropriate if people over 45 constitute an important part of the target market.

3. If the strategist's aim is to influence mature consumers, strategies based on self-perception theory are likely to be more effective than the traditionally used persuasion approaches. Persuasion entails providing the message recipient with arguments for engaging in a particular behavior. It is predicated on the assumption that individuals' attitudes can be influenced by facilitating processing through its cognitive precursors—exposure, learning, and acceptance. In contrast to persuasion strategies, which seek to change an individual's view of a

product, self-perception involves changing individuals' views of themselves so that a product is considered to be congenial with their needs.

One self-perception based strategy that may be appropriate to reach the elderly is labeling. It involves interpreting the behavior of individuals for them. Klein and Birren (1973) used this procedure in labeling their subjects as either competent or not competent at a judgment task on the basis of their past performance. The limited evidence comparing the two influence strategies indicates that self-perception strategies are more influential than persuasion strategies in situations where people are uncertain about their attitudes. Because older individuals experience substantial shifts in the roles they must perform and because they find new roles difficult to learn, they are often uncertain as to what constitutes appropriate behavior in newly acquired role situations. In these instances self-perception strategies are likely to be particularly effective.

4. A substantial portion of the mature consumer market thrive on remaining active and involved. They want to be part of the mainstream of society. If the strategist's goal involves this group, products and services should be presented portraying enjoyment.

5. The mature consumer is also sensitive to the problems of aging. This group needs and seeks security, but they are generally lacking in self-confidence when making decisions. And they are cautious about spending money. Communication appeals that emphasize security are ways to approach this group of mature consumers. Strategists should emphasize product and service reliability with heavy use of testimonials and documentation.

6. Another group of mature consumers are highly suspicious. They are fixed in their patterns of shopping behavior, and it is difficult to induce them to change. Generally, only relatively easy-to-use products that deliver on promises will be accepted by this group of mature consumers. Appeals should be direct and should emphasize immediate satisfaction from use.

OTHER MARKETING MIX VARIABLES

Mature consumers are likely to show differential sensitivity to other marketing variables. For example, because many have fixed incomes mature consumers are more price sensitive than other segments of the population. Evidence reported in other studies seems to corroborate this inference. McCann (1974) found that the over-55 group was at least twice as responsive as other age segments to price changes in the consumer nondurable category he examined; and evidence reported by Bucklin (1969) and Howell and Loeb (1975) indicates that the price sensitivity of older adults extends across a variety of frequently purchased consumer products.

If personal selling strategies are used, special problems in interpersonal interaction with mature consumers should be recognized. The older consumer may be unable to process what seems to be an ordinary sales conversation because it resembles an externally paced task. Thus, direct salespeople and telephone salespeople who are in frequent contact with mature consumers should convey an unhurried impression to avoid any misunderstanding.

PRESENTATION STRATEGIES

Presentation often determines whether a message is successfully communicated. Because reading and hearing are in part physical actions, the physical aspects of a printed work or audiovisual production define to whom your communication is accessible. If people cannot read it or hear it, they can never be part of the audience.

Layout, graphics, color, and fonts, as well as pacing and sound in films, video, and slide shows are just some of the choices made in putting together a presentation. In making the choices, budget and time constraints are weighed against aesthetic content, targeting, and image criteria. As a result, selections may be made that inadvertently exclude millions of people from the audience. These are the people of all ages who have a visual, hearing, or other physical impairment.

Impairments of the senses are surprisingly common and occur in people of all ages. Not surprisingly, because eyes and ears age with the rest of the body, vision and hearing problems are more prevalent in older persons. About half of those with visual or audio handicaps are older.

Even with corrective lenses or medical treatments, millions of Americans have less than 20/20 vision. The causes vary. Some are congenital, but no one is immune. By about age 30, everyone's sight will have begun deteriorating. By age 65, virtually every person will suffer some loss in ability to focus, to resolve images, to discern colors, and to adapt to light. Over 60 percent of those considered visually impaired are older persons.

These people need not be written off. The lack of perfect vision can, to a degree, be compensated for in presentation without impairing the budget or style.

Contrast is the first element in seeing, and the greater the contrast, the easier an image is to discern. Contrast depends upon light and definition. If there is a spot on a large sheet of paper, it must be sufficiently different—either brighter or darker—than the background or it will not be perceived and the process of seeing essentially stops.

Color is identified by the amount and frequency of light reflected back to the eye. For instance, black, the absence of color, is the least reflective and absorbs light from across the spectrum. Since white is most reflective, the contrast is greatest between black and white. Because all colors absorb some light, the use of color reduces the level of brightness contrast. Maintaining good contrast is even more difficult when using both colored ink and paper.

The level of contrast is critical to visually impaired persons because many impairments, particularly those that result from age, affect light sensitivity. Opacities in the eye, including clouding of the lens and cataracts, reduce significantly the amount of light that passes through the eye.

Reduced light sensitivity lowers the contrast threshold at which impaired persons begin to "see." In choosing colors, then, the contrast between red ink on pink paper versus red ink on white paper clearly points to the selection of red on white.

Because of the yellowing of the eye, images to older persons may appear as if seen through a yellow veil. This phenomenon can be readily duplicated by using a yellow filter to check the contrast and appearance of your work to older readers. Another result of yellowing is that less violet light is registered by the eye; it becomes progressively more difficult to match blues and greens. It is, therefore, often easier for older persons to discriminate among reds, oranges, and yellows than among blues, greens, and purples.

Awareness of this reduced color sensitivity is especially important in the selection of colors for bar graphs and drawings where understanding is contingent upon distinguishing between colors. Using colors from different ends of the spectrum or amplifying the difference with dots or crosshatches helps ensure clarity.

Along with the comparative contrast in light and dark of the image to its background, the crispness of the edge determines the visibility of an image. Image formation, the recognition of a form or letter, occurs at the edge and is dependent upon the edge gradient—the rate of change between light and dark. Any factor that actually blurs, or appears to blur, the edge hampers vision. For instance, glare or dazzle greatly reduces the seeming contrast at the edge, which suggests shiny paper and metallic inks be used sparingly. Enlarging and poor printing quality muddy the edge of an image, again reducing contrast.

Because colors have varying degrees of visibility, color selection and interaction also affect image definition. Yellow, for instance, has a very high velocity, hence visibility. For distance viewing, on billboards, films, and slides, yellow—particularly against a black background—is an excellent choice. If not toned down, however, yellow's intensity at close range can cause the edge to dance or vibrate, thereby reducing the apparent contrast and making reading difficult.

If the contrast is sufficient for an image to be perceived, identification, the next step in seeing, is controlled by the *size* and *detail* of the image. In reading, this depends on the choice of font—type style and size—and the spacing—*leading* and *proportion*.

The ability to focus declines with age, impairing a person's ability to distinguish small interstices and variations in form. Many visually impaired persons suffer a loss of central vision. In both cases, larger print and more sizeable images are easier to see.

The size of the type, although crucial, is not the sole consideration.

Style is important to readability. Ornate faces, italics, and styles with extraneous squiggles are more difficult to discern. They tend to clutter the image without imparting any useful information, a principle that applies to all visuals. In general, serif type has been shown to be preferred by readers. But in the selection of type, it is perhaps most useful to look at the size and frequency of the smallest dimension of the letters (including interior white spaces) because it is this dimension that largely determines visibility.

The "free" or white space around a letter or image is as important as the letter itself. Proportional spacing, where the white space between letters is kept constant regardless of letter width, should always be used.

Also, the leading or spacing between lines of type combined with the font make copy readable. Within reasonable limits, tradeoffs between the two—smaller types with an additional point or two of leading, and vice versa—can be used to create the desired effect, conserve paper space, and maintain readability. There are limits to the benefit of leading; over three points is almost as difficult to read as unleaded copy.

Reading continuous copy or following a coherent sequence of images makes fewer demands on the visual ability of the audience because context and perceptual clues aid understanding. In print, indentation of paragraphs and the use of standard capitalization also provide visual clues, which improve reading.

When faced with single words or phrases or nonsequential images these context clues are lost. The labeling of graphs, schematic drawings, and other visual aids—whether on a page or screen—require particular attention to ensure they really aid understanding. The type should be clean, perhaps bold-faced, as large as possible, and set against a high contrast background. Additionally, when the reader's ability to understand a figure depends on being able to differentiate between various lines, the lines should be made to look very different from one another. A thin dashed line and a thin solid line can be readily confused; the use of dashes divided by small triangles or circles is much clearer to the viewer.

The food industry has learned well the attraction of bite-sized snacks. People have a similar reaction to the written word. Smaller blocks of *copy* are much more agreeable and easier to read. Divisions, both horizontal and vertical, are effective and can be achieved by using shorter lines of type and more paragraphs.

The optimum line length is not set. It depends on the type size and leading, although it appears that the maximum comfortable length is from five to six inches. Columning frequently affords maximum use of available space and may improve readability.

Margins are, of course, necessary, but other than aesthetic relief afforded by "white space," the use of margins wider than one-quarter inch appears to have little impact on readability. The sole exception is the interior margin of a bound publication, especially large paperbacks. If the print "comes into" the binding, it is exceedingly difficult to read because of the curve, the reduction in available light, and the physical adjustments that need to be made in order to see.

Maintenance of a straight left-hand margin helps readers follow the copy, whereas it appears that justification of the right-hand edge has little effect.

Surprisingly, side bars are truly more readable. Not only do they tend to be "bite size," but many readers prefer a vertical line on either side of the copy.

Time and *environment* are two additional factors that affect one's ability to see. A reader can, if desired, adjust the lighting, hold a book closer or further away, and spend hours reading only one passage. These options are not available to the viewer of most audiovisual presentations.

In film strips, slide shows, movies, and television, time is controlled by the producer. Generally, a viewer with sensory loss is unable to compensate for a bit more time on a scene. This makes the audience even more dependent on the quality of the image and awareness of the producer.

With the exception of television, the environment for watching most audiovisual products is beyond the control of both the viewer and producer. Unfortunately, the normal environment—a darkened room with a limited range of viewing distance—compounds the problems of the visually impaired, particularly older persons. In this situation, one of "dark adaptation," sensitivity to brightness contrast and visual acuity (the ability to distinguish detail) are both reduced.

The ability to adapt to changes in lighting usually decreases with age, but problems of impaired viewers can be minimized by keeping a fairly constant and high, but not excessively bright, level of lighting on the screen. The use of gradual transitions from scene to scene or slide to slide (where possible) greatly aids viewing. Finally, when a sudden dramatic change in light is desired, the difficulties can be alleviated by holding the new scene long enough for impaired viewers to adjust and by avoiding crucial visual action in the first few minutes unless accompanied by sufficient audio clues.

Even for younger people and those without visual impairments, adapting to changes in light still takes time. For instance, after walking into a dark theatre from bright sunlight, it takes from two to four minutes before reasonable sensitivity is regained. Total adaptation takes about twenty minutes.

As we age, it takes us longer to register a new image clearly. There is a carryover of the previous image's form and color that interferes with seeing the "new" image. When green and red are flashed in quick succession, an older person is more likely to integrate the colors and "see" yellow. In essence, a new scene starts a second or so later for older persons, which again suggests delaying any crucial visual action for several seconds after a major scene shift.

By definition, the success of an audiovisual presentation depends on another physical ability of its audience: *hearing*. For over 15 million Americans, less than half of whom are 65 or older, this physical ability is significantly impaired. In fact, most people's hearing is less than "perfect." By age twenty, sensitivity to sound, particularly of a high frequency, begins to diminish and continues to diminish with age.

Aside from volume control, captioning, and stereo, there are other variables a producer can control to maximize the audience's understanding of the audio presentation.

First and foremost is awareness and control of background noise because, more than anything else, it interferes with the dialogue or narrative. The higher the ratio of narrative to ambient noise, the better the understanding of the audience. For instance, an outside scene can be established by traffic sounds which are then dropped as the dialogue begins. For news broadcasts, relatively quiet sites should be selected for stand-ups and interviews.

The dialogue or narration itself also deserves attention. Good diction, clear tones in the lower ranges, and a natural rate—speaking not too fast and not too slowly—all measurably increase the ability to hear and understand. Mumbling, "fast talk," and other vocal devices ideally should only be used if they are necessary for artistic purposes. In contrast, the ability to understand accented speech, unless it is overly heavy, depends primarily on a person's individual experiences. Generally, it also helps hearing-impaired persons to be able to see the speaker's face.

Finally, if off-screen sound is important to the action, a visual cue helps understanding. This is particularly applicable when the sound is in the higher frequency range, such as a whistle or sounds with an "f," "th," "s," or "z," as in "sh-sh-sh" for "quiet."

PRICING STRATEGIES

There appear to be two general mature consumer segments: price-quality market and a lower-to-moderate price appeal group (Loudon 1976). Goeldner and Munn (1964) concluded that lower incomes due to retirement result in the mature market becoming price-sensitive. Retired consumers therefore prefer products in the low or moderate price range. McCann (1974) reported that consumers over 55 were three times as responsive to price changes as the middle-aged group and about twice as sensitive as younger consumers. Other studies have found that older consumers are price sensitive across a wide variety of consumer goods (Howell and Loeb 1975; Bucklin 1969). Mason and Bearden (1978b) reported that mature consumers generally compare prices before making purchase decisions.

While Tongren (1976) suggests that the older consumer does not necessarily have as low an income as generally thought, owing to such factors as tax breaks, reduced costs of medicine (although they certainly do buy more medicine), and paid-off mortgages, Gelb (1978) found mature consumers, nevertheless, were economy-conscious. However, this economy-consciousness has not generated cost-cutting behavior such as increased usage of generic products. This buying behavior may be due more to reluctance to adopt innovations than to lack of economy-consciousness (Strang, Harris, and Hernandez 1979).

On the other hand, there appears to be a subsegment of the mature market that prefers quality over price. *Forbes* magazine (1969), in an article entitled "The Forgotten Generation," reported that a large number of mature consumers prefer to buy the best. One study reported that mature consumers do not seek out discounts preferring to patronize higher-priced department stores (Schewe 1984). Lumpkin and Greenberg (1982) reported that mature consumers were not price sensitive when purchasing apparel. The high propensity to be brand loyal also appears to support this position.

Numerous price discounts are granted to mature consumers (e.g., bus fares, shopping discounts, entertainment). In an examination of mature consumers' unmet needs and wants, pricing discounts were the number one concern of the older respondents (Lambert 1979). Over 50 percent wanted the discounts applied to a wider variety of products. There was also a number of respondents who wanted discounts increased above the customary 10 percent. Gelb (1978) suggests that marketers offering discounts to mature consumers should simultaneously convey the message of saving and special attention.

The evidence with respect to credit has been mixed. One study reported that only one in six mature consumers possessed a credit card (half that of the general population) (Howard 1967). Tongren (1974) suggests this lack of credit use reflects that the mature feel that debt carries a stigma and the payment of interest a lack of thrift. He also reported that the over-65 age group is generally being ignored by credit grantors. Lumpkin and Greenberg (1982) found credit to be less important to mature consumers when purchasing apparel than to younger shoppers. On the other hand, Hawes, Talarzyk, and Blackwell (1976) found mature consumers more likely to hold credit cards than younger consumers.

LABELING AND PACKAGE SIZE

There are some strategic actions marketers can implement to meet the special needs of mature consumers with respect to labeling and package size. By changing the packaging of certain products, especially grocery and drug items, marketers could better service the needs of mature consumers. Because of poor eyesight, many mature consumers experience difficulty in identifying products in catalogues. Mature consumers with poor eyesight have difficulty reading print on green or blue backgrounds. Marketers could make packages more readable by the following changes: Use dark background colors and highly reflective printing (e.g., white); print vital directions in as large a print as possible and contrast them against the background color; small print information (e.g., product use) should be repeated in a large-print package insert; avoid script type or other stylish forms of print; clearly identify the packaging's opening feature by a contrasting color; and use a large distinctive logo and package shape to easily identify the brand and type of product (Silvenis 1979). These suggested changes are especially important for mature consumers who are prescribed to take one or more medications. They may forget their medicine or take an improper dose. Prescriptions and over-the-counter drugs should be packaged in unit doses to fit a uniform administration schedule. Packages could be designed to remind senior citizens of the proper administration schedule (e.g., seven pills on a card, one for each day of the week) (Silvenis 1979).

Mature consumers are often on restricted diets (e.g., low sodium or low cholesterol) and have difficulty finding the amounts of these ingredients listed on product labels. Grocery stores should group special diet foods in one place or "flag" these foods with large, colorful stickers. Mature consumers prefer smaller-sized packages of perishable items and other goods because of their smaller appetites, fewer family members, tighter short-term budgets, and easier handling for public transportation or walking (Mason and Bearden 1979).

Examining mature consumers' unmet needs in the marketplace, Lambert (1979) reported that 9.4 percent in the 55 to 64 age category and 8.2 percent in the 65 and older category suggested a need for smaller packages of perishable products. In the same study, 9.4 percent of the 55 to 64 year old respondents and 10.3 percent of the age 65 and over respondents indicated having problems reading price information because the numerals were too small or blurred.

CONCLUSIONS AND RECOMMENDATIONS

Sociologists, psychologists, and marketers have documented older persons' resistance to change. Studies have revealed that the mature resist relocation and changes in work situations (Kasteler, Gay, and Caruth 1968; Pollman and Johnson 1974). Compared to younger people, mature consumers tend to be more cautious and to seek greater certitude before they act (Botwinick 1973). As consumers, older adults have been shown to be among the last to adopt a product, service, or idea innovation (Robertson 1971; Uhl, Andrus, and Poulson 1970). Kerschner and Chelsvig (1981) found age to be related to attitudes toward and adoption of technology:

the older the consumer, the more negative the view toward technology and the lower the use of various technologies. In two other studies, mature consumers were shown to be more resistant than younger consumers to the item price removal associated with scanner technology (Harris and Mills 1981" Pommer, Berkowitz, and Walton 1980).

However, the literature also suggests certain strategies for gaining more rapid and greater acceptance among older adults. While the findings from this study do not indicate that mature consumers are significantly more resistant to direct-marketing/selling modes than any other age group, the use of these strategies may be helpful in developing the potential that still exists. Though the strategies suggested are applicable in gaining adoption among all age segments, the ways in which these strategies are implemented differ when the elderly are of focal concern.

One such strategy entails minimizing the *complexity* that the mature consumers perceive in the buying process. Simple order forms and easy-to-read catalogues are two possible suggestions. Complex ordering procedures may discourage mature consumers from making any attempt to place an order. Minimizing the number of products in a seller's line is also a way to reduce complexity for the mature consumer. They should be given presentations of only those products that are tailored to fit their needs.

A second product strategy is to aim marketing efforts toward increasing the *divisibility* of the buying process for older consumers. In comparison with other age groups, the elderly have fewer economic resources and are more cautious in making decisions. As a result, the degree to which they can try a new product or buying mode on a limited basis (i.e., its divisibility) is likely to be a crucial factor in determining adoption of new purchasing modes. Providing introductory coupons or a free gift for placing an order might facilitate trial by the mature consumer.

Previous research studies on senior citizens have concluded that: (1) this older age group is frequently among the last to adopt, in general, and is more cautious in making decisions due to limited financial resources appeared to have less impact on older age segments than on younger age experience and less on promotional messages to learn more about a new product (Schiffman 1971); and (3) susceptibility to promotional efforts appeared to have less impact on older age segments than on younger age segments (Phillips and Sternthal 1977).

Interesting results have emerged from the examination of trial and adoption patterns of mature consumers and younger consumers. While smaller percentages of mature consumers than the younger consumers often adopt an innovation, higher usage rates are often associated with the mature consumers. Thus it behooves both direct marketers and direct sellers alike to design special strategies in an effort to gain the patronage of the mature consumer market.

Table 9.1
Information Source Typology

	Mature Consumer			Younger Consumer	
	Dimensions	Source		Dimensions	Source
(1)	Advertisement	Newspaper, Radio, TV, Magazine	(1)	Advertisement	Newspaper Radio, TV, Magazine
(2)	Product/Store Reputation	Brand Reputation, Country of Manufacture, Store Reputation	(2)	Product/Store Reputation	Brand Reputation, Country of Manufacture, Store Reputation
(3)	Family	Spouse Family	(3)	Family	Spouse Family
(4)	Guarantees	Money-back, Other warranties	(4)	Guarantees	Money-back, Other warranties
(5)	Salespeople	Salespeople	(5)	Salespeople	Salespeople
(6)	Friends and Experience	Friends, Neighbors, Experience	(6)	Personal Evaluation	Price/Quality Evaluation, Experience
(7)	Evaluation at Home and Store	Price/Quality Evaluation, Point-of-Purchase Information, Catalogues	(7)	Friends	Friends, Neighbors
(8)	Independent	Endorsement, Trade Publications	(8)	Independent and In-Store Information	Trade Publications, Endorsement, Point-of-Purchase Information

Appendix A

Figure A.1
Demographic Profile of Sample

Geographic Division	Percent	Education of Spouse	Percent
New England	6%	1-7 Years Grade School	1%
Middle Atlantic	11%	8 Years Grade School	5%
East North Central	22%	1-3 Years High School	8%
West North Central	14%	4 Years High School	22%
South Atlantic	16%	1-3 Years College	12%
East South Central	6%	4 Years College	6%
West South Central	9%	5-8 Years College	4%
Mountain	5%	Did Not Attend School	41%
Pacific	11%		

Population Density		Household Size	
Non-MSA	37%	One	33%
Central City	17%	Two	49%
(50,000 to 500,000)		Three	8%
Outside Central City	20%	Four	6%
Central City	6%	Five	2%
(500,000 to 2,000,000)		Six	1%
Outside Central City	9%	Seven	1%
Central City (2,000,000+)	4%	Eight or More	1%
Outside Central City	6%		

Type of Dwelling Unit		Employment Status of Respondent	
Mobile Home or Trailer	8%	Works for Someone Else	17%
1-Family Home Detached from any Other House	76%	Temporarily Unemployed	1%
		Self-Employed	7%
1-Family Home Attached to 1 or More Houses	2%	Work for Someone Else: Part-time Only	7%
A Building for 2 Families	4%	Retired and Not Employed	50%
A Building for 3 or More Families	9%	Disabled, Student, Etc. and Not Employed	1%
Other	1%	Full-time Homemaker	15%

Figure A.1 (continued)

Ownership of Residence	Percent		Employment Status of Spouse	Percent
Owned by You or Someone Else in Household	85%		Works for Someone Else	11%
			Temporarily Unemployed	41%
Rented for Cash Rent	12%		Self-Employed	6%
Occupied with no Cash Rent Paid	2%		Work for Someone Else: Part-Time Only	4%
			Retired and Not Employed	27%
			Disabled, Student, Etc. and Not Employed	2%
			Full-Time Homemaker	8%

Education of Respondent			Occupation of Respondent	
1-7 Years Grade School	1%		Professional/Technical	7%
8 Years Grade School	4%		Managers & Administrators, Except Farm	6%
1-3 Years High School	11%			
4 Years High School	37%		Clerical and Kindred Workers	8%
1-3 Years College	24%		Sales Workers	2%
4 Years College	11%		Craftsman and Kindred Workers	3%
5-8 Years College	11%		Operative Except Transport	1%
Did Not Attend School	< 1%		Transport Equipment Operatives	1%
			Laborers, Except Farm	1%
			Farmers Laborers	< 1%
Marital Status			Service Workers, Including Private Households	4%
Married	58%		Farmer or Farm Mgr. Workers	2%
Widowed	15%			
Divorced	5%			
Separated	< 1%		Occupation of Spouse	
Never Married	22%			
			Professional/Technical	3%
			Managers & Administrators, Except Farm	4%
Race				
			Clerical and Kindred Workers	3%
White	97%		Sales Workers	1%
Black	2%		Craftsman and Kindred Workers	3%
Asian/Pacific Islander	< 1%		Operative Except Transport	2%
Other	< 1%		Transport Equipment Operatives	1%
			Laborers, Except Farm	1%
			Farmers Laborers	< 1%
Sex of Panel Member			Service Workers, Including Private Households	2%
Male	11%		Farmer or Farm Mgr. Workers	2%
Female	89%			

Figure A.1 (continued)

Sex of Respondent (Reported)	Percent	Age of Respondent	Percent
Male	33%	20-34	7%
Female	67%	35-49	7%
		50-64	20%
		65+	66%

Age of Spouse	Percent
20-34	6%
35-49	9%
50-64	23%
65+	62%

Household Income	Percent
Less Than $ 5,000	6%
$ 5,000 to $ 7,499	7%
$ 7,500 to $ 9,999	10%
$10,000 to $12,499	10%
$12,500 to $14,999	9%
$15,000 to $17,499	6%
$17,500 to $19,999	8%
$20,000 to $22,499	7%
$22,500 to $24,999	5%
$25,000 to $27,499	4%
$27,500 to $29,999	4%
$30,000 to $32,499	4%
$32,500 to $34,999	4%
$35,000 to $39,999	5%
$40,000 to $44,999	3%
$45,000 to $49,999	3%
$50,000 to $59,999	3%
$60,000 to $74,999	1%
$75,000 and over	2%

Figure A.2
Customer and Job Orientation Scales for Salespeople

Scale Name and Item	Alpha
S1: Customer Orientation	.816

Salespeople have my best interests in mind.
Salespeople try to influence me with
   information, not pressure.
Salespeople offer me products suited to my
   needs.
Salespeople provide accurate representations
   of products.
Salespeople show their concern by following
   up on the sale to see if I am satisfied.
Salespeople genuinely enjoy helping me.
Salespeople are easy to talk to.
Salespeople also seem interested in me as
   a person.
Salespeople want to do their job well.

S2: Job Orientation .777

Salespeople try too hard to complete a sale.
Salespeople's primary concern is to complete
   a sale.
Salespeople try to sell me as much as they
   can rather than trying to satisfy me.
Salespeople are more interested in what they
   have to say than in what I have to say.
Salespeople try to dominate the conversation.
Salespeople try to impress me with their
   achievements.

Technical Appendix B: Discriminant Analysis

Discriminant analysis is an appropriate statistical technique when the dependent variable is categorical and the independent variables are not. It involves deriving a linear combination of the two (or more) independent variables that will best discriminate between predefined groups.

The objectives of discriminant analysis are threefold: (1) to determine if statistically significant differences exist between the average scores of two or more predefined groups, (2) to establish a procedure for classifying individuals into groups, and (3) to determine which independent variables account for the most differences.

Before attempting to interpret the discriminant function, the careful analyst will check on its statistical significance. A statistically significant function means that there is a meaningful differentiation of the groups on the discriminant scores. This implies that the investigation of the discriminant function can be worthwhile. The investigation is typically carried out by checking the statistical significance of Mahalanobis' D^2 statistic, which is a squared distance measure that is similar to the standard Euclidian distance measure. More specifically, it measures the distance from each case to the group mean while allowing for correlated axes and different measurement units for the variables. Fortunately, the F statistic for testing the significance of the D^2 statistic is routinely printed out by most computer programs. If it turns out that the discriminant function is statistically significant, the interpretation of the function can proceed.

Discriminant coefficients are interpreted in much the same way as regression coefficients, in that each coefficient reflects the relative contribution of a unit change of each of the independent variables on the discriminant function. A small coefficient means that a one-unit change in that particular variable produces a small change in the discriminant function score, and vice versa. To remove scale-of-measurement effects that are arbitrary, the discriminant weights that would be applied to the predictors in *standardized form* are employed when comparing the contributions of the individual variables. The relative magnitudes of these standardized weights are determined by multiplying each raw score weight by the *pooled standard deviation* of the corresponding variable.

Define v_k^* as the standardized weight; v_k^* is related to the raw score weight v_k by the formula

$$v_k^* = v_k s_k,$$

where s_k is the pooled sample standard deviation of the kth variable.

In essence, discriminant analysis multiples each independent variable by its corresponding weight and adds these products together. The result is a single discriminant score for each individual. The absolute size of the standardized weights can be compared to determine the relative contribution of the variables.

For example, in Table 6.6 in Chapter 6, the indicated variable, persuasive (coefficient = .62), is the most important, followed by well-organized (coefficient = .40) and customer orientation (coefficient = .40) variables. Variables with positive coefficients exert a positive impact. That is, consumers who perceive salespeople as sincere are more likely to be in Group 1: direct-selling users who are 65 years of age or older.

The standardized weights agree with what intuition might suggest regarding the importance of the variables when there is relatively little correlation among the predictors. For example, one very common intuitive assessment of the relative importance of the various variables in distinguishing between the groups is a comparison of their means. Large differences in the means on a particular variable suggests that the variable is an important discriminator between the groups, and vice versa. When there is little correlation among the predictors, the relative size of the coefficients in the discriminant function will yield the same ranking of importance of each variable in discriminating between the groups as ranking the size of their mean differences. When there is a high degree of correlation among the predictors, the ordering is not necessarily the same, and, as a matter of fact, the coefficients in the discriminant function need to be interpreted with a good deal more caution. A small standardized weight may then mean either that the variable is irrelevant in discriminating between the groups, or, alternatively, that its impact has been partialed out of the relationship because of the high degree of multicollinearity in the data.

Discriminant loadings can also be used as a basis for interpretation. These loadings measure the simple correlation between each independent variable and the entire discriminant function. They represent the relative contribution of each independent variable to the discriminant function, but suffer from some of the same instability problems as discriminant weights. When using the loadings approach, generally any variables with a loading larger than $\pm .30$ are considered significant, although variables that have large loading differences are considered significant by many.

CLASSIFYING INDIVIDUALS USING THE DISCRIMINANT FUNCTION

To assist in interpretation, we could also calculate the mean discriminant score for each group. To do this it is simply necessary to substitute the mean values of the variables for each group into the calculated discriminant function. Thus, the mean discriminant score for Group 1, direct-selling users 65 years of age and older, would be

$$Y_w = V_1X_1 + V_2X_2 + V_3X_3 + \ldots V_{18}X_{18}$$

where V_1 = customer orientation discriminant coefficient
X_1 = customer orientation mean for Group 1
V_2 = job orientation mean discriminant coefficient
X_2 = job orientation mean for Group 1
and so on

To determine whether the discriminant function provides meaningful, practical differentiation (versus statistical differentiation) between the two groups, it is possible to apply the discriminant function to each individual to predict the person's score and, on the basis of the generated score, to classify the respondent into one of the dependent categories. We could then compare this prediction with the individual's known actual classification to determine whether the function provides meaningful discrimination. When the groups are equal in size, the cutting score, Y_{es}, is given as the simple average of the mean discriminant scores for the groups. When the groups are not equal, the formula needs to be modified to take the size of each group into account. The appropriate formula is then

$$Y_{es} = n_2\bar{Y}_1 + n_1\bar{Y}_2 / n_1 + n_2$$

where Y_1 and Y_2 are the mean discriminant scores and n_1 and n_2 the sizes of Groups 1 and 2, respectively.

CLASSIFYING RESPONDENTS

As is indicated in Table 6.6, the discriminant analysis accurately predicted 29.7 percent of the respondents' group membership. This is slightly better than chance, or 16.7 percent.

The functions have the following interpretation. Of all the linear combinations of the four variables that could be developed, the linear combination given by the first function provides maximum separation. Maximum separation is understood, of course, to be defined on the discriminant scores; the customers within a group are very similar with respect to their Y_1 scores, while the customers in different groups have very dissimilar Y_1 scores. Given the first linear combination, the second function provides maximum separation among all linear combinations that could be developed that were uncorrelated with the first set of scores. Thus, the second function provides maximum separation on a contingent set of scores, provided that they are uncorrelated with the first set of scores; that is, $r_{Y_1Y_2} = 0$.

Technical Appendix C: Perceptual Mapping

Because the findings discussed in Chapter 7 are presented with minimal technical support, this appendix supplies the interested reader with the analysis plan and a nonmathematical presentation of the analysis procedures employed.

The focus of Chapter 7 is the perceptions of consumers regarding each of the direct-marketing and direct-selling modes compared to each other and to retail stores. This is accomplished through the technique of Multidimensional Scaling (MDS). As noted in the chapter, it is of interest whether the perceptions of one mode versus another are dependent upon consumer familiarity (i.e., made a recent purchase) with a particular mode. It is also of interest whether age influences the perceptions of the various modes. To test for differences in the perceptual maps across "user" groups and age groups, confirmatory factor analysis was used. If no differences are found across groups, it is appropriate to use the perceptions of the total sample regardless of user or age group to study perceptual differences.

The third phase of the analysis plan was to combine the perceptual map with preferences to establish an "ideal" mode of purchase for each of the three "typical" products. To accomplish this, paired comparisons of preferences are converted to scale values via the Thurstone Case V Scaling procedure. Each of these procedures is discussed briefly below.

MULTIDIMENSIONAL SCALING

Multidimensional Scaling (MDS) is a useful technique for measuring perceptions of respondents to stimuli which are represented as points in geometric space. The axes of this space are assumed to represent perceived attributes that characterize that stimuli (Green and Carmone 1969). MDS allows more complete insight into viewing behavior by transforming unidimensional expressions of relationships into multidimensional expressions of these same relationships. It shows relationships that underlie a unidimensional measure (Hair et al. 1979, p. 287).

Or, putting it another way, Shepard states that MDS:

reconstruct[s] the metric configuration of a set of points in Euclidean space on the basis of essentially nonmetric information about that configuration. A minimum set of Cartesian coordinates for the points is determined when the only available information specifies for each pair of those points—not the distance between them—but some unknown, fixed, monotonic function of that distance. The [MDS] program is proposed as a tool for reductively analyzing . . . measures of inter-stimulus similarity . . . by making explicit the multidimensional structure underlying such data (1962, 126).

The basic idea of MDS, then, is using similarities between pairs of stimuli to find a psychological distance between the stimuli. If one pair of stimuli are deemed more similar than another pair, then the psychological distance between the first pair is less than between the second pair. MDS programs take this set of distance data and try to find a spatial configuration or pattern of points in some number of dimensions whose distance best matches the input data (Green and Tull 1978; Kruskal 1964).

The underlying objective of MDS is to find the dimensionality and configuration of the points whose distances *best* fit the input data. A measure of fit between the MDS configuration and the input data has been suggested by Kruskal (1964). His goodness-of-fit measure, stress, is described as a positive residual sum of squares which is dimensionless, although it can be expressed as a percentage. The smaller the stress, the better the fit. Based on experimentation with synthetic data, the following evaluation of various levels of stress was provided by Kruskal (1964):

Stress	Goodness of Fit
20%	Poor
19%	Fair
5%	Good
2.5%	Excellent
0%	Perfect

He points out that by "perfect" we mean that there is a perfectly monotonic relationship between dissimilarities (or similarities in this case) and the distances.

The correct number of dimensions is found by identifying the smallest possible number of dimensions that still have satisfactory stress levels.

Because of the key role that visual inspection plays in interpretation of the dimensions, Green (1975) suggests that the number of dimensions be limited to three or fewer regardless of the stress values. The problem that confronts the researcher, then, is the trade-off between a better fit with a higher dimensionality and the more easily interpretable dimensions if fewer dimensions are retained.

After the number of dimensions has been determined, the next step is to identify the dimensions. The MDS technique has no built-in procedure for labeling the dimensions. Green and Carmone, in discussing several methods to aid in identifying the dimensions, note:

Probably the most usual approach to axis interpretation is based on the more or less ad hoc judgments of the researcher, as formed by examining the configuration itself. Candidate axes may be suggested by having respondents list—at completion of the task—main criteria which they believe they used in making the similarity judgments (1970, 331).

Respondents are usually asked to describe how the stimuli were "alike and/or different" after they completed the similarity scale for each pair. The information gained from these comments is used along with the researcher's evaluation of the configuration itself, the procedure used in this research. The MDS routine used in this analysis is the TORSCA 9 nonmetric MDS program (Young 1968).

CONFIRMATORY FACTORY ANALYSIS

To determine if the perceptual map of one user group (or one age group) was significantly different from another, confirmatory factory analysis was used. The procedure employed was CMATCH developed by Cliff (1966). In this procedure the MDS configuration (e.g., the two-dimensional coordinates) for each group can be rotated to congruence either by rotating each to a compromise position or by taking one as a target and rotating the other to maximum congruence with it. The former method is particularly useful in MDS where the basic assumptions about the psychology of the response processes require the dimensions to be orthogonal (i.e., uncorrelated).

Using CMATCH, each user or age groups' MDS solution is compared on a pair-wise basis for congruence. A goodness-of-fit measure is provided for each comparison. If none of groups differ, it is appropriate to use the MDS solution (perceptual map) from the total sample.

IDEAL POINTS

MDS provides a means to evaluate the underlying dimensions and the respondent's positioning of direct-marketing/selling modes along those dimensions. However, this information is somewhat limited because even if the respondents perceive the modes on a set of common dimensions, the dimensions may not have the same degree of saliency to each individual. In short, similarity of perception does not necessarily lead to similar behaviors (Singson 1975). Because differing amounts of importance are attached to the perceived attributes, *preferences* may differ among individuals or groups of individuals.

On another level, it is informative to know, given the position of each direct-marketing/selling mode on the established dimensions, which mode is *most preferred* when purchasing a specific product. Because no one mode may be "ideal," a composite ideal mode can be inferred through a series of pair comparisons where, for each product, the preferences for each mode, two at a time, are determined.

These pair-wise preferences are converted to interval scale values through application of the Thurstone Case V Method (Thurstone 1959). Consider an example to illustrate this procedure. Suppose almost all of our respondents prefer mode A over mode B. Then the proportion of total comparisons in which A is preferred to B will be close to 100 percent. Suppose, however that when mode B is compared to mode C, only 55 percent of the respondents prefer B to C. Intuitively, we could assume that the scale value associated with A and B will be much greater than the difference between the scale value associated with B and C. Therefore, the greater the percentage of respondents who prefer a particular mode over another, the greater the difference in scale value and the greater the separation between the two modes. The larger the scale value, the greater the preference for the mode. From the relationship among the preferences for the various modes and the relationship to the underlying dimensions, the "ideal" mode can be identified. When this ideal point is added to the MDS perceptual map, each of the modes studied can be compared to this "ideal mode."

The program used to combine the most preferred mode to the perceptual map of the existing modes is PREFMAP. This program was developed by Chang and Carroll in the Bell Laboratories.

References

Barnes, Nora Ganim, and Michael P. Peters. 1982. "Modes of retail distribution: Views of the elderly." *Akron Business and Economic Review* 13 (Fall): 26-31.

Bartos, Rena. 1980. "Over 49: The invisible consumer market." *Harvard Business Review* (January-February): 140-49.

Bearden, William O., and J. Barry Mason. 1979. "Elderly use of in-store information sources and dimensions of product satisfaction/dissatisfaction." *Journal of Retailing* 55 (Spring): 79-91.

Bearden, William O., Jesse E. Teel, and Melissa Crockett. 1980. "A path model of consumer complaint behavior." *Proceedings of The American Marketing Association*, Chicago, 101-4.

Bellenger, Danny N., Dan H. Robertson, and Barnett A. Greenberg. 1977. "Shopping center patronage motives." *Journal of Retailing* 53: 29-38.

Berkowitz, Eric N., John R. Walton, and Orville C. Walker. 1979. "In-home shoppers: The market for innovative distribution systems." *Journal of Retailing* 55 (Summer): 15-33.

Bernhardt, Kenneth L. 1981. "Consumer problems and complaint actions of older americans: A national view." *Journal of Retailing* 57 (Fall): 107-23.

Bernhardt, Kenneth L., and Thomas C. Kinnear. 1975. "Profiling the senior citizen market." *Proceedings*, Association for Consumer Research: 449-52.

Birren, James E. 1969. "Age and decision strategies." In *Interdisciplinary Topics in Gerontology*, edited by A. T. Welford. Vol. 4. New York: Korger.

_____. 1974. "Translations in gerontology—from lab to life—psychophysiology and speed of response." *American Psychologist* 29: 808-15.

Blake, R. R., and J. S. Mouton. 1970. *The grid for sales excellence.* New York: McGraw-Hill.

Botwinick, J. 1973. *Aging and behavior.* New York: Springer.

Bovée, Courtland L., and William F. Arens. 1986. *Contemporary advertising.* 2d ed. Homewood, Ill.: Richard D. Irwin, Inc., 469-70.

Brotman, Herman B. 1977. "Population projection part I: Tomorrow's older population (to 2000)." *Gerontologist* 17: 203-9.

Bucklin, L. 1969. "Consumer search, role enactment, and market efficiency." *Journal of Business* 42 (October): 416-38.

Buzzotta, V. R., R. E. Lefton, and M. Sherberg. 1972. *Effective selling through psychology.* New York: John Wiley and Sons.

Christie, R., and F. L. Geis. 1970. *Studies in Machiavellianism.* New York: Academic Press.

Cliff, Norman. 1966. "Orthogonal rotation to congruence." *Psychometrika* 31 (March): 33-42.

Cox, Donald F., and Stuart U. Rich. 1964. "Perceived risk and consumer decision-making: The case of telephone shopping." *Journal of Marketing Research* 1 (November): 32-39.

Cronbach, Lee J. 1951. "Coefficient alpha and the internal structure of tests." *Psychometrika* 16: 297-334.

Cunningham, Isabella C. M., and William H. Cunningham. 1972. "The urban in-home shopper: Socioeconomic and attitudinal characteristics." *Journal of Retailing* 49: 42-50.

Direct Marketing. 1987. "Direct marketing—What is it?" 50 (July): 24.

Doody, Alton F., and William R. Davidson. 1967. "Next revolution in retailing." *Harvard Business Review* 45 (May-June): 4-20.

Fishman, Arnold. 1987. "The 1986 mail order guide." *Direct Marketing* 50 (July): 50-53, 124-25.

Forbes. 1969. "The forgotten generation." 103 (January): 22-29.

Fowles, Donald G. 1975. "Estimate of the size and characteristics of the older population in 1974 and projections to the year 2000." *Department of Health, Education and Welfare*, 31.

French, John R. P., and Bertram Raven. 1959. "The Bases of Social Power." In *Studies in Social Power*, edited by D. Cartwright, 150-67. Ann Arbor: Univ. of Michigan Press.

Gelb, Betsy D. 1978. "Exploring the gray market segment." *MSU Business Topics* 26 (Spring): 41-46.

Gillett, Peter L. 1970. "A profile of urban in-home shoppers." *Journal of Retailing* 49: 38-50.

Goeldner, Charles R., and Henry L. Munn. (1964. "The significance of the retirement market." *Journal of Retailing* 40 (Summer): 43-52, 60.

Green, Paul E. 1975. "Marketing applications of MDS: Assessment and outlook." *Journal of Marketing* 39 (January): 24-31.

Green, Paul E., and Frank J. Carmone. 1969. "Multidimensional scaling: An introduction and comparison of nonmetric unfolding techniques." *Journal of Marketing* 7 (August): 330-41.

————. 1970. *Multidimensional Scaling and Related Techniques of Marketing Analysis.* Boston: Allyn and Bacon, Inc.

Green, Paul E., and Donald S. Tull. 1978. *Research for marketing decisions.* Englewood Cliffs, N.J.: Prentice-Hall.

Hair, Joseph F., Ralph E. Anderson, Ronald L. Tatham, and Bernice F. Grabblowsky. 1979. *Multivariate data analysis.* Tulsa, Okla.: Petroleum Publishing Company.

Harris, Brian F., and Michael K. Mills. 1981. "The acceptance of technological change in retailing: The case of scanners and item price removal." In *The marketing environment: New theories and applications*, Series No. 47, edited by Kenneth Bernhardt et al., 66-69. Chicago: American Marketing Association.

Harris, Brian F., and U.S. Department of Health, Education, and Welfare. 1978. *Health United States 1978*. Washington, D.C.: GPO, 217.

Hawes, Douglass K., W. Wayne Talarzyk, and Roger D. Blackwell. 1976. "Female and male possession of bank credit cards: A psychographic-demographic profile." *Proceedings* American Marketing Association: 87-93.

Howard, John A. 1967. "Remarks on consumer interests of the elderly." Hearings before the Subcommittee on Consumer Interests of the Elderly of the Special Committee on Aging, United States Senate, 90th Congress, First Session, Washington, D.C.: GPO.

Howell, J., and D. Loeb. 1975. "Income, age and food consumption." *Gerontologist* 15: 7-16.

Kasteler, Josephine M., Robert M. Gay, and Max J. Caruth. 1968. "Involuntary relocation of the elderly." *Gerontologist* 8: 276-79.

Kerschner, Paul A., and Kathleen A. Chelsvig. 1981. "The aged user and technology." Paper presented at the Conference on Communications Technology and the Elderly: Issues and Forecasts, Cleveland, OH.

Klein, R. L., and J. E. Birren. 1972a. "Age differences in susceptibility to social influence: A search for general tendencies of social conformity." Ninth International Congress of Gerontology, Kiev, USSR.

_____. 1972b. "Age differences in social conformity on a task of auditory signal detection." *Proceedings of the 80th Annual Convention* American Psychological Association: 661-62.

_____. 1973. "Age, perceived self-competence, and conformity: A partial explanation." *Proceedings of the 81st Annual Convention* American Psychological Association: 584-87.

Klippel, Eugene, and Timothy W. Sweeney. 1974. "The use of information sources by the aged consumer." *Gerontologist* 14: 163-66.

Korgaonkar, Pradeep K. 1982. "Consumer preferences for catalog showrooms and discount stores." *Journal of Retailing* 58 (Fall): 76-88.

Kruskal, J. B. 1964. "Multidimensional scaling by optimizing goodness of fit to a nonmetric hypothesis." *Psychometrika* 29 (March): 1-27.

Lambert, Zarrell V. 1979. "An investigation of older consumers: Unmet needs and wants at the retail level." *Journal of Retailing* 55 (Winter): 35-57.

Loudon, David L. 1976. "Senior citizens: An underdeveloped market segment." *Proceedings* Southern Marketing Association: 124-26.

Lumpkin, James R. 1984. "The effect of retirement vs. age on the shopping orientations of the elderly consumer." *Gerontologist* 24: 622-26.

_____. 1985a. "Health versus activity in elderly persons' locus of control." *Perceptual and Motor Skills* 60: 288.

_____. 1985b. "Validity of a brief locus of control scale for survey research." *Psychological Reports* 57: 655-59.

_____. 1985c. "Shopping orientation segmentation of the elderly consumer." *Journal of the Academy of Marketing Science* 13 (Spring): 272-89.

Lumpkin, James R., and Marjorie Caballero. 1985. "Locus of control and the information sources of the elderly." *Proceedings* Southern Marketing Association, edited by David M. Klein and Allen E. Smith: 28-31.

Lumpkin, James R., and Troy Festervand. 1987. "Development of a factory based typology of information sources as a segmentation basis for the elderly: An investigation of the homogeneity of the elderly." Working paper.

Lumpkin, James R., and Barnett A. Greenberg. 1982. "Apparel shopping patterns of the elderly consumer." *Journal of Retailing* 58 (Winter): 68-89.

Lumpkin, James R., Barnett A. Greenberg, and Jac L. Goldstucker. 1985. "Marketplace needs of the elderly: Determinant attributes and store choice." *Journal of Retailing* 61 (Summer): 75-105.

Lumpkin, James R., and Jon M. Hawes. 1985. "Retailing without stores: An examination of catalog shoppers." *Journal of Business Research* 13 (April): 139-52.

Lumpkin, James R., and C. William McConkey. 1984. "Identifying determinants of store choice of fashion shoppers." *Akron Business and Economic Review* 15 (Winter): 30-35.

Manzer, Lee, James W. Gentry, and Teresa L. Wilson. 1982. "Shopping and personal characteristics of the discontented elderly consumer." *Proceedings of the Southwestern Marketing Association*, Dallas, 63-65.

Martin, Claude R. 1975. "A transgenerational comparison: The elderly fashion consumer." *Proceedings* Association for Consumer Research: 453-56.

Mason, J. Barry, and William O. Bearden. 1978a. "Profiling the shopping behavior of elderly consumers." *Gerontologist* 28: 454-61.

———. 1978b. "Elderly shopping behavior and marketplace perceptions." *Proceedings* Southern Marketing Association: 290-93.

———. 1981. "Elderly consumer post-transaction satisfaction and actions taken as a result of bad buying experiences." *Proceedings* Southern Marketing Association: 97-101.

Mason, J. Barry, and Brooks E. Smith. 1974. "An exploratory note on the shopping behavior of the low income senior citizen." *The Journal of Consumer Affairs* 8: 204-9.

Mayer, Barbara. 1982. "Mail-order sales are on the upswing." *Akron Beacon Journal* (July): 57.

McCann, John. 1974. "Market segment response to the marketing decision of workers." *Journal of Gerontology* 18: 66-70.

McNair, Malcom P., and Eleanor G. May. 1978. "The next revolution of the retailing wheel." *Harvard Business Review* 56 (September-October): 81-91.

McQuade, Walter. 1980. "There's a lot of satisfaction (guaranteed) in direct marketing." *Fortune* 100 (April 21): 110-24.

Peter, J. P. 1979. "Reliability: A review of psychometric basics and recent marketing practices." *Journal of Marketing Research* (November): 6-17.

Phillips, Lynn W., and Brian Sternthal. 1977. "Age differences in information processing: A perspective on the aged consumer." *Journal of Marketing Research* 14 (November): 444-57.

Pollman, A. William, and Alton C. Johnson. 1974. "Resistance to change, early retirement and managerial decisions." *Industrial Gerontology* 1 (1): 33-41.

Pommer, Michael D., Eric N. Berkowitz, and John R. Walton. 1980. "UPC scanning: An assessment of shopper response to technological changes." *Journal of Retailing* 56 (Summer): 25-44.

Reinecke, John A. 1964. "The dialectics of human development." *American Psychologist* 31: 689-700.

———. 1975. "Supermarkets, shopping centers and the senior shopper." *Marquette Business Review* 19 (3): 105-7.

Reynolds, Fred D. 1974. "An analysis of catalog buying behavior." *Journal of Marketing* 38 (July): 47-51.

Robertson, T. S. 1971. *Innovative behavior and communication.* New York: Holt, Rinehart and Winston.

Robinson, J. P., and P. R. Shaver. 1973. *Measures of Social Psychological Attitudes.* Ann Arbor, Mich.: Survey Research Center, Institute for Social Research.

Samli, A. Coskun. 1967. "The elusive senior citizen market." *Business & Economic Dimensions* 3 (November): 7-16.

Samli, A Coskun, and Feliksas Palubinskas. 1972. "Some lesser known aspects of the senior citizen market—A California study." *Akron Business and Economic Review* 11 (Winter): 47-55.

Saxe, R. 1979. "The customer orientation of salespeople." Ph.D. diss. UCLA Graduate School of Management 1979.

Saxe, Robert, and Barton A. Weitz. 1982. "The SOCO scale: A measure of the customer orientation of salespeople." *Journal of Marketing Research* 19 (August): 343-51.

Schewe, Charles. 1984. "Research dispels myths about elderly; suggests marketing opportunities." *Market News* 18 (May 25): 12.

Schiffman, Leon G. 1971. "Sources of information for the elderly." *Journal of Advertising Research* 11 (October): 33-37.

———. 1972. "Social interaction patterns of the elderly consumer." *Proceedings* American Marketing Association Fall Conference, Houston.

Schneider, Robert L. 1976. "A discount program for older persons: A limited method for expending income." *Gerontologist* 16: 257-63.

Schneiderman, Ron. 1980. "Non-store shopping growing as consumer habits change." *Merchandising* 5 (September): 60-61.

Shepard, R. N. 1962. "The analysis of proximities: Multidimensional scaling with an unknown distance function." *Psychometrika* 27 (June): 125-39.

Sherman, Edith M., and Margaret R. Brittan. 1973. "Contemporary food gatherers: A study of food shopping habits of an elderly urban population." *Gerontologist* 13: 358-63.

Silvenis, Scott. 1979. "Packaging for the elderly." *Modern Packaging* 52 (October): 38-39.

Singson, Ricardo L. 1975. "Multidimensional scaling analysis of store image and shopping behavior." *Journal of Retailing* 51 (Summer): 38-52.

Spence, Homer G., James F. Engel, and Roger O. Blackwell. 1970. "Perceived risk in mail order and retail store buying." *Journal of Marketing* 38 (April): 54-60.

Strang, Roger A., Brian F. Harris, and Allan L. Hernandez. 1979. "Consumer trial of generic products in supermarkets: An exploratory study." *Proceedings* American Marketing Association: 386-88.

Strong, E. K., Jr. (1925). "Theories of selling" *Journal of Applied Psychology* 9 (January): 75-86.

Thomas, K. W. 1976. "Conflict and conflict management." In *Handbook of industrial and organizational psychology*, edited by P. A. Dunnette. Chicago: Rand-McNally.

Thurstone, L. L. 1959. *The measurement of values*. Chicago: University of Chicago Press.

Tongren, Hale N. 1974. "Consumer credit and the over-65 age group." *Journal of Consumer Credit Management* (Spring): 117-23.

_____. 1976. "Imputed income as a factor in purchasing power of the over-65 age group." *Proceedings* Southern Marketing Association: 127-29.

_____. 1981. "Retailing to older consumers." *Proceedings* Southern Marketing Association: 93-96.

Uhl, K., R. Andrus, and L. Poulson. 1970. "How are laggards different? An empirical inquiry." *Journal of Marketing Research* 7 (February): 51-54.

U.S. Department of Commerce. 1980. *Statistical Abstracts of the U.S.*, 101st edition.

Waddell, Frederick E. 1975. "Consumer research and programs for the elderly—The forgotten dimension." *The Journal of Consumer Affairs* 9: 164-75.

Warland, Rex H., Robert O. Herrman, and Jane Willits. 1975. "Dissatisfied consumers: Who gets upset and who takes action." *Journal of Consumer Affairs* 9 (Winter): 148-169.

Weiner, Steve. 1981. "Sears beams life into summer catalog for video shopping." *Wall Street Journal* (May 1): 10.

Welsh, G. S. 1956. "Factor dimensions A and R." In *Basic Readings on the MMPI in Psychology and Medicine*, edited by G. S. Walsh and W. G. Dalstrom. Minneapolis: University of Minnesota Press.

Young, Forrest W. 1968. "TORSCA 9, an IBM 360-75 FORTRAN 4 program for nonmetric multidimensional scaling." *Journal of Marketing Research* 5 (August): 319-21.

Subject Index

Advertisements, 34, 39-41, 45-47, 120, 121, 122, 198; as an information source, 116, 117

Aging, 11, 189

Alterations/Repairs, 92, 101

Ambition, 98

American Association of Retired Persons (AARP), 1, 21

Attitudes, influence of, 188; learning, 188; acceptance, 188; exposure, 188

Baylor University, 29

Cash on delivery (C.O.D.), 51, 52, 65, 93, 102, 179

Call/postage when ordering, 55

Charge, purchases, 54, 55, 56, 65, 66, 67, 68-74, 93, 101, 102, 179, 185, 195

Communication, 187, 189; exposure to, 5, 188; multiple, 188

Conformity, 94, 180, 181, 182

Considerateness, 98

Cosmetics, 34, 36, 38, 42-47, 91, 120, 127-30, 135-38

Creativity, 98, 99

Customer orientation, 96, 97, 98, 109, 202

Database marketing, 1

Delivery, direct to home, 51, 54, 56, 59, 62, 63, 64, 65, 66, 67, 68-74, 75, 77, 79-89, 92, 101, 102, 183

Demographic profiles, 5, 11, 13, 14, 15, 16, 17, 18, 19, 20, 21, 22, 23, 26, 27

Department stores, 30, 35, 183

Determinant attributes, 49

Direct mail, 2, 3, 9, 28, 34, 38, 39-41, 45-47, 49, 54, 55, 56, 57, 58, 79, 80, 116, 118, 120, 121, 122, 123, 124, 126, 131-34, 143, 165, 178

Direct marketing, 2, 5, 7, 8, 24, 25, 29, 30, 32, 33, 34, 36, 37, 39-41, 45, 46, 49, 51, 52, 53, 54, 56, 115, 116, 120, 121, 123, 124, 139, 140, 142, 147, 148, 149, 153, 154, 155, 156, 157-62

Direct Marketing Association, 2

Direct Marketing magazine, 3

Direct modes, 37; access to salesperson, 50, 51, 65, 179; accuracy, 53, 55; competitive prices, 66, 67, 68-74, 100; complaint number, 54, 65, 66, 67, 68-74, 101, 102; convenience, 50, 51, 54; credible product claims, 54, 55, 56, 66, 67, 68-74, 100, 177; direct delivery, 51, 54; experience with brand/product/company, 50, 59, 61, 62, 65, 102, 179; information, 54, 66, 67; money-back guarantee, 50, 54, 65, 66, 67, 68-74,

101, 102; postage/call, 5, 6, 55, 57, 65, 66, 67, 68-74, 92, 101; post-purchase follow-ups, 93, 96, 179; price matches quality, 66, 67, 68-74, 100; quality products, 53, 55, 67, 68-74, 100; samples, 52, 65, 103; selection, 179; trialability, 50, 52, 65, 179, 185; well-known brands/products, 51, 53, 60, 65, 66, 67, 68-74, 75, 77, 79-89, 101, 102

Direct selling, 2, 4, 5, 7, 24, 25, 29, 32, 33, 36, 37, 42-47, 49, 51, 52, 53, 55, 68, 85-86, 91, 92, 93, 94, 96, 100, 102, 115, 116, 118, 119, 121, 139, 140, 142, 145, 147, 153-55, 156-62, 168, 178-79

Distrust of in-home shopping, 95, 177

Door-to-Door, 2, 28, 34, 35, 38, 42-47, 49, 55, 61, 71, 91, 99, 116, 117, 118, 119, 122, 127-30, 135-38

Economics, 9, 49, 50, 52, 65

Elderly, 11, 12, 14, 15, 19, 23, 24, 27, 30, 180, 183, 184, 185, 187, 197

Electronics, 34, 38-44

Entertainment, 33, 34, 38-44, 195

Family as an information source, 14, 185, 186

Family composition, 13

Focus groups, 28

"Forgotten Generation," the, 195

Geographical distribution, 12

Gray market, 26

Guarantees, 56, 58, 59, 60, 75, 77, 79-89, 185, 186, 198

Hardware, 33, 34, 38-44, 115

Health, 13, 30

Household items, 6, 33, 34, 38-44

Ideal points, 116, 117, 118, 119, 120, 209

Income, 141, 143, 144, 154, 158, 161, 164-70, 189; distribution of, 12, 22, 29; sources of, 11, 16

Influenceability, 181, 182, 187

Information, 187, 188; formal sources, 186; informal sources, 186; sufficiency of, 55, 68-74, 100

In-home demonstrations, 2, 28, 34, 38, 42-47, 49, 55, 59, 63, 64, 73, 89-90, 91, 92, 99, 116, 118, 119, 121, 122, 127-30, 135-38, 146, 170, 178

In-home shopping, 2, 6, 7, 24, 30, 31, 32, 34, 35, 36, 51, 56, 57, 58, 59, 60, 61, 62, 63, 64, 75, 76, 78, 92, 96, 143, 144, 145, 146, 147, 148, 149, 177, 178

Knowledge of store product, 49, 50

Labeling, 195

Leisure, 56, 57, 60, 64, 75, 77, 79-89, 178

Loyalty, 183; to local merchants, 98, 99, 102, 111, 113, 147, 171-75, 178

Mail order, 3, 4, 24, 30, 35, 56

Mail panels, 27

Mail surveys, 25, 27

Marital status, 12, 17, 20, 28, 29, 140, 141, 142, 143, 144, 146, 152, 155, 158, 162, 163, 164-70, 200

Market facts consumer mail panel, 29

Marketing, 2, 96

Mature consumers, 1, 6, 7, 11, 13, 14, 15, 23, 24, 25, 26, 27, 28, 91, 177, 185, 186, 188

Media advertisements, 2, 28, 38, 51, 54, 55, 69, 81-82, 123, 124-26, 131-34, 144, 166, 178, 179

Men's apparel, 34, 38-41

Migration, 12, 13

Mobility, 35, 95, 102, 139, 147, 149, 171-75, 179, 182, 183

Multidimensional scaling (MDS), 115, 116, 207, 208, 209

National Consumer Assistance Center, 24

Newspapers, 186, 188, 198

Packaging, 34, 195

Party plans, 28, 33, 34, 37, 38, 42-47, 49, 55, 56, 57, 58, 59, 60, 62, 63, 72, 75, 77, 79-89, 91, 92, 99, 116, 119, 121, 122, 127-30, 135-38, 145, 146, 169, 178, 179

Patronage decision, 49

Persistence, 95, 98, 99

Personal contact, 58, 59, 117, 118, 139

Personalizing shopper, 95, 110, 147, 148, 149, 171-75, 178

Persuasion, 94, 95, 96, 98, 180, 181, 188

Poverty, 12, 15, 18

Power, 97, 98, 99, 107, 108, 109; coercive, 97, 104, 106, 107, 108, 111-12; expert, 95, 97, 98, 104, 105, 106, 107, 108, 111, 112; of sales-person, 105; legitimate, 94, 95, 97, 104, 105, 106, 107, 108, 111, 112; referent, 95, 97, 104, 105, 106, 107, 108, 111; reward, 95, 97, 98, 99, 104, 105, 106, 107, 108, 111, 112

Presentation of message, 190

Price, 56, 57, 117; discounts, 195

Price consciousness, 139, 171-75

Print labels, 196

Promotion, 5, 197

Reputation of product, 186; of store, 186

Retail shopping, 55, 56, 74

Retail stores, 3, 116, 119, 120, 178, 184

Risk, 35, 56, 142, 144, 148, 178, 186, 187; functional, 142; psychological, 142; social, 142

Risk reducers, 49, 50, 52, 53

SOCO, 96, 97

Salesperson, 104, 185, 198; as an infor-mation source, 30, 50, 97

Salesperson, ambition, 105, 106, 110, 111, 112; attributes, 94, 95, 98, 99, 104, 112, 113; considerate, 104-6, 110-13; enthusiasm, 95, 104, 106, 110; experience, 104-6, 110-12; friendly, 104-6, 110-11; organized,

95, 104-6, 110-11, 113; persuasion, 98, 104-6, 110-11, 113; sincerely,

Sample, 187 104-6, 110-11, 113; verbal skills, 104-6, 110-11

Selection, 49, 50, 51, 52

Self-confidence, 6, 102, 139, 147, 148, 149, 177, 189

Self-perception theory, 189

Shoes, 3, 4, 38, 41

Shopping, 36, 50, 58, 59; innovation, 139, 171-75; orientation, 97, 98, 108, 147, 148; propensity, 111, 139; recreational, 149; social, 95, 102, 110, 111

Sincerity, 94, 95, 98, 99, 112

Social shopping, 57, 149, 171-75

Standard Metropolitan Statistical Areas, 25

Suggestibility, 180, 181

Suspicious nature, 95, 139, 171-75

Telephone shopping, 35, 61

Telephone solicitation, 2, 28, 34, 35, 37, 38, 39-41, 45-47, 49, 55, 60, 70, 83, 84, 116, 117, 118, 120, 121, 122, 123, 124-26, 131-34, 144, 145, 167, 178

Time pressure, 102, 147, 171-75

Toiletries, 34, 38, 42-44

Transportation, 14, 35, 183, 184

Trial period, 52

Trust, 5

Tupperware, 33, 34, 38, 42, 43, 51

U.S. Census, 11, 15, 16, 18

U.S. Department of Commerce, 23

Users, 32, 36, 49, 52, 143, 207; heavy, 57, 142; light, 57, 142

User categories, 37, 45-47, 50

Wide selection, 50, 51, 55, 65, 66, 67, 68-74, 92, 100, 102, 178, 179

Willingness to purchase, 35, 36, 45-47, 99, 149

Wise buymanship, 24

Women's apparel, 33, 34, 38-41

Author Index

Andrus, R., 2, 196

Baier, Martin, 8
Barnes, Nora Ganim, 35
Bartos, Rena, 23
Beardon, William O., 7, 23, 24, 31, 32, 35, 184, 186, 194, 196
Bellenger, Danny N., 32
Berkowitz, Eric N., 6, 197
Bernhardt, Kenneth L., 26, 32, 35, 186
Birren, James E., 179, 180, 181, 182, 189
Blackwell, Roger D., 35
Blackwell, Roger O., 195
Blake, R. R., 96
Botwinick, J., 196
Bovee, Courtland L., 2
Brittan, Margaret R., 35
Brotman, Herman B., 23
Bucklin, L., 189, 194
Buzzorta, V. R., 96

Caballero, Marjorie, 25
Carmone, Frank J., 207
Caruth, Max, J., 196
Chelsvig, Kathleen A., 196
Christie, R., 96
Cliff, Norman, 209
Cox, Doald F., 35
Crockett, Melissa, 186
Cronbach, Lee J., 96

Cunningham, Isabella C. M., 6
Cunningham, Wiliam H., 6

Davidson, William R., 6
Donnelly, R. L., 29
Doody, Alton F., 6

Engel, James F., 35

Festervand, Troy, 185
Fishman, Arnold, 9
Forbes, 195
Fowles, Donald G., 23
French, John R. P., 94

Gay, Robert M., 196
Geis, F. L., 96
Gelb, Betsy D., 23, 35, 184, 195
Gilette, Peter L., 6
Goldstucker, Jac L., 25
Green, Paul E., 207, 208, 209
Greenberg, Barnett A., 7, 23, 25, 31, 32, 35, 184, 195

Harris, Brian F., 183, 195, 197
Hawes, Douglass K., 195
Hawes, Jon M., 6
Hernandez, Allan L., 195
Hoke, Henry R., Jr., 8
Howell, J., 189, 174

Johnson, Alton C., 196

Kasteler, Josephine M., 196
Kerschner, Paul A., 196
Kinnear, Thomas C., 26, 32, 35
Klein, R. L., 181, 182, 189
Klippel, Eugene, 186
Korgaonkar, Pradeep K., 6
Kruskal, J. B., 208

Lambert, Zarrell V., 23, 25, 35, 183,
    184, 195, 196
Lefton, R. E., 96
Loeb, D., 189, 194
Loudon, David L., 194
Lumpkin, James R., 6, 23, 25, 26, 31,
    35, 184, 185, 195

Martin, Claude R., 26, 31, 32, 177
Mason, J. Barry, 7, 23, 24, 31, 32, 35,
    184, 186, 194, 196
May, Eleanor G., 6
Mayer, Barbara, 3
McCann, John, 189, 194
McConkey, C. William, 6
McNair, Malcolm P., 6
McQuade, Walter, 6
Mouton, J. S., 96
Munn, Henry L., 194

Palubinskas, Feliksas, 183
Peter, J. P., 96
Peters, Michael P., 35
Phillips, Lynn W., 26, 197
Pollman, A. William, 196
Pommer, Michael D., 197
Poulson, L., 196

Reinecke, John A., 23, 183
Reynolds, Fred D., 6

Rick, Stuart U., 35
Robertson, Dan H., 32
Robertson, T. S., 196

Samli, A. Coskun, 183
Saxe, Robert, 96, 97
Schewe, Charles, 195
Schiffman, Leon G., 23, 185, 186, 197

Schneider, Robert L., 24
Schneiderman, Ron, 3
Sherman, Edith M., 35
Silvenis, Scott, 195
Singson, Ricardo L., 210
Smith, Brooks E., 7, 31, 32, 35
Spence, Homer G., 35
Sternthal, Brian, 26, 197
Stone, Robert, 8
Strang, Roger A., 195
Sweeney, Timothy, 186

Talarzyk, W. Wayne, 195
Teel, Jesse E., 186
Thomas, K. W., 96
Thurstone, L. L., 210
Tongren, Hale N., 23, 195
Tull, Donald S., 208

Uhl, K., 196

Waddell, Frederick E., 24
Walker, Orville C., 6
Walton, John R., 6, 197
Weiner, Steve, 6
Weitz, Barton, 96
Welsh, G. S., 96

Young, Forrest W., 209

About the Authors

JAMES R. LUMPKIN is the Phil B. Hardin Professor of Marketing at the University of Mississippi.

MARJORIE J. CABALLERO is Associate Professor and Executive Director at the Center for Professional Selling at Baylor University.

LAWRENCE B. CHONKO is the Holloway Professor of Marketing at Baylor University.